PUTTING *the* SUPERNATURAL IN ITS PLACE

Putting the Supernatural
in Its Place

Folklore, the Hypermodern, and the Ethereal

EDITED *by* JEANNIE BANKS THOMAS

THE UNIVERSITY OF UTAH PRESS
SALT LAKE CITY

The Defiance House Man colophon is a registered trademark of the
University of Utah Press. It is based on a four-foot-tall Ancient Puebloan
pictograph (late PIII) near Glen Canyon, Utah.

19 18 17 16 15   1 2 3 4 5

Library of Congress Cataloging-in-Publication Data

Putting the supernatural in its place : folklore, the hypermodern, and the ethereal/
edited by Jeannie Banks Thomas.
      pages   cm
Includes bibliographical references and index.
ISBN 978-1-60781-449-8 (pbk. : alk. paper)—ISBN 978-1-60781-450-4 (ebook)
1. Supernatural.
2. Folklore.
3. Ghosts.
I. Thomas, Jeannie B., editor.
II. De Caro, F. A., 1943– Lalaurie haunted house, ghosts, and slavery.
GR500.P88 2015
398.2—dc23   2015017701

Printed and bound by Sheridan Books, Inc., Ann Arbor, Michigan.

CONTENTS

FIGURES

ACKNOWLEDGMENTS

The authors of the chapters in this volume made my job as an editor a pleasure. My terrific colleagues Annie Nielson, Lori Hyde, Rebecca Sanders, Kuniko Poole, Carol Nicholas, Robin Wheelwright, and Pat Gantt provided assistance with the text and were gracious about sharing their thoughts in the face of my endless musings about all things spooky and weird. Annie Nielson worked wizardry with the Kate Fox interview. Kate Fox, Erik Rodenhiser, Marietta Goodridge, Jim McAllister, David Johnson, and Christian Day were kind enough to share their knowledge of Salem with me. Julie Mullis provided some North Carolinan perspective on the Tom Dooley (Tom Dula) legend. John Alley, Burt Feintuch, and Nancy Banks made insightful editorial suggestions. Finally, Paden Carlson just happens to be the best research assistant that a folklorist could want.

I hope this book finds many readers like Nancy Banks, who inspires me with her writing, interest in chicken sweaters, playful wit, and attention to fine and arcane detail. My parents John Banks and Dorothy Pingree Banks should take credit for the best parts of me, but they should not be held responsible for my faults as an author or otherwise. They tried, God help them. Despite preferring strathspeys to the supernatural and not actually knowing—or wanting to know—a zombie from a vampire, Burt Feintuch took this journey with me. He is a patient, irreverent, and insightful partner in the field; he is both my fellow traveler and my home. Madison and Rio Thomas are unsurpassed as my spies in the millennial generation. They continually help me find the very best in both the ordinary and the extraordinary.

Introduction

JEANNIE BANKS THOMAS

Just where do we find the supernatural in the contemporary world? The answer is simple: everywhere. It still exists in the oral tradition, and it is pervasive in digital and mass-mediated forms as well. The dominance of scientific and technological narratives has not meant the eradication of supernatural accounts (Goldstein, Grider, and Thomas 2007, 3-4; Pew Research 2009; Bader, Mencken, and Baker 2010, 44). Everyday life is full of uncertainties and mysteries. Otherworldly narratives excel at speaking to our anxieties, and they also contain cultural truths.

Consider the popularity of just one exemplar of the supernatural in the early twenty-first century: the zombie. For starters, take a look at all of the *Night of the Living Dead* movies. Don't forget *Pride and Prejudice and Zombies*, a novel with the tagline, "The Classic Regency Romance—Now with Ultraviolent Zombie Mayhem!" Then peruse the Center for Disease Control and Prevention (CDC) webpage that is devoted to the Zombie Apocalypse. It began as tongue-in-cheek, but the CDC soon discovered their zombie page (where you can "log on, get a kit, make a plan, and get prepared!") was an effective way to engage the public. CDC Director Dr. Ali Kahn notes, "If you are generally well equipped to deal with a zombie apocalypse you will be prepared for a hurricane, pandemic, earthquake, or terrorist attack" (Centers for Disease Control and Prevention 2013).

On a lighter, more athletic note, games of "Humans versus Zombies" engulf entire college campuses. The game is a form of moderated tag wherein "human players must remain vigilant and defend themselves with socks and dart blasters" (yes, they did say *socks*) from an ever-growing mass of their zombie/residence hall peers. According to its website, it is "the antidote for the ailments of a generation" (HvZ: HumansVsZombies 2013). Students say that playing the game can cause them to bond with each other and their campus, so the game can function as a form of student retention.[1]

Those less athletically inclined can attend a more leisurely "Zombie Walk," or its even-less-ambitious variant the zombie pub crawl, wherein humans dressed up as zombies gather in public and stagger around the city in "an orderly fashion" for good, clean zombie fun or for a worthy cause such as the local food bank.[2]

Additionally, we have popular video games such as *Call of Duty*, in which "first-person shooters" (i.e., our children and spouses) can ruthlessly mow down Nazi zombies. Who knew there were Nazi zombies? I didn't—at least not until I started the research for this book—but it's clear that an entire generation not only knows about them but has also pondered in some detail the apocalyptic and apocryphal future they pose. My own son is part of this generation. He and his friends routinely ask me moderately alarming questions such as, "Mom, during the zombie apocalypse, can I use the big weed whacker? The snow blower? Your Hori-Hori garden knife?"

Zombies certainly are relevant to our time, as *New Yorker* movie critic David Denby noted when he reviewed *World War Z*:

> Vampirism, as everyone says, is about sex and violation. But what is the fascination with the hungry undead about? The origins of zombie lore in Africa and the Caribbean . . . have long been appropriated by the modern media. The undead really do keep on coming; they are taking over our bookstores, our movie theaters, our cable channels. Every neighborhood has a zombie or two. Are they what we fear we might become if we let ourselves go—soulless vessels of pure appetite, both ravaged and ravaging? Do they represent our apprehension of what hostility lies behind all those blank faces in the office, at the mall, across the dinner table? (2013, 1)

FIGURE 0.1. Zombie family, including a zombie hunter, at the Logan, Utah, Zombie Walk, which is a benefit for the local food bank. (Photo by Jeannie Banks Thomas)

Finally, consider Max Brooks, who has capitalized on the cultural relevance of zombies. A former *Saturday Night Live* writer and the son of comedian Mel Brooks and actress Anne Bancroft, Brooks is the world's leading zombie expert. He is the author of *The Zombie Survival Guide* and the previously mentioned *World War Z*, which was turned into a movie in 2013 and stars the ubiquitous Brad Pitt. The *New York Times* describes Brooks as the nation's "zombie public intellectual," and his thinking encompasses enough depth, historical analysis, and contemporary anxiety that he has actually lectured at various army bases on zombie preparedness (Brodesser-Akner 2013, 20). In his lectures, Brooks brings an audience member on stage to demonstrate the best zombie-fighting move. He assumes a karate stance. Then he just runs.

Brooks' zombies capture the particular fears of our age. But his response to them is a variation on an old, traditional (and wise) behavior: *Run from scary things!*

When haven't we done this?

Granted, some ages appear higher in anxiety than others; the September 11th terrorist attacks, Hurricane Katrina, climate change, and the global economic meltdown alone have whipped early twenty-first century worries into a frenzied froth. However, consider history as a whole. While people couldn't "tweet" or "Facebook" about it, death rates in the fourteenth century (or just pick a century, any century, from one to nineteen) were devastating and fueled by events such as the bubonic plague—or other diseases like tuberculosis, which later gave rise to some vampire legends—or just plain old childbirth, which killed thousands and thousands of women and children and gave rise to some witch legends. Things probably felt awfully apocalyptic back then, too.

PLACE AND THE SUPERNATURAL

However, like some of our ancestors, we don't just run *from* scary things. We run *to* them as well—and some of us do this commonly. Given the Internet and the relative ease of travel, we can also seek out frightening places on a much larger scale than was historically possible. This book is about some of those places.

The title of this collection, *Putting the Supernatural in Its Place*, is meant literally: the chapters place and consider the supernatural in the locations

FIGURE 0.2. Tour guide at Marie Laveau's tomb, New Orleans. (Photo by Jeannie Banks Thomas)

from which it emerges. Also, this book argues that the place of the supernatural is important, not trivial. The chapters, when taken together, show that the supernatural in various forms—including ghosts, zombies, vampires, and witches—is culturally and individually meaningful enough to be found in a large variety of places, which is an indication of just how relevant supernatural stories are.

The subtitle of this book references the "hypermodern" and the "ethereal." *Ethereal* and *otherworldly* are simply used as synonyms for *supernatural* in this book. These terms are meant to encompass all the supernatural beings mentioned in this book. *Ethereal*, in general use, can mean lightness and insubstantiality, and—as with the first part of the book's title—the chapters in this book work against that faulty assumption to demonstrate that the ethereal is, indeed, a realm of cultural substance. Hypermodern folklore is discussed in detail later in this introduction, but its presence in the title points to the idea that some of the supernatural folklore in this book relates to specific characteristics prevalent in our time.

Supernatural folklore is the stuff of everyday life, and folklorists pay attention to it. Folklore can be defined succinctly as that which is traditionally and informally learned.[3] It is a kind of cultural oxygen: that is, a necessary, highly functional part of everyone's culture. Folklore is often appealing, intriguing, or fun. It is also full of meaning and vitality (Jones 1983, viii). Yet, like oxygen, it is often taken for granted, even overlooked. We don't think much about it because it typically works so well. But it is worth pondering on occasion, especially if we want to better understand the worlds we create and inhabit, so this book uses otherworldly folklore as an entrée into some of these places.

One of the folkloric genres frequently associated with the supernatural is the legend. Briefly defined, a legend is a story that is believed or believable. It is often localized and historicized (Tangherlini 1996, 437); it can be factual or fictitious. The chapters in this book reference a variety of supernatural legends attached to specific places.

While we can't write about every site associated with the otherworldly— there are just too many—we have written about a variety of supernatural locations, including New Orleans; Salem, Massachusetts; Lily Dale, New York; a Catholic retreat in Utah; and a cave in Japan. Our chapters present an expanded sense of place appropriate for our hypermodern era. We also include a couple of supernatural-themed media and digital sites: zombie movies and vampire fan sites on the Internet. It is our intent to illuminate the meanings and uses of these supernatural places in a way that reveals why the site and its stories captivate.

HYPERMODERN FOLKLORE

Some of the chapters in this book present a particular kind of folklore, which, borrowing from the work of philosopher Gilles Lipovetsky (2005), I call *hypermodern folklore*. This term recognizes the intermingling of folk, popular, consumer, and digital cultures. I like the word *hypermodern* for its clarity—you get an immediate sense of what the word means. Unlike the complicated (although useful) term *postmodern*, you don't need to put in a couple of semesters of graduate work to unpack the word's meaning. More specifically, Lipovetsky uses the word to encompass characteristics of contemporary life. He notes the pervasiveness of hypercapitalism, hyperclass, hyperpower, hyperindividualism, and hyperconsumption. He says we live in times that are modern to the *n*th degree, and it is easy to find excessiveness in every part of life (2005, 30, 32).[4]

We have what I call accessible excess, which means that forms of excess are available to more people—not just to the elite—than in the past. Lipovetsky says our times are notable for the "Internet galaxy and its deluge of digital streams: millions of sites, billions of pages and characters, doubling in numbers every year; tourism and its cohorts of holiday-makers; urban agglomerations and their over-populated, asphyxiated, tentacular megalopolises" (2005, 32). He maintains that we have "socially consecrated" the consumerist present (37).

Several of the chapters in this collection point to what I call—following Lipovetsky—hypermodern folklore, which proliferates in our time. Folklore continues to circulate as it has through the ages, but its medium for transmission varies. Under the folklore umbrella, hypermodern folklore in our day is a subset or type that is distinguished by the impact, even to an excessive degree (etymologically, *hyper* means "over"), of digital technology and other trends of our time. Many elements of the modern age give hypermodern folklore its character, including the presence of some forms of mass media (think zombie movies) or digital technology, especially those which facilitate communication (think vampire fan sites on the Internet) or mass consumption or consumerism (think witch tourism in Salem), or any combination of these. Simply stated, then, hypermodern folklore is lore that emerges from, deals with, or is significantly marked by contemporary technology and media (including the omnipresent Internet) or consumerism (with all its accessible excesses and its ability to generate pleasure mixed with anxiety).

Such folklore is often marked by the speed and pervasiveness of its proliferation and distribution (think memes on the Internet). So when something "goes viral" on the Internet, it circulates via a hyper version of the folk process. Hypermodern folklore is distinctive and ubiquitous enough that it deserves to be delineated and recognized as a separate category. However, more conventionally transmitted folklore exists together with hypermodern folklore in our world. Both kinds of folklore are significant, and both appear in this book.

In summary, the hypermodern era is defined by the dominance of the market, consumption, constant movement, an emphasis on the individual, technology, a mixture of pleasure and anxiety, and excess (Lipovetsky 2005, 40, 45–47). Hypermoderns feel continuous pressure to do more: "Women more than men, thanks to the constraints of the 'double day,' complain about being overwhelmed, of 'running to stand still,' of being overworked. And now there is no age category that seems to be able to escape this headlong rush: pensioners and children too now have an overloaded timetable. The faster we go, the less time we have" (51).

Lipovetsky gives us a very good description of our times, but when he turns to tradition, folklorists—who have devoted their careers to the documentation and study of tradition—may not find his conclusions so apt. He says, "The world of consumption and mass communication appears like a waking dream, a world of seduction and ceaseless movement. . . . No longer, as in traditional societies, do we see a repetition of the models of the past, but quite the opposite: systematic novelty and temptation act to regulate and organize the present" (2005, 37). He argues that we replace tradition with movement (37).

Lipovetsky also posits that hypermoderns pay a problematic kind of attention to heritage: "The past no longer provides a social foundation or structure: it is revamped, recycled, updated, exploited for commercial ends. Tradition no longer calls for the faithful repetition and revival of the ways things were always done: it has become a nostalgic product to be consumed, a piece of folklore, a wink and a nod at the past, an *object of fashion*" (2005, 60; emphasis original). This is definitely where I part ways with Lipovetsky. First, there's the all-too-common and all-too-inaccurate approach to

folklore—or tradition, as he puts it—as the opposite of modernism. Equally
reductive is his characterization of new folklore as fashionable nostalgia.
Robert Glenn Howard and Trevor Blank note the "long history of foibles"
that emerges from the false distinction between modernity and folklore
(2013, 8). They say, "While change is certainly the only constant, that does
not mean that traditions have disappeared. . . . the processes of tradition
remain, even as their modes of expression and transmission change" (10).
When I use the term *hypermodern folklore*, it references traditions that are
dynamic. Of course, dynamism is a long-recognized characteristic of folklore
(Toelken 1979). Folklore is created and propelled by movement and change.
It is not a static, wrinkled entity that occasionally chirps out a Child ballad
when not quietly dozing in a corner rocking chair.

Lipovetsky deserves credit for including discussions of heritage, especially heritage tourism, in his consideration of hypermodern culture, but
did he really say "piece of folklore" in that dismissive way? As in "a piece of
junk" or "a piece of something untrue and valueless," except as commodified
nostalgia? For the record: folklore is not old, untrue, unchanging, or lacking
in value. It can be old or new. It can be true or false. But whatever form it
takes, it will tell you something worth knowing about the group from which
it emerges.

I find much that is relevant and insightful in Lipovetsky's formulation
of the hypermodern, but I disagree with a couple of his assertions about it.
Despite that, I think that identifying some contemporary folklore as hypermodern is a succinct and useful way to recognize the stew of folk, popular,
consumer, and tech culture that we cook up and ingest on a daily basis.

Obviously, not all of today's folklore is hypermodern—nor is all the
folklore examined in this book hypermodern. Hypermodern folklore is just
one tributary of the river of contemporary folklore. In this book, we spend
some time drawing attention to it because it is common and important in
the current folkloric transmission of the supernatural. Yet, we also want
this book to acknowledge and demonstrate that it's not the *only* type of
folklore (supernatural or otherwise) that we see in our times. Indeed,
as Bill Ellis said to me in an email exchange, one thing that folklore often
accomplishes "is to maintain a distinct, individualist quality in life in the
face of the homogenizing influence of mass culture. While there is indeed
'hypermodern folklore,' in the sense of people using new technologies and
modes of communication, there is also a contrarian instinct of maintaining
emic ways, even in the face of mass media." Ellis notes that in his studies

of Internet groups (2012, 2015) he finds some of the emergent lore is a response to the dehumanizing nature of virtual communication. According to his emails, he sees a "stubborn individualist streak" that shows up in choices of quirky avatars, handles, signatures, and private customs. He says that, in some ways, folk groups "being by definition small enough to maintain individual identities" are at odds with hypermodern tendencies.

In this book, specifically, we included the chapter about St. Ann's Retreat to illustrate a contemporary but non-hypermodern (yet) form of supernatural folklore. The St. Ann's legend doesn't need to exist in a hypermodern mode in order to circulate. It doesn't require mass media attention to be relevant or to have an impact on human behavior. It was vital before the Internet and continues to be spread in face-to-face contexts. This is a straight-up folk tradition: a legend and subsequent legend trips that emerge from at least the mid-twentieth century, with aspects that are sometimes hundreds of years old. In 1997, tragic events took place at St. Ann's Retreat, and the site was not immune to the hypermodern then (tabloid television ran accounts of the drama at the site); however, the story is not reliant on the hypermodern. The legend has not been largely commodified, but it does have an Internet presence, so, today, it has some elements of hypermodern. Still, the St. Ann's lore relies on a legend shared face-to-face, a storied place, and the impact of both on individuals within a community—all classic aspects of folklore throughout the generations.

This book begins by introducing the concept of the hypermodern, its usefulness, and some of its limitations. This introduction also discusses the relation of each chapter to the hypermodern—an element whose presence or absence is worth pointing out. However, the focus of the chapters themselves remains on supernatural legends and place. Finally, the hypermodern appears again in Bill Ellis's chapter at the end of the book. Along with his analysis of Japanese legends and place, he takes up the concept in order to show— in relation to Lafcadio Hearn's ([1894] 2012; 1899; [1903] 1971) nineteenth-century rendition of legends—that the hypermodern is not limited to our day and age. Ellis argues that the term hypermodern can reference any aspect of a given cultural era in which innovations in media may have led to sudden changes in consumer behavior. In an email exchange with me, he notes as examples the emergence of "race" and "hillbilly" 78 rpm records in the early twentieth century, the rapid adoption of radio in the 1930s, and the similar embrace of television in the 1950s. All of these can be understood, in his words, as "hypermodern in nature with important impacts on folk culture."

It's also worth recognizing that, like the St. Ann's Retreat legends, some of the older Japanese legends and sites that Hearn writes about do not escape today's hypermodern processes. For example, the Cave of the Children's Ghosts is the site of commercially led legend trips (Madeinmatsue 2013). Hearn's book of legends was also made into a movie by the same name, *Kwaidan*, in the twentieth century. Ellis describes Hearn as antimodern in an anti-industrial sense. Yet, one of Hearn's astute descriptions shows us that folklore is simultaneously something "immemorially old" and something very "contemporary." In folklore, the past contains the stuff of the future (Howard and Blank 2013, 10). This Janus-faced quality of folklore is the foundation that allows it to move into new eras with ease. Indeed, folk culture adapts so well to our hypermodern times that it is currently proliferating on the Internet in a way that Merrill Kaplan argues could be the greatest boon to the documentation and preservation of folkloric materials in history (2013, 122, 143).

The supernatural folklore examined in this book is both of its time and of the places from which it emerges. As David Denby says, supernatural beings really do keep on coming—and to a location near you. The tenacity of the ethereal, even as the times and places change, is an indicator of the way in which it is culturally significant. Just as Claude Lévi-Strauss famously wrote in *Totemism* that animals are "good to think" with (1962, 89), so are ghosts, witches, zombie movies, vampire fanlore, legend quests, and "delightful, old customs," as Hearn ([1894] 2012, vii) refers to them. Thinking on the supernatural reminds us that it comes from landscapes that have the potential to alter reality. Sometimes, like Max Brooks, we should run from what these places offer. However, that doesn't mean we should always run—especially if a supernatural landscape can help us remember important, if difficult, histories; re-enchant us; or lead us to a better understanding of the places we inhabit.

INDIVIDUAL CHAPTERS AND OVERARCHING THEMES

New Orleans is the grand dame of supernatural locales. The city is not only famous for Mardi Gras, brass bands, and beignets; it boasts several supernatural tours and consistently shows up on lists of the "most haunted cities in America" (Nixon 2013). The Lalaurie Mansion is one of the city's most famous haunted locales, and its legends are the subject of the first chapter.

The house is inhabited by the ghosts of grotesquely mistreated, enslaved, nineteenth-century African Americans, including a phantom child who repeatedly plunges from the roof of the mansion. Frank de Caro, the chapter's author, says that many ghost stories, including this one, have a "dual structure": one part focuses on the appearance and actions of an apparition, and the other part is historical and explains the background that creates the haunting.

The popular but disturbing Lalaurie legends are both revelatory about New Orleans as a specific place and also hypermodern. They complicate and challenge the city's tourist identity as a romantic place. In a city famous for its elegant mansions in the Garden District, the Lalaurie legends serve as a harsh reminder of a definitive quality of the place: many of the Crescent City's palatial homes were built on profits wrenched from the horrors of slavery. While this legend emerged in the nineteenth century, it has become a type of hypermodern folklore due to its prominence in the New Orleans tourism industry, especially in ghost tours, and its presence on the Internet, where, for example, it has its own TripAdvisor site with rankings. It has also been interpreted in the mass media: in 2013, Madame Lalaurie appeared as a character in the television series *American Horror Story: Coven*.[5]

Salem, Massachusetts, also routinely shows up on "most haunted" lists (TopTenz.net 2013). Tourists in Salem can learn about the Witch Trials of 1692. However, witches and their attendant tourists do not always thrill locals. The supernatural is both good business and a controversial aspect of local identity. In chapter two, I explore why the witch manages to be such a vexed and, at the same time, beloved figure in Salem. I also examine how Salem tourism commodifies legend tripping and grapples with the conflicted meanings of the witch. In addition, the chapter introduces two new terms. The first is *invasive narrative*: a story from which those who live in the place cannot escape. In Salem, witch narratives are invasive. The second term is *simulacrum trip* or *sim-ostension*: a legend trip to a site that is manufactured and has no material or historical ties to the events described in the legend. Salem's tourism is based heavily on simulacrum trips.

The supernatural shapes Salem as a specific place, and its supernatural folklore is also hypermodern. Salem's well-known identity as a supernatural place has some outward ripple effects: it's helped make the witch iconic in the U.S., contributed to the multiple meanings of the witch, and repeatedly demonstrated not only the marketability of the witch but also the didactic potential of this supernatural figure. Today, Salem's witch legends are

FIGURE 0.3. Zombie merchandise, including a zombie sleep mask, breath mints, and a zombie family sticker to put on a car's rear window. (Photo by Jeannie Banks Thomas)

good examples of hypermodern folklore. Consumerism has taken over the legends, and they are now a major component of the local tourist industry. Salem's witches also have a strong media presence, ranging from early movies, such as *I Married a Witch* (1942), to television, such as the *Bewitched* series (1964-72) or the more recent *Salem* series (2014) on the WGN network. Unsurprisingly, Salem's witches of all types have a large Internet presence, too. Along with Salem's pervasive witch commercialism and tourism, the city is also shaped by an irrepressible didacticism that commercialism, like legendry, sometimes amplifies.

In tourist Salem and New Orleans, not only do we allow ourselves to be seduced by the scary but we're also willing to pay good money for it. We can also buy spookiness closer to home—in movie theaters. In chapter three, Mikel Koven traces the proliferation of the cinematic zombie horde, starting with pre-Brad Pitt gems like *White Zombie* in 1932 or *Zombies on Broadway* in 1945. He takes a folkloric approach to these movies in order to demonstrate that cinema is continually creating new zombie storylines and lore.

He argues that zombie films have become the basis for a "neo-oral tradition." Drawing parallels between the films and the folktale, Koven uses and modifies the Historic-Geographic Method—a venerable folklore approach that relies on place—because it traces narrative through time and space. He also discusses what he, borrowing from Italian film studies, calls the *filone*, or a tradition of narrative expression.

The cinema is both a real space as well as an ethereal space. It is simultaneously a concrete space (the theater, or the room in which a viewer watches a film) and an imaginative space (the film and its world as it is understood by a viewer). Koven's chapter demonstrates the international scope of zombie film traditions and shows how these movies use place to advance the films' (perhaps surprisingly) political messages. As a place, the theater often takes us out of ourselves, yet Koven's chapter reveals that even some of the most outrageous zombie tales provide a discourse, which often relies on place, to comment on cultural and political issues.

Fundamental zombie concepts can be found in Benin, Cameroon, Ghana, the Ivory Coast, Nigeria, Togo, Tanzania, and Zaire (Ackermann and Gauthier 1991, 469). In the eighteenth century, enslaved Africans brought their zombie beliefs with them to Haiti, where zombie lore flourished. In the twentieth century, the zombie horde easily took to and took over the theater, thus becoming a form of hypermodern folklore in the process. As figure 0.3 illustrates, the market found zombies to be extremely useful servants in many commercial forms, ranging from video games and movies to coffee mugs and mints. Now the oral tradition draws on media zombies (which have departed from much of the earlier Haitian zombie oral tradition) to create new verbal traditions. For example, children, teens, and even adults participate in casual and lighthearted, "What will you do during the zombie apocalypse?" discussions. Appearing in a wide variety of contexts, hypermodern zombies are one of the tense pleasures of our time.

But we don't even have to go out to the movies to find fear, dread, and the undead. We can locate all of this right in our own homes just by watching a vampire series on television and then joining a vampire fan site on the Internet, which is Lynne McNeill's subject in chapter four. McNeill argues that a thriving, contemporary folk culture has grown up around vampires. Movies, television shows, and books—such as *Dracula*, *Interview with the Vampire*, *Buffy the Vampire Slayer*, the *Twilight* movies, and *True Blood*—have provided the raw material for a rich online fan culture. According to McNeill, fans now have unprecedented technological capacity through easy-to-use computer audio, visual, and image editing tools. Therefore, they have a much greater ability to interact with media. The folk process of change and variation is enabled by technology and draws on popular culture. She also argues that the Internet allows for widely accessible, ostensive interaction with the supernatural, despite non-belief.

Like the cinema, the Internet is also a more ethereal place than other sites in this book. Yet, it relies on the language of place (i.e., "Internet sites"), and McNeill argues that it allows for the creation of places where fictions like vampires can become more real. By its very nature, the Internet lends itself particularly well to the creation of supernatural places. The vampire and the zombie follow similar hypermodern paths; they move easily from oral tradition to movies and television to the Internet. This mix of the traditional, the commercial, the mass-mediated, and the digital firmly places McNeill's topic in the realm of hypermodern folklore.

Unlike the two aforementioned chapters, Lisa Gabbert's chapter explores a place that is not reached via "plugging in." St. Ann's Retreat is in northern Utah, but it is a type of place recognizable to many legend trippers. It's that site just outside of town to which teens, in particular, travel (Tuan 1979, 137), hoping to experience what Lafcadio Hearn describes thusly: "There is charm indefinable about the place—that sort of charm which comes with a little ghostly thrill never to be forgotten" ([1894] 2012, 109).

Drawn to the place by legends about swimming pools, pregnant nuns, and drowned babies, sometimes the teens traveling to St. Ann's find the thrill that Hearn describes. But on a cold October night in 1997, they found something much darker and more of this world. Thirty-eight legend tripping teenagers were tied up, held hostage, and left in the bottom of the retreat's unused swimming pool by armed men who were self-appointed vigilante "caretakers" of the site.

In her discussion of the incident, Gabbert maintains that the landscapes of legends can be performative (Gabbert and Jordan-Smith 2007, 220); that is, they "gather together" people, narratives, and events and change reality. We often consider place to be passive; however, the landscapes of legends are not merely acted-upon sites. Instead, the place helps people transform themselves into story characters. While this lore has some hypermodern threads, including a small Internet footprint, it is instructive to consider it in contrast to the other sites that are hypermodern. At this time, the St. Ann's folklore is not yet hypermodern, but the difference is a matter of degree. It lacks the heavy influence or shaping of the marketplace, the

FIGURE 0.4. Empty swimming pool at St. Ann's Retreat. (Photo by Jeannie Banks Thomas)

media, and the Internet. St. Ann's lore could move into hypermodern realms in the future, or it could stay as is.

While today's supernatural folklore is often hypermodern, it bears repeating that it is not our intent to imply that *all* of it is. Hypermodern folklore is significant, but it is important to recognize that, despite the many ways in which we are culturally smitten with and bound to the digital and the mass-mediated, we still leave room in contemporary life for a good story told in a face-to-face context. After all, story has worked for people for centuries. Some argue that our brains are wired to understand things through narrative (Carey 2007). St. Ann's Retreat reminds us that sometimes a compelling legend linked to a place—no batteries, electricity, or digital media needed—is enough to move people to action.

Elizabeth Tucker's chapter also looks at interactions with a supernatural place: Lily Dale, New York. Historically, the town was a spiritual retreat; now people travel to Lily Dale—made famous by its Spiritualist origins and currently the home of many mediums—to get chills that are family-friendly. Literally. As in "I think I just got a message from my favorite deceased

FIGURE 0.5. Forest Temple, Lily Dale. (Photo by Elizabeth Tucker)

aunt." Because it is seen as an unusual—even a magical or spiritual—place, "the Dale," as locals call it, understandably becomes the site of legend trips, or more specifically what Tucker terms "legend quests." For Tucker, "legend trip" refers to a journey, while "legend quest" points to the search for meaning and the varied reasons for visiting supernatural sites, such as an attempt to understand death or to feel a thrill in a relatively safe environment (Tucker 2007, 182). Folklore studies have commonly focused on the legend tripping of teenagers. However, Tucker's chapter looks at legend quests by older people: specifically, middle-aged women.

Destinations like Lily Dale, which speak to spiritual and human yearnings for meaningful contact with other worlds, show us how important place can be in what Sabine Maglioccio refers to as process of re-enchantment (2004, 121). Such places fortify us through their wonders (whether small or large), which we hope will sustain us in the everyday world.

Due to the way in which the market (the tourism and mediums' fees that are a significant part of the town's economy) is so much a part of the place, Lily Dale also represents a kind of hypermodern folklore that can be traced back to its nineteenth-century Spiritualist pilgrimages and commerce. But, like St. Ann's Retreat, Lily Dale also maintains some of the classic feel of a legend-tripping destination. Today, information about the town circulates within various digital and electronic mediums, which reach a large audience. It has an Internet presence and a definite tourist profile, including a Trip-Advisor page. Media depictions of it exist (see, for example, the 2011 HBO documentary, *No One Dies in Lily Dale*). All of these sources feed into the lore about the town.

Beguiling places are also the subject of the last chapter. Bill Ellis takes as his focus nineteenth-century writer Lafcadio Hearn's depiction of Japanese supernatural legends and places. Hearn was intrigued by stories and locations that were home to faceless humans, kimonos that killed their wearers, and shrines where the ghosts of children left tiny, poignant footprints in the sand. In Hearn's view, these places scared people just a bit but also captured the "rare" charm of rural Japanese places and everyday life. According to Ellis, Hearn was ahead of his time in the ethnographic and contextual detail that he provided in his legend texts, and place was important in his writings about Japanese legends. Ellis believes Hearn's genius was his ability to illuminate the emotionally powerful aspects of places and their supernatural folklore.

Ellis argues that the context for a legend includes the manner in which we "socially construct the space around us," including the landscape. We experience place not just in terms of the sensory information we take in but also as the "unfolding of the spot's ongoing history." Because of how we process place, legendry should be understood more dynamically than it is. Understanding a legend involves the ongoing social history of the location of the legend, the culture's definitions of the supernatural, and the manner in which we respond emotionally to the site of the legend. One of the fascinating things about Hearn is that anti-industrial though he was, he was also hyperactive in using the newly forged international publishing networks to communicate what he found in Japan to a hugely expanded audience, which allowed them to engage in a kind of cultural tourism. That is, Hearn was hypermodern in his use of the day's mass media.

Finally, when taken together, all the chapters in this book raise at least two overarching ways of understanding supernatural places: as sites of memory and as locations of the weird (strange, uncanny, eerie, or creepy). The supernatural places discussed in this book can serve as sites of memory, which means they are associated with recollection and history. These sites serve our need to mark and capture transitory human experiences, including the painful history of slavery (Lalaurie House), the tragic history of witches in Massachusetts (Salem), the loss of loved ones (Lily Dale), a rural and earlier time (Old Japan), and prejudices about a cultural "other" (St. Ann's Retreat). Our era's hypermodern zombies and vampires, while perhaps less overtly connected to historical places, still retain traces of their Haitian or European roots, respectively. The latter two hypermodern creations often recall the past in ways that are malleable to remaking, personalizing, and fictionalizing. All of the places in this book contain history and human stories that we decide to mark and remember in some way. The sites often serve as tangible prompts for recalling the history and stories associated with them.

It is worth noting that many sites of memory recall historical facts that are known—as is the case with Salem, New Orleans, and Old Japan—but others have histories that are mainly personal, such as the deaths of loved ones that become the impetus for trips to Lily Dale, although the distinction is not always hard and fast. Spiritualism as a movement had national, historic significance, after all. However, St. Ann's Retreat shows us a kind of "remembering" that sometimes has little to do with factual, historical events. The same can be said of films and the Internet, though any of these can be informed by or reference history.

Scholar Kenneth Foote says these places "play an active role in their own interpretation. What I mean is that the evidence . . . left behind often pressures people, almost involuntarily, to begin debate over meaning" (1997, 5). The legends about St. Ann's do record the reality of nuns decked out in full habits and wimples camping in cabins and relaxing by a pool in the wilds of Mormon Utah. More recent versions of the legend also contain details— such as kidnappers with guns—that recall the controversial events that happened at the site in 1997. However, the body of the legend contains variable details, and one can hear accounts that don't include any direct or clear historical references. Today, people are not familiar with the actual history behind the site, but they do debate the site's meaning and history, as Foote says. Often what is "remembered" in the legend are very old beliefs and prejudices about nuns—so much so that some people think St. Ann's actually was a nunnery, although it wasn't, or that murders occurred at the retreat, although they didn't. The stories about the nuns of St. Ann's remind us that collective memories don't always emerge from factual history.[6]

Supernatural places also create, appropriately enough, weird space. The term "weird space" draws on geographer Edward Soja's notion of third space.

For Soja, first space is material, mappable space (the real; what is seen and experienced). Second space is how we conceive of the space (the imagined). Third space is his attempt to collapse the binaries between first and second space (the space as it is both experienced and imagined). He argues that third space is how we actually understand place; it's how we "practice" place. It is both objective and subjective, concrete and abstract, real and imagined, of the moment and historical (Soja 1996, 56–57). Thus, place is made and remade on a daily basis (Cresswell 2004, 38–39). Supernatural places, then, are everyday, third spaces that lean heavily toward the weird.[7]

All of the places the authors discuss in this book can be seen as weird spaces. They are places that are strange or uncanny. St. Ann's Retreat, with its swimming pool in the middle of largely wild landscape, immediately registers as weird in the context of its surroundings. Vampire fans find that creating websites on the Internet is an effective way to make more real the weird, fictional spaces that are important to them. As many tellers of ghost tales know, a darkened room can help to open the door to the creepy, which is why this kind of space is relied upon in Salem's storefront haunted houses. Similarly, the darkened theater helps makes zombie movies vivid enough to frighten. A legend accompanying a cave with mysterious piles of rocks, or a tree stump around which mediums gather in Lily Dale, or a nineteenth-century mansion in New Orleans can also generate a sense of the uncanny.

Supernatural places become both a repository and a trigger for memories, desires, and cultural concerns—as well as something stranger. And, while these places are often anxiety-producing, many of us go to them actively seeking weirdness. Why? Why do people visit a haunted mansion in New Orleans? Why do people want to spend time creating vampire spaces and lore on the Internet? Why do people seek the dead in Lily Dale?

People visit these places because the narratives associated with them are compelling, and these sites can allow for some kind of transformation. They are locations where we hope to achieve a heightened or altered awareness. Visitors to Lily Dale often seek to connect to dead loved ones. Fans embrace the *Twilight* and *Buffy* stories. Their creation of related Internet sites and memes allows them to connect with characters they care about, and they can escape from the everyday and enter into a more storied space. Tourists at the Lalaurie Mansion seek entertainment and a rush of adrenaline.

Weird, supernatural spaces allow for movement and the subversion of norms, which facilitates feelings of transformation and difference. Otherworldly places allow us, like doppelgangers, to be in two places at once.

We are still in and of this world, but we are simultaneously in another, more ethereal, space as well. This is an anxious and uncanny pleasure that shows every sign of remaining in place.

NOTES

1. A student participant explains the attraction of HvZ thusly: "What's so incredibly profound about a game with pretend humans and zombies, who chase each other around campus with children's toys for a week? The answer is simple: Humans vs. Zombies transcends awkward social barriers and brings people together in a way that no other event, tradition, or organization on campus can. . . . Put simply, neither side can survive the game alone. Because of this, humans are constantly looking out for other survivors to team up with, and zombies are constantly looking for other zombies to form a 'horde' with. In these groups, friendships are made instantly" (Smith 2013, 199).
2. This information comes from the Facebook page for the Zombie Walk (2012), as well as from the "Zombie Walk" Wikipedia entry (2013).
3. Mine is a basic definition of folklore that allows for expansion and additions, including Oring's notion that folklore is a "process of cultural reproduction" (2013, 43).
4. Presumably, then, in our times Jean Baudrillard's "hyperreal" (a real without origin or reality) would be even more hopped up on the digital, the mass-mediated, and consumerism.
5. Not content with just the Lalaurie ghost story, like many mass-mediated traditions, the show uses multiple supernatural story lines: it manages to incorporate "descendants of Salem witches," who now reside in New Orleans. Madame Lalaurie (played with gory aplomb by Kathy Bates) has three zombie daughters, and Marie Laveau (Angela Bassett) commands an entire zombie horde.
6. Pierre Nora's work on *les lieux de mémoire* discusses the place of commemoration that exists when a tradition, a history, has ended. Commemorative places mark discontinuity, loss, and change (1989).
7. Historically, the word "weird" has strong connections to the supernatural. Its meaning is rooted in notions of fate, magical power, and enchantment, and it was linked to witches, most famously those in Shakespeare's *Macbeth* (*Oxford English Dictionary* 2013).

WORKS CITED

Ackermann, Hans-W., and Jeanine Gauthier. 1991. The Ways and Nature of the Zombi. *Journal of American Folklore* 104: 466–94.

Bader, Christopher D., F. Carson Mencken, and Joseph D. Baker. 2010. *Paranormal America: Ghost Encounters, UFO Sightings, Bigfoot Hunts, and Other Curiosities in Religion and Culture*. New York: New York University Press.

Brodesser-Akner, Taffy. 2013. "I Can't Think of Anything Less Funny Than Dying in a Zombie Attack." *New York Times*, June 23, 18–21.

Carey, Benedict. 2007. "This Is Your Life (and How You Tell It)." *The New York Times*, May 22. http://www.nytimes.com/2007/05/22/health/psychology/22narr.html ?pagewanted=all&_r=0.

Center for Disease Control and Prevention. 2013. "Preparedness 101: Zombie Apocalypse." http://blogs.cdc.gov/publichealthmatters/2011/05/preparedness-101 -zombie-apocalypse/.

Cresswell, Tim. 2004. *Place: A Short Introduction*. Malden, MA: Blackwell Publishing.

Denby, David. 2013. "Life and Undeath." *The New Yorker*, July 1, 1–2. http://www .newyorker.com/arts/critics/cinema/2013/07/01/130701crci_cinema_denby.

Ellis, Bill. 2012. "Love and War and Anime Art: An Ethnographic Look at a Virtual Community of Collectors." In *Folk Culture in the Digital Age*, edited by Trevor J. Blank, 166–211. Logan, UT: Utah State University Press.

———. 2015. "What Bronies See When They Brohoof: Queering Animation on the Dark and Evil Internet." *Journal of American Folklore* 128: 298–314.

Facebook. 2012. Zombie Walk. https://www.facebook.com/events/373103479435836 /permalink/373103482769169/.

Foote, Kenneth. 1997. *Shadowed Ground: America's Landscapes of Violence and Tragedy*. Austin, TX: University of Texas Press.

Gabbert, Lisa, and Paul Jordan-Smith. 2007. "Space, Place, Emergence." *Western Folklore* 66.3–4: 217–32.

Goldstein Diane E., Sylvia Ann Grider, and Jeannie Banks Thomas. 2007. *Haunting Experiences: Ghosts in Contemporary Folklore*. Logan, UT: Utah State University Press.

Hearn, Lafcadio. [1903] 1971. *Kwaidan: Stories and Studies of Strange Things*. Rutland, VT: Tuttle Publishing.

———. 1899. *In Ghostly Japan*. Boston: Little, Brown, and Company.

———. [1894] 2012. *Glimpses of an Unfamiliar Japan: First Series*. Auckland, NZ: The Floating Press.

Howard, Robert Glenn, and Trevor J. Blank. 2013. "Introduction: Living Traditions in a Modern World." In *Tradition in the the Twenty-First Century: Locating the Role of the Past in the Present*, edited by Trevor J. Blank and Robert Glenn Howard, 1–21. Logan, UT: Utah State University Press.

HvZ: HumansVsZombies. 2013. http://humansvszombies.org/.

Jones, Louis C. 1983. *Things That Go Bump in the Night*. Syracuse, NY: Syracuse University Press.

Kaplan, Merrill. 2013. "Curation and Tradition on Web 2.0." In *Tradition in the Twenty-First Century: Locating the Role of the Past in the Present*, edited by Trevor J. Blank and Robert Glenn Howard, 123–48. Logan, UT: Utah State University Press.

Lévi-Strauss, Claude. 1962. *Totemism*. London, UK: Merlin Press.

Lipovetsky, Gilles, with Sébastien Charles. 2005. *Hypermodern Times*. Cambridge, UK: Polity Press.

Madeinmatsue. 2013. "Caves of Kaga, Kaga-no-kukedo." *YouTube*. http://www .youtube.com/watch?v=eQZiNz6_TvI.

Magliocco, Sabina. 2004. *Witching Culture: Folklore and Neo-Paganism in America*. Philadelphia: University of Pennsylvania Press.

Nixon, David. 2013. "The 6 Most Haunted Cities in America." http://www
.insidermonkey.com/blog/the-6-most-haunted-cities-in-america-159175/.

Nora, Pierre. 1989. "Between Memory and History: Les Lieux de Mémoire." *Representations* 26: 7–24.

Oring, Elliott. 2013. "Thinking through Tradition." In *Tradition in the Twenty-First
Century: Locating the Role of the Past in the Present*, edited by Trevor J. Blank and
Robert Glenn Howard, 22–48. Logan, UT: Utah State University Press.

Oxford English Dictionary. s.v. "weird," accessed August 10, 2013, http://www.oed
.com/view/Entry/226915?rskey=FxnIYT&result=1&isAdvanced=false#eid.

Pew Research. 2009. "Religion and Public Life Project." http://www.pewforum.org
/2009/12/09/many-americans-mix-multiple-faiths/.

Smith, Braden. 2013. "Don't Nerf the Zombies!" In *Voices in Print: An Anthology of
Student Essays*, edited by Susan Anderson and Bonnie Moore, 195–203. Logan,
UT: Utah State University Publication Design and Production.

Soja, Edward W. 1996. *Thirdspace: Journeys to Los Angeles and Other Real-and-
Imagined-Places*. Malden, MA: Blackwell Publishing.

Tangherlini, Timothy R. 1996. "Legend." In *American Folklore: An Encyclopedia, edited
by Jan Harold Brunvand*, 437–39. New York: Garland Publishing, Inc.

Toelken, Barre. 1979. *The Dynamics of Folklore*. Boston: Houghton Mifflin Harcourt.

TopTenz.net. 2013. "Top 10 Most Haunted Cities in the U.S." http://www.toptenz.net
/top-10-most-haunted-cities-in-the-u-s.php?wpst=1.

Tuan, Yi-Fu. 1979. *Landscapes of Fear*. Minneapolis, MN: University of Minnesota
Press.

Tucker, Elizabeth. 2007. *Haunted Halls: Ghostlore of American College Campuses*. Jackson, MS: University Press of Mississippi.

Zombie Walk. 2013. http://en.wikipedia.org/wiki/Zombie_walk.

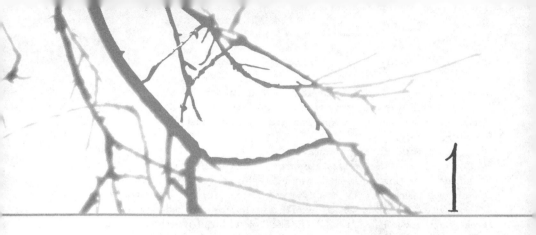

The Lalaurie Haunted House, Ghosts, *and* Slavery

New Orleans, Louisiana

FRANK DE CARO

The mansion located at 1140 Royal Street in New Orleans has long been associated with stories of haunting ghosts who appear to those who enter or even pass by the house. In particular, the ghost of a small African American child plunges from the roof, and that of an adult African American male comes down the interior staircase in chains. Both of these ghosts promptly disappear, but others are said to be in the house as well. These ghosts of legend have been widely interpreted to be slaves who were tortured by the white mistress of the house, Madame Delphine Lalaurie, in the nineteenth century; her own ghost may, according to oral tradition, also be in residence. The whole story of Delphine Lalaurie, how her evil deeds were discovered, and how ghosts have been associated with the house has long been recounted in both oral and written accounts.

The building at 1140 Royal is a nineteenth-century structure of stuccoed-over brick. Built in 1831 and having undergone major renovations later in the nineteenth century, such that the current structure looks little like the original, it looms as a very grand mansion. Unlike many others in the French Quarter, it has not been converted to condominiums or a hotel, although it has served several commercial and institutional purposes and has at times contained rental apartments. Recently owned by actor Nicolas

24

FIGURE 1.1. Lalaurie mansion, New Orleans. (Photo by Nick Bocher)

Cage until he lost possession of it in 2009 because of unpaid taxes, it is situated at the corner of Royal and Governor Nicholls Streets, a part of the "lower" Quarter that is still primarily residential in what is otherwise a part of the city given over to hotels and tourism. In recent years Governor Nicholls Street has acquired the local, whimsical nickname "the Hollywood Hills," not only because of Cage's presence but also because Brad Pitt and Angelina Jolie purchased a house on the street and other film-world celebrities— including Cage's director uncle Francis Ford Coppola—are at least rumored to have houses along Governor Nicholls. The fame of 1140 Royal, however, long predates Cage's ownership, and for decades the building was simply known as The Haunted House and identified as the "most haunted" structure in the Crescent City. Its very designation as *the* haunted house suggests how it was, for many decades, pointed out as the central focus for ghost stories and hauntings in a city in which tourism had become increasingly prevalent. Even in the nineteenth century, visitors looked for interesting bits and pieces of information,[1] including those having to do with the supernatural. The house served as *the* ghostly place in New Orleans, and if visitors encountered any one story about ghosts in the Crescent City, it was likely the Lalaurie story, with Delphine Lalaurie as the house's owner and the

FIGURE 1.2. Actor Nicolas Cage, former owner of the Lalaurie home. (Photo by Nicolas Genin)

principal actor in the house's narrative tradition. This story was the premier supernatural legend to be found in New Orleans, and probably the only one widely disseminated.

Indeed, in the 1930s the Louisiana Writers' Project—the state affiliate of the Federal Writers' Project, part of the New Deal Works Progress Administration—collected folklore that included ghost legends. When it came to publishing these, a number were briefly retold in *Gumbo Ya-Ya: A Collection of Louisiana Folk Tales*, one of the very few publications to come out of New Deal-era folklore collecting activities. Lyle Saxon, Edward Dreyer, and Robert Tallant are listed as the compilers of *Gumbo Ya-Ya*, but the book was a group project, and it is difficult at best to determine who wrote what parts of it. They indicate that by this time the Lalaurie story was so well known that they could simply ignore it: "The famous 'Haunted House' of Madame La Laurie [an alternate, not uncommon spelling], undoubtedly the best known of those in this oldest section of the city [i.e., the Vieux Carré, or the French Quarter], has been so much publicized that there is no use repeating here its controversial tale of slave-torture, flight and envy" (Saxon, Dreyer, and Tallant 1945, 293).[2] And the writers say no more, assuming the story to already be so thoroughly familiar by that time that it needed no further recounting.

THE DUAL STRUCTURE OF GHOST LEGENDS

Many ghost legends have a dual structure. There is the "ghostly" part, which recounts a haunting or the appearance of an apparition, possibly even to the narrator of the story. Then there is the "historical" part, which comments on the background of the apparition, possibly explaining why the haunting is taking place or why the apparition is making its presence known, often because of some past event in the "real" world. The extent to which verifiable historical events may have a reputed connection to a ghost legend varies, and by "historical" I mean only some connection to real or supposed past happenings. The Madame Lalaurie story has such a dual structure that—though I have referred to it as a story or legend—we might speak of it as a little complex of interrelated narratives, multiple ghostly accounts amplifying the historical but with the historical enjoying a semi-independent existence. Its historical aspect, which works to explain legend-ary accounts of supposed encounters with haunting spirits, would appear to be a combination of historical legend, actual historical events recounted in contemporary newspapers and documentary sources, and suppositions made about those events.

THE LALAURIE GHOST NARRATIVES

The ghostly narratives about the Lalaurie house may have begun to emerge in or just after the 1870s, although the key, actual historical events of rele-vance took place in 1834. According to the *New Orleans City Guide*, a volume in the American Guide Series that also came out of the Federal Writers' Proj-ect and that was also edited by Lyle Saxon and Edward Dreyer, the house was occupied during the Civil War as the Union headquarters in the city (with no ghostly happenings reported at the time), and it became a gam-bling house in the 1870s:[3]

> Stories were told and retold of the strange lights and shadowy
> objects that were seen flitting about in various apartments, their

forms draped with sheets, skeleton heads protruding. "Hoarse
voices like unto those supposed to come only from the charnel
house floated out on to the fog laden air on dismal and rainy nights,
with the ominous sound of clanking chains coming from the servants' quarters where foul crimes are said to have been committed."
(*New Orleans City Guide* 1938, 249; the reason for using quotation
marks is not made clear)[4]

A few years earlier, in his 1928 book *Fabulous New Orleans*, Lyle Saxon wrote
about what he called The Haunted House: "The real story [that is, the historical events of 1834 and their aftermath] is interesting enough, but the cred-
ulous have added many a supernatural touch: blue lights at the windows,
a skeleton hand at the door, hoarse screams in the night, and the sound
of jangling chains as they drag down an empty staircase . . ." (Saxon [1928]
1943, 202; ellipsis original).

In their recent timeline for the house's "alleged hauntings," Victoria Cosner Love and Lorelei Shannon suggest that ghostly phenomena may have
been reported as early as 1837, after the house was sold by a Lalaurie agent
to a man who kept the property for only three months and who "tells friends
and family that the house plagued him with awful noises, cries and groans
in the night and that he was driven to flee the place" (2011, 109). This man
then tried to rent out rooms in the house, but no one would stay for long,
not even businesses that were renting space—"It is rumored that there is a
curse on the location and that no endeavor can or will succeed there" (109).
The timeline holds that in 1882 a teacher attempted to open a school in the
building but that it was shunned after a newspaper printed a story accusing
the owner of "improprieties with female students." When the school closed,
"it is rumored that the spirits of the Lalaurie house hold a wild carnival to
celebrate their triumph" (111). For the year 1920, Love and Shannon say,

> There are many reports of ghosts. "There were no other families
> living here at the time and one night, on the third floor, I saw a
> man walking carrying his head on an arm," reported one resident.
> Another resident saw a large black man wrapped in chains on the
> main stairs, confronting an Italian tenant [by this time the French
> Quarter had become a slum, and many of its residents were poor
> Sicilian immigrants]. The chained man disappeared on the last step.
> A young Italian mother found the apparition of a wealthy white

woman bending over her sleeping baby. The ghostly woman was later identified as Delphine Lalaurie herself. In some versions of the story, Delphine is attempting to suffocate the infant. (112)

Love and Shannon, however, do not indicate their sources other than "websites and articles about the mansion" (108).

In fact, New Orleans ghost legends have been little collected or investigated in a systematic manner, and the supernatural traditions associated with the Lalaurie house tend to be reported rather vaguely in print; they may only be loosely referred to ("hoarse screams in the night") and may be lacking in true narrative structure, and their sources, whether oral or otherwise, may not be indicated. There are virtually no published texts taken down from oral tradition—though one ghost tour guide's account given by Cosner Love and Shannon seems to be a notable exception—and it is difficult to determine which stories come from which sources. Probably much of the Lalaurie story passed on today is done so in the context of ghost tours, though in the past the printed accounts of the story have been important, and the Lalaurie story as a whole has likely been communicated through oral accounts among local residents and from residents to visitors, particularly in the context of organized tourism, as well as through published accounts. Almost certainly, these oral and printed accounts have influenced each other, and such books as Saxon's *Fabulous New Orleans* have been widely popular both locally and with visitors. Indeed, Jeanne deLavigne's 1946 book *Ghost Stories of Old New Orleans* has been particularly important in shaping perceptions of the Lalaurie narrative as a ghost story. DeLavigne gives an especially full and rather sensationalistic recounting of ghost motifs associated with the Lalaurie house:

> It became impossible to find tenants for the mansion [following its abandonment by the Lalauries after 1834]. Those who did rent it told of being constantly awakened from sleep at night by hollow voices whispering in the corners and down the chimneys; by horrible noises of heavy bodies being dragged across floors; of chandeliers falling with a crash of glass and metal; of terrified Negro chatter from the dark and deserted kitchens; of shrieks from the courtyard; of wails and prayers and poundings under the floors; of mad jibberings from the empty garret; of a murderous whip flailing the air in awful rhythm, cutting human flesh to ribbons while a Negro throat

shrieked agonized supplications; of jeers and taunts and threats and unprintable filth screamed in a clear, cultivated soprano; of the rustle of silks and the scent of exquisite perfume and the touch of soft, frenzied fingers, clutching and clawing in demoniacal fury.

A colored servant, having been induced to sleep in a room above the old stable at the rear of the courtyard, awoke one night to find firm hands throttling him, and a woman's voice babbling curses in rapid French. For a moment he saw her face bending over him— a pale face with black eyes and a white forehead, the hair done in old-fashioned bands, and a snarl of rage on the twisted lips. Then black hands tore the white fingers away, forcing the assailant back and back. Then the two vanished through the wall. . . . In the morning a long gash at one side of the Negro's neck gaped bloody and burning with fever. . . .

[Some time later] one night a gentleman, somewhat tipsy, passed on the opposite side of the street. As he came abreast of La Maison Lalaurie he chanced to look upwards. There, poised on the very edge of the roof, was a small dark figure. Over into space it plunged shrieking, all but striking another pedestrian.

The slightly inebriated one crossed over. In the moon's bright light the two men paused beside the still form of a young Negress, crushed and broken. The newcomer bent to touch her, but she vanished as his hand descended. . . .

Others began to see this grisly sight. Every moonlight night the young Negress came shrieking down through the still air, to vanish the moment anyone ventured to touch her crumpled body. . . .

When the Italians began to seep into the Old Quarter, they needed housing space. . . . The forty rooms of La Maison Lalaurie meant shelter for dozens. So they swarmed into it. . . . And then they began to complain to the landlord.

Ghosts were besieging them, they declared. Black ghosts and white ghosts. A fruit peddler was going upstairs one night, and he met a giant Negro on the landing. [He] was naked and his limbs were bound with chains which rattled and clanked as he descended the staircase. While the Italian gazed after him he melted into a skeleton, the chains still hanging from his dry white leg bones, and a smell of scorched flesh trailing in his wake. When he reached the bottom of the stairs he vanished. . . .

Italian women claimed a sheeted figure stood in their door-
ways, stole their children's food and switched them until great welts
showed on their backs. (deLavigne 1946, 252–254)

Victor C. Klein, whose *New Orleans Ghosts* and *New Orleans Ghosts II*
and *New Orleans Ghosts III* (1993; 1999) are almost the only volumes on
New Orleans spooks to appear in print since deLavigne's, also includes
accounts of ghostly encounters in the house:

[Following the abandonment of the house by the Lalauries] the
house remained vacant for many years. It fell into decay and disre-
pair. Its feral state was maintained by ghastly rumors. Many a solid
citizen swore that ungodly screams could be heard in the dark of
the moon. Witnesses came forth to testify that parades of mutilated
Negroes could be seen gliding along the creaking balconies. Or, that
a white woman with a whip accompanied by a blood-encrusted man
with wolf-like eyes could be glimpsed peering from the attic windows. Stories also circulated about vagrants who, seeking shelter in
the forbidden fortress, were never seen again—in one piece. . . .
[In the 1890s, after the waves of Sicilian immigration into the
city] almost as soon as the Italians had taken up residence [in the
Lalaurie house] then did a whole new generation of hauntings
appear. Men on their way to labor on the waterfront found their
mules and horses agonizingly butchered. Decapitated dogs and cats
appeared on the dark staircases. Children were occasionally attacked
by a white female phantom swinging a blood soaked whip. (Klein
1993, 10–11)[5]

Klein then retells the story of the Italian resident of the house, no longer
a fruit peddler but "a burly longshoreman" returning home from work and
meeting a black man in chains on the stairway.

THE HISTORICAL STORY OF MADAME LALAURIE

There are plenty of ghostly events, then, associated with the Lalaurie house,
though it is difficult to determine what forms these narrative elements have
taken as legends in oral tradition. The written accounts tend to be vague

or lean toward literary embellishment; writers like Jeanne deLavigne (who also published novels and short stories) may have even created some of the larger written narrative. The ghosts seem either to be black people or a threatening white woman, in at least one case identified as Madame Lalaurie and possibly otherwise assumed to be her. The ghosts stem from the historical events or historical legend of Madame Lalaurie—the events of 1834. Indeed, those events themselves have been the subject of various retellings and clearly were well known locally.

The accounts of the Lalaurie incident in some ways overshadow the ghost stories, and several important written accounts of the incident— by Harriet Martineau, Fredrika Bremer, George Washington Cable, and Henry Castellanos—have little or nothing to do with ghosts and hauntings. Even Lyle Saxon, who wrote to entertain a wide, popular audience, includes in his sixteen pages only that part about ghosts quoted above, a bare sentence—and Saxon seems rather disparaging of the supernatural side of the story at that. Martineau, whose writings appeared in 1838, mentions no ghosts. Cable, publishing in 1888, was aware that the Lalaurie house was the "haunted house," but he tells no ghost stories, and he mentions only metaphorical ghosts and the story of a woman who thinks she sees a mysterious figure in one window of the house only to realize after rational reflection that it is a trick of the moonlight. Castellanos, who published *New Orleans As It Was: Episodes of Louisiana Life* in 1895, mentions at the very end of his account that the house "has been named by some the 'Haunted House,'" and goes on to note that he has spoken to occupants of the house who say there certainly are no hauntings, no spirits who "wander through its wide halls and open corridors" (Castellanos [1895] 1961, 62). All of these writers concentrate on the events of 1834, giving similar accounts that only differ in the details. Lyle Saxon, in writing his 1928 account, had access to earlier published accounts, and what follows extensively quotes his recounting in *Fabulous New Orleans*, although it is based on other sources as well.

Delphine Maccarthy—or McCarty or Macarty—Lalaurie was a descendent of a prominent French family, originally Irish, and a person of high social standing in creole New Orleans. She married three times: to Ramon López y Ángulo, a Spanish colonial official; to Jean Blanque, a shady character involved in smuggling and slave-trading; and finally to Dr. Louis Lalaurie, who studied medicine in France and who was much younger than Delphine. Her first two husbands have been said to have died mysteriously, although this idea may stem only from the fact that their death records

FIGURE 1.3. Daguerreotype of a slave owner and an enslaved young woman, mid-1800s, New Orleans. (The Burns Archive, www.burnsarchive.com)

could not be found by earlier researchers; Long (2012, 33, 48) has located death records for both.

Evidently there were rumors circulating that Delphine mistreated her slaves. Except for a robust coachman, her slaves were noticed to be "surprisingly thin and hollow chested [who] moved like shadows, never raising their eyes" (Saxon [1928] 1943, 205), and there appears to have been a legal proceeding in which she was fined and had her slaves taken from her and sold, although she is said to have conspired with friends and relatives to have them returned to her. On one occasion a neighbor observed Delphine pursuing a small black child across the rooftop of her house with a whip in her hand, and then saw the child lose her footing and fall to her death in the courtyard below. According to Cable's account, this neighbor continued to observe and eventually saw adult slaves emerge and take away the tiny body and bury it in the courtyard. This story clearly relates to later ghost stories about the phantom child plunging from the roof.

Eventually, on the morning of April 10, 1834, a fire broke out in the Lalaurie house. According to Saxon, the cook, who was found chained in the kitchen, later admitted to setting the fire because Delphine was torturing her slaves and the cook "preferred to be burned alive rather than continue her life" under such circumstances (Saxon [1928] 1943, 209). But firemen arrived and neighbors and other citizens arrived to help. They burst into the house and began carrying out valuables as well as looking for the source of the fire and for people to assist. The Lalauries, when asked about the presence of slaves who might need to be rescued, responded with indifference and even hostility, as though the slaves did not matter so much as the valuables. Saxon writes:

> Mme. Lalaurie was at her best. She was composed, calm. She directed workers who were carrying out the handsome paintings, the bronzes, the brocades, the lighter pieces of furniture. She stood at the head of the stairs, near the carved door which lead into the main salon: "This way!" she cried, "this way, please! Yes, take that. . . . Oh, thank you!" And men went down the stairs, laden with beautiful things. Dr. Lalaurie was in the background. But he was there. The fact was testified to by many who saw him, including Judge Canonge [called Judge Canongo in other accounts], who gave out an interesting statement the same day.
>
> M. Montreuil, the same neighbor who had made a complaint against Mme. Lalaurie before [leading to the abovementioned legal proceeding], was present. He asked if the slaves were in danger from the fire. The Lalauries answered that he would be better if he did not meddle in the affairs of his neighbors. M. Montreuil then appealed to Judge Canonge. A Mr. Fernandez joined them. They made an attempt to reach the third story, but found locked doors barring their way. As Dr. Lalaurie refused to open the doors, these three men broke them down. Slaves were found mutilated, starved, bound down with chains. Now, let me quote from the newspaper of that day, "L'Abeille" (*The Bee*). The article is by Jerome Bayon, the editor:
> *We saw where the collar and manacles had cut their way into their quivering flesh. For several months they had been confined in those dismal*

dungeons, with no further nutriment than a handful of gruel and an insufficient quantity of water, suffering the tortures of the damned and longingly awaiting death as a relief from their sufferings. We saw Judge Canonge, Mr. Montreuil, and others, making for some time fruitless efforts to rescue these poor unfortunates, whom the infamous woman Lalaurie had doomed to certain death and hoping that the devouring element might thus obliterate the last traces of her nefarious deeds.

The search went on. Two negresses were brought out with heavy, spiked iron collars and irons on their feet; they could not walk, and were supported. An aged negress was found, bound in a kneeling position. She had been in this cramped posture for so long that she was hopelessly crippled. Her head had been laid open by a blow from a sharp instrument. (Saxon [1928] 1943, 209–210)

The slaves were taken to the Cabildo—the local building for government administration—for safekeeping and, according to Saxon, another local newspaper said that at least 2,000 people came to observe them there. A table in the jail yard, part of the Cabildo, held the instruments that had been used to torture them. According to other accounts, some of the rescued slaves died soon afterwards. Meanwhile, an irate mob gathered at the house, incensed at this inhumane treatment of slaves:

Late in the afternoon, the doors of the high-walled courtyard swung open, and the crowd in the street saw a carriage emerge. It came furiously forward, directly into the mob. The black horses plunged, and the men fell back before their hoofs. On the box was the mulatto coachman, lashing the horses. His whip fell across the faces of the men nearest him. And the horses plunged through and were gone, with a clatter of hoofs, out Hospital Street, toward Bayou Road [at the time Governor Nicholls Street was called Hospital Street, and it led directly into Bayou Road, the "shell road" that led out to Bayou St. John and Lake Pontchartrain]. (Saxon [1928] 1943, 213–214)

Delphine was in the coach; the coachman was her confederate and her spy among the slaves. The coach raced along Bayou Road, a thoroughfare used for fashionable outings, dashing past many out to enjoy the day and reaching the lake. There Delphine boarded a sailing vessel, a schooner according to some accounts, and the captain was bribed by the coachman to take off at once. Delphine sailed across to the north shore of the lake, where ten days later she executed a legal document giving her business affairs into the hands of someone with power of attorney. The coachman returned to the city, but he was met by the mob. Sources are uncertain as to the coachman's fate,[6] but the mob killed the horses and destroyed the coach. Then they broke into the house and virtually destroyed it and its furnishings until the sheriff arrived to restore order. The Lalauries abandoned the house and eventually sold it, and for many years the Lalaurie house sat in a ruined state.

The threatening ghost of a white woman is clearly meant to represent the evil Delphine Lalaurie, although Delphine's actual death has been shrouded in mystery—some traditions say that she died after being gored by a wild boar while hunting in France, where she was hiding out; others say she secretly returned to New Orleans and lived there quietly for a number of years; another states she died in France but was secretly buried in New Orleans.[7] The ghosts identified as African American are clearly those of the slaves who perished in the house, and rumors and legends of discovering bodies buried on the property have circulated at various times. Although ghosts are commonly conceived as bearing chains, the chained African American ghost encountered by a Sicilian on the Lalaurie stairway represents the literal chaining of slaves in the house.

The Lalaurie incident—the fire, the discovery of maltreated slaves, Delphine's exit, the sacking of the Lalaurie house—is a historical event described in contemporary newspaper accounts and in documents such as a statement by Judge Canonge, quoted by Saxon. But the event also entered the realm of hearsay, rumor, oral history, and legend. When English traveler Harriet Martineau came to New Orleans later in the 1830s, many people were able to tell her about the incident. She herself noticed the derelict mansion and, asking about it, got the story, eventually inquiring for further details from others (for her account, see Martineau 1838, 263–267). Saxon ([1928] 1943, 208) writes that "stories [about the house and the incident] have been told to me by old people who have heard them from their fathers." And Cable (1889, 193, 21) says that "fifty people in this old Rue Royale . . . can tell you their wild versions of this house's strange true story," and that the "history of the house is known to thousands in the old French quarter" (the second comment is drawn from Cable's discussion of how he came by the stories in his book).

Today ghost tour stories include the 1834 incident because of its presumed connection to the ghost legends, though evidently a popular variant

FIGURE 1.4. 1920 Frank Schneider painting of New Orleans "voodoo queen" Marie Laveau. (Louisiana State Museum, New Orleans)

of the story with the guides has it that the fire broke out at night while a grand party was taking place. The party may have even lingered in the street, the Lalaurie servants continuing to pass delicacies to the displaced guests. Of course, the idea of the party's continuing is further suggestive of Madame Lalaurie's indifference to the circumstances, including those that are about to undo her. But the nighttime setting for the fire seems appropriate to the time of day of the tours themselves, when guides set out with their groups into the comparative darkness of the French Quarter (which even today is lit by antique-looking street lamps). The physical darkness is a factor that suggests not only haunting but also the moral darkness associated with old New Orleans, whether it be Madame Lalaurie's supposed evil, the former existence of voodoo, the violence leading up to the deaths that produce haunting (the tour guides seem especially sensitive to accounts of violence), or slavery itself (which tourists may or may not be thinking of but is evoked by the guides' stories, which may remind those on the tours of the centrality of race in New Orleans).

In addition to the ghost stories about the house, other stories emerged about the Lalauries. It was said that slaves had been discovered who seemed to be the subject of hideous experiments, such as body parts being removed and reattached in grisly ways. Dr. Lalaurie, it was suggested, exercised his scientific curiosity by engaging in bizarre medical experiments (see Long 2012, 106ff.), possibly even experimenting with the use of zombie powder as a means of controlling slaves. And Delphine has been associated with that other famous frightening New Orleans woman, the "voodoo queen" Marie Laveau, who had given Madame a "devil baby," a hideous monster that Delphine cared for.[8]

PLACE, SOCIAL COMMENTARY, AND LEGEND

But why has the historical legend of the Lalaurie incident attracted so much attention? Why has it been one of the central stories of nineteenth-century New Orleans? The story is a dramatic one, full of rather grisly details and including a fortuitous escape and mob violence. But legends often are a form of social commentary, and I argue that the story is in fact a key comment on slavery, serving to express important attitudes toward the chattel bondage that was an essential element in New Orleans life up until the Civil War. It is a central story not because it is a dramatic tale about a historically unimportant Creole woman and her husband and household, but because it comments on a key historical issue and serves to say something about how a particular place, New Orleans, dealt with this issue, as well as to perhaps separate the city from a larger region, the slave-holding American South. That is, it is a story about place in the context of a particular historical situation—a historical situation that has significant moral implications— and it has had great appeal in that place for those very reasons.

Harriet Martineau, who had abolitionist sentiments, tells us that, even as she listened to the story in the late 1830s, she was asked "on the spot to *not* publish it as exhibiting a fair specimen of slaveholding in New Orleans" (Martineau 1838, 263; emphasis added). Cable, a New Orleans native and former Confederate cavalryman who developed sympathies toward African Americans that eventually contributed to his exile from his hometown, says "that a public practice [slavery] is answerable for whatever can happen easier with it than without it" (Cable 1889, 202). That is, the Lalaurie incident, with its details of oppressive cruelty, easily lends itself to an anti-slavery message, something Martineau's interlocutors feared she might present. But why, then, would the story continue to be so popular in New Orleans, where the institution of slavery was an important presence? The story would seem to be the narrative of an incident better forgotten, despite the appeal of its sensationalism and drama. Yet this was a story told to locals and outsiders alike, told till the present day. The reason for this, I suggest, lies in the great deal of attention the story gives to the local non-slave populace's insistence on providing humane treatment for slaves and its militant disapproval of the Lalauries doing otherwise.

Even before the events of April 1834, the Lalauries were suspected of mistreating their slaves, and neighbors tried to interfere.[9] Cable tells of a lawyer who sent his clerk to tell Delphine that she is suspected, hoping that she will mend her ways, though instead the young man is merely charmed by her. One account claims there was a legal proceeding after which her slaves are taken away from her; or, according to another account, she was at least fined for her reprehensible behavior.[10] When, during the fire, her true treatment of her slaves was discovered, not only did thousands go see the mistreated slaves, but an angry anti-Lalaurie mob formed that sought to bring Delphine and her husband to rough justice. "The rage of the crowd . . . was excessive," writes Martineau (1838, 266). When Delphine escaped, the mob was enraged and tried to pursue her, though without success. Later, the mob destroyed the coach, killed Delphine's fine horses, and ransacked and virtually destroyed her house; her daughters are said to have barely escaped the fury, but they too sneaked away.

Martineau (1838, 267) says the Lalaurie house "stands, and is meant to stand, in its ruined state," implying that it is left that way as a grim reminder, perhaps even a warning, to those who might mistreat their slaves. Indeed, Cable (1889) notes that, following the incident, some local citizens sought to warn others suspected of mistreating their slaves that they too could meet such a fate. Delphine herself remained a pariah who had to hide out in France. New Orleans was clearly full of people who wanted slaves treated properly and humanely and who even became enraged when the enslaved population was not so treated. The story shifted from one that was potentially about the horrors of slavery to one in which slavery was, perhaps uneasily, seen in a more positive light, at least so far as the situation in New Orleans.

As a place, New Orleans certainly has plenty to feel guilty about so far as slavery is concerned. Not only did the city exist as part of the larger slave-holding South, but it was a major emporium for slave trading, especially after states in the upper South, suffering from over-cultivation, began to sell off their enslaved populations into the Lower Mississippi Valley beginning in the late 1790s and continuing throughout much of the first half of the nineteenth century. A number of slave markets existed throughout the town, sometimes little more than places on the street where it was known slaves could be bought, although two of the major ones actually existed right in the confines of two important hotels, the St. Louis in the Vieux Carré and the St. Charles in the American section.[11] Solomon Northup wrote *Twelve Years a Slave* in 1853, and it was made into an Academy Award winning movie in 2013. It is one of the few published antebellum slave narratives from Louisiana—though, since Northup was a free man of color kidnapped into slavery, it is a somewhat atypical one. He writes of the slave pen

REBECCA, AUGUSTA and ROSA.
Slave Children from New Orleans

FIGURE 1.5. Slave children, New Orleans, 1863. (Albumen print carte-de-viste by M. H. Campbell)

in which he was held, most likely across the street from the St. Charles. Here he witnessed the "mournful scene" of a slave mother being forced to part from her children, and he notes slaves being kicked and threatened by whips cracking near them (see Northup [1853] 1991, 51–60).

In his earlier slave narrative, Henry Bibb ([1849] 2005) writes of being confined in a slave trader's "yard" in New Orleans "on the corner of St. Joseph Street," and of how the slaves being sold were beaten if they failed to present themselves in a manner that would contribute to their saleability; he also writes of his wife being taken away for a beating (61–62). Although the Lalauries may have been accused of mistreating their slaves, it was perfectly acceptable to punish slaves in various ways, including whipping them; indeed, slaves could be sent to the local jail by a master or mistress to be whipped, for a fee. Cable (1889) points out that the slaves supposedly seized from Delphine were hardly liberated but merely sold, something that enabled her to get them back. Certainly, any action taken against her was not meant to undermine the institution of slavery itself.[12] Christine Vella (1997, 18) notes that "a fear of [slave] revolt . . . obsessed" Louisiana, and—although she is referring to earlier, colonial times—there was a major revolt in 1811, well into the period of American control. Long (2012, 15) notes that fear of slave revolts gripped New Orleans in the late eighteenth century (as Delphine, born in 1787, was growing up), and the massive slave revolt in Saint-Domingue, Haiti, which began in 1791 and went on for many years, was much on the minds of people in Louisiana.

Hence, because slavery was not a benign institution, it seemed important to view it as such, and so it was seen. This was not limited to New Orleans, of course, but New Orleans has always viewed itself as a particularly cosmopolitan and unique place in the South. So far as slavery is concerned, New Orleans prominently had the *Code Noir* (1724) to regulate the institution, this having been a legal document going back to Spanish and French colonial times that was seen as insuring—to some degree—slaves' rights, although more stringent laws came into effect under American administration, laws "increasingly tilted toward repression" (Palmer 2009, 110). Both Cable and Saxon call attention to the provision of the *Code* that insists slaves must be "properly fed, clad, and provided for" and can complain to the attorney general if they are being subjected to "wrongs."[13]

Castellanos, though writing after the abolition of slavery, was born in 1827 and knew about slavery firsthand. "Slavery was a social device," he insists, "patriarchal in its character, not essentially tyrannical. The master was not unlike the 'pater familias' of the Roman Commonwealth" (Castellanos [1895] 1961, 61). That is, there was an idealized view of slavery that certainly prevailed after its abolition, and possibly before. The Lalaurie story, with its outraged mob rescuing mistreated slaves and demanding justice from those doing the mistreating, supports such a view and serves to assuage guilt felt over the existence of the real "peculiar institution." Although the story does not specifically suggest that slavery in New Orleans was different from and happier than that of the rest of the South, references in literary accounts to the local *Code Noir*, as well as those accounts calling attention particularly to actors with known French and Spanish Creole names, may reflect an attitude that New Orleans treated slaves better.

Certainly, the story serves to exonerate one place, New Orleans, from having maintained the horror of slavery by emphasizing local intolerance of masters who do not behave properly and humanely toward the enslaved. Because slavery had been abolished only the year before in the British Empire when Parliament passed the Abolition of Slavery Act in 1833, which stipulated that slavery would cease to exist within much of the Empire in 1834—including the British Caribbean Islands, with which Louisiana maintained close cultural and economic ties—New Orleanians might have felt particular anxiety over slavery and the treatment of slaves.

But why the ghost stories? "It's all about the *haunted* house, isn't it" write Love and Shannon (2011, 106; emphasis added); "That is why people visit the epicenter of the legend—they're hoping to see a ghost." Certainly the status of the Lalaurie house as haunted has kept interest in the historical legend alive; without the ghosts, the larger Lalaurie story, including the basis for the hauntings, conceivably might have been forgotten. However, I would argue that the ghosts are there for another important reason: because of what they communicate.

They are there to make the statement that New Orleans, the place, is indeed haunted by slavery. Though the centrality of slavery to antebellum New Orleans may be overlooked and conveniently ignored by local residents and present-day tourists alike (may be, so to speak, hidden in the attic like Madame Lalaurie's mistreated slaves), the ghosts are there to remind us of this and, indeed, of the horrors that slavery wrought. These ghosts, appearing at the most famous haunted place in the city, are clearly meant to be understood as those of mistreated slaves and of the white woman who brought about their mistreatment. They are standing in for the greater specter of what we understand today as a sinister institution, and for the horrors that were a part of it, something that, along with decades of post-slavery racism, literally haunts New Orleans in such arenas as local politics and social conditions.

The ghost legends—of a grown man chained, of a tiny girl who dies while trying to escape a whipping—symbolically express a "haunting" past to a particular place. It is no coincidence that the ghost stories probably post date the abolition of actual slavery, seeming to be more a phenomenon of the later nineteenth (and subsequent) centuries than of actual slavery times. That is, they come into play as an aspect of New Orleans memory, and they, in effect, explain why the exculpatory story of the mob seeking justice in the wake of Madame Lalaurie's transgressions has been so important to New Orleans.

As tourists became more significant as an element in New Orleans life, the city sought more and more to project a romantic self-image. The prior existence of slavery and the memory of it could interfere with that image. The legends of the Lalaurie house could, of course, add the romanticism of ghosts and even suggest the recognition of being haunted by slavery, but the historical traditions of Madame Lalaurie's exposure and the subsequent demand that slaves be treated humanely created a self-image that negated slavery's barbarity and established New Orleans as a civilized, kindly place. Hence, the legend became an important indicator of a more positive image, whether this was simply projected to outsiders or taken to heart by locals as part of an internalized sense of identity.

Of course, it is possible that the Lalaurie story has served a variety of purposes. At the time of the incident, the city's French Creoles—that is, those of French and Spanish descent who maintained the older, French-based culture and society—were feeling pressed by the arriving Americans, those flooding into the newly acquired Louisiana territory from the United States. There were years of conflict between these groups,[14] and the story may have served to suggest that Creoles expected better of slaveholders than did the arriviste Americans, or it may have suggested to the Americans that Latin Creoles, who needed to be socially displaced, were a cruel people who mistreated slaves. Whether either of these were the case is impossible to say without further information about who circulated the story, how, and what their actual attitudes were toward it. However, with the American acquisition of Louisiana, the slave laws operative in New Orleans were brought more in line with American law, whereas the old *Code Noir* (1724), with its provisions giving slaves certain minimal rights, is mentioned by writers on the Lalaurie incident (though it was not even operative in 1834). This might conceivably indicate a Creole desire to use the story to suggest their greater kindness toward slaves than the Americans could exhibit. Fredrika Bremer, the Swedish traveler whose book on her American sojourns appeared in English in 1853 and who wrote of the Lalaurie story that she heard in New Orleans (though she refers to "Madame Lallorue"), says that she was told the "severest slave-owners . . . are French" (249). Long (2012) says the French-language press in New Orleans was more critical of Madame Lalaurie than the English press, however.

It is also worth noting that the villain of the story is a woman, though the control of slavery and the general exercising of operations in the institution of slavery were in the male domain. Although several writers note that Delphine Lalaurie was thought to be charming and had a prominent social position, they also point out that she married a much younger man, and consequently may have been seen as a deviant woman. The use of the *charivari*, whereby gangs of men would provide a "rough" serenade with raucous music and other noise to a newlywed couple when the match was publically thought inappropriate because of the respective ages of the bride and groom, was not uncommon in New Orleans (de Caro 1990). By shifting the blame for cruelty to a woman, who might be thought deviant anyway, the story does tend to relieve the burden of guilt from the white men who were actually most involved in slavery.

Bremer notes that in South Carolina she was told (1853, 243) that women were known to be "the cruelest slave-owners"; of course such a statement might represent merely the same attempt to pass the burden of guilt from the men who were most involved. Long (2012, 74) states that such sources as "family letters, travelers' accounts, newspaper stories, and court cases from the colonial period until just before the Civil War . . . indicate that Creole women were most likely to mistreat their bondspeople." However, it may simply be that Madame Lalaurie had her misdeeds publicly revealed and her mangled slaves actually put on display; surely this was at least a factor in her becoming a symbol of slavery's horrors.

However, the Lalaurie story is clearly about slavery itself. Though not the case in the Lalaurie narrative, legends of cruel masters who are punished by what appear to be supernatural means are not uncommon. In another Louisiana legend recorded by the Louisiana Writers' Project and noted in *Gumbo Ya-Ya* (Saxon, Dreyer and Tallant 1945), for example, a master who hanged a number of his slaves is found dead, floating in the air and looking as though he himself has been hanged. Though the Lalauries are not punished by ghosts, legends of the ghosts of slaves haunting places because of the ill treatment that slavery spawned are by no means limited to New Orleans, a fact that suggests the Lalaurie legends are part of a larger trend by which ghost stories can be used to call attention to the horrors of slavery and how we are still haunted by a past that has not simply been left behind. For example, George Carey (1971) recorded a Maryland legend from a white woman who lived in a house haunted by Aunt Betsy, "an old slave who was chained and beaten until she died right in the basement here," where there was actually a whipping post. Among other things, Aunt Betsy drags her chain down the front steps of the house.[15]

Some supernatural legends are not tied to a specific place—though the Maryland ghost does, like the Lalaurie ghosts, haunt a particular house. Haunting in and of itself does, of course, imply a connection to place, the place where the ghosts are encountered. The Lalaurie house is a particular place that, like other haunted sites, has ghosts. But the Lalaurie story is tied to place in a larger sense, as embodying the most widely known ghost story in New Orleans and the best-known haunted site in the city. By calling attention to the ghosts of people injured and killed because of slavery, these ghosts stories are a statement that this city is "haunted" by slavery, an institution that may be gone but whose results and whose memory linger in important ways.

The "historical" Lalaurie story, which provides the background for the haunting, probably predates the ghost stories by some years. Not only did the events recounted in this story have to happen as a precondition to the ghosts, but this story had to become well-known as a narrative—indeed, that part of the story was well-known when Martineau visited the Crescent City only a few years after the events of 1834.

Because the historical story became important as a statement that New Orleans did try to mitigate slavery by insisting on the humane treatment of slaves, the ghost stories exist to remind us that this place is nonetheless haunted by that very slavery and its horrors. The community outrage that was part of the historical incident—or, at any rate, the narrative about it—stands as a sort of counternote to the moral darkness that the ghosts remind us of and that the ghost tours may evoke in the literal darkness. There is a kind of duality in which the place is projected as titillatingly evil but nonetheless having a moral center that caused citizens to stand up to assert the rights of an oppressed population. However, these ghost stories connect to and play on the earlier narrative, amplifying historical events by using the supernatural to indicate how those events (and the institution from which they stemmed) continue to haunt a whole city, haunt with a memory not merely of particular events in 1834 but of an evil way of life.

NOTES

1. S. Frederick Starr suggests that the writer Lafcadio Hearn "invented" the romantic image of New Orleans that has appealed to locals and tourists alike (see Starr 2001). Hearn came to New Orleans in 1878 and stayed about ten years. Although he published *Some Chinese Ghosts* (Hearn 1887) while in New Orleans, he did not take any great note of New Orleans ghosts; however see *Occidental Gleanings* for more of the supernatural (Hearn 1925, 192ff.).
2. It has been pointed out that, despite its subtitle, this book is not a collection of folktales at all, but rather a popular account of folklore and life in Louisiana,

particularly in New Orleans. For discussion of the book, see de Caro and Jordan (2004, 73ff.).

3. In their recently published book about Madame Lalaurie, Love and Shannon (2011, 109) say they "have been unable to verify that General Butler used the Lalaurie mansion as his headquarters." Benjamin Butler was the Union commander in occupied New Orleans. Love and Shannon do not mention the possibility that the house was used for gambling in the 1870s, but they do note that the house became a school for girls around 1872. Carolyn Morrow Long (2012, 157ff), whose scholarly work on Lalaurie should be seen as definitive, does not list a Union headquarters or a gambling den, but she does note the school in 1872. Because the school admitted students of African descent, it became a focus for controversy and even assault by whites.

4. No editors are actually listed for the volume, though Saxon and Dreyer both signed the preface as the state director and assistant state director of the Louisiana Writers' Project. The only personal name appearing on the title page is that of New Orleans mayor Robert Meastri as "co-operating sponsor."

5. In his second volume, Klein (1999, 3) complains that Jeanne deLavigne's book did not seem "an anthropologically significant effort . . . [and] included no bibliography, footnotes nor index"; in Klein's first book he had all three, including, he points out, 131 notes. Although Klein indicates his fondness for library research, his sources are not always clearly cited; he did, however, speak with informants.

6. According to Long (2012, 113–114), the coachman may simply have been sold by Madame Lalaurie's agents and manumitted late in life by a subsequent owner.

7. Long (2012) found Delphine Lalaurie's death records in France, where she died in 1849, and determined that her body was later returned to New Orleans and probably interred in St. Louis No. 1 cemetery in a tomb owned by the family of her son, Paulin Blanque; the cemetery burial records for the relevant year no longer exist, however.

8. Jeanne deLavigne (1946, 52–66) recounts another ghost story, which she dates to 1893, as being set in the Lalaurie mansion, though it seems to have no connection to Madame Lalaurie.

9. Mary Gehman (1988, 37–38), citing research done by journalist Meigs Frost in the 1930s, suggests that a single neighbor, a relative of Delphine, who was involved in a financial dispute with her may have "planted rumors about mistreatment of slaves." Long (2012, 103–5), however, indicates that Frost's determination of the facts was "inaccurate" and "mistaken."

10. I say "claims" because, though this is part of the Lalaurie story as recounted by Cable and Saxon, I have seen no documentation of an actual proceeding. Cable (1889, 205) says that "an investigation was made, and some legal action was taken against Madame Lalaurie for cruelty to her slaves," but he does not cite any records. Saxon ([1928] 1943, 207) says only that "the court record is vague," suggesting that he has seen some sort of record, but he does not quote it or indicate its location. Long (2012, 84ff), a talented student of Louisiana historical documents, indicates that the records for the relevant court and years no longer exist, but she argues that several sources make it clear that Madame Lalaurie was suspected of odious behavior toward her slaves. Long also discovered a receipt from noted attorney John Randolph Grymes, acknowledging receiving

payment for having defended her in the relevant criminal court in 1829. Long does conclude that Delphine Lalaurie mistreated her slaves.

11. The Swedish traveler Frederika Bremer describes her visit to New Orleans slave markets in her 1853 work *The Homes of the New World: Impressions of America*, reprinted in de Caro and Jordan (1998, 195–99).

12. Cable (1889) notes that the initiative to warn others who were reputedly cruel to their slaves petered out because of the fear that the slaves might "be thereby encouraged to seek by violence those rights which their masters thought it not expedient to give them" (217).

13. The *Code Noir* (1724) contained the French colonial law regarding slavery. In 1806–1807, the American Territorial Legislature passed three statutes that came to be collectively called "the Black Code." Cable (1889, 204) quotes from the colonial code, which would not have been in force in the 1830s, and Saxon may have also had this outdated version of the *Code* in mind.

14. However, Vella (1997, 269) suggests that stories of Creole–American conflict are more "myth" than history.

15. The Maryland legend appears in Carey (1971, 7); it was also reprinted in de Caro (2009, 198–99). Additionally, Zora Neale Hurston (1931) published a legend about a Georgia planter who kills a young black servant (this seems to be set in post-slavery times) in a fit of pique when she "sasses" him. He is then punished through magical means by the girl's father, who practices hoodoo and who pursues the planter as he flees to several places (it appears in Hurston 1931, 408–10). The "hanged" planter story appears in Saxon, Dreyer, and Tallant (1945, 234); it was reprinted in de Caro (2009, 229–247). All of these legends suggest that folk narratives of the supernatural have been used, whether by whites or by African Americans, to call attention to the horrors of slavery and racism.

WORKS CITED

Bibb, Henry. [1849] 2005. *Narrative of the Life and Adventures of Henry Bibb, an American Slave*. Mineola, NY: Dover Publications.

Bremer, Fredrika. 1853. *The Homes of the New World: Impressions of America*, vol. 2. Translated by Mary Howitt. New York: Harper and Brothers.

Cable, George Washington. 1889. *Strange True Stories of Louisiana*. New York, NY: Scribner's.

Carey, George. 1971. *Maryland Folk Legends and Folk Songs*. Centreville, MD: Tidewater Publishers.

Castellanos, Henry C. [1895] 1961. *New Orleans As It Was: Episodes of Louisiana Life*. New Orleans, LA: Pelican.

de Caro, Frank. 1990. "Charivari in Nineteenth-Century New Orleans." *Louisiana Folklore Miscellany* 6.3:78–83.

———, ed. 2009. *An Anthology of American Folktales and Legends*. Armonk, NY: M. E. Sharpe.

———, ed., and Rosan Augusta Jordan, assoc. ed. 1998. *Louisiana Sojourns: Travelers' Tales and Literary Journeys*. Baton Rouge, LA: Louisiana State University Press.

————, and Rosan Augusta Jordan. 2004. *Re-Situating Folklore: Folk Contexts in Twentieth-Century Literature and Art.* Knoxville, TN: University of Tennessee Press.

deLavigne, Jeanne. 1946. *Ghost Stories of Old New Orleans.* New York, NY: Rinehart.

Gehman, Mary. 1988. *Women and New Orleans: A History,* second edition. Photography Nancy Ries. New Orleans, LA: Margaret Media.

Hearn, Lafcadio. 1887. *Some Chinese Ghosts.* Boston, MA: Roberts Brothers.

————. 1925. *Occidental Gleanings,* vol. 1. Edited by Albert Mordell. New York: Dodd, Mead.

Hurston, Zora Neale. 1931. "Hoodoo in America." *Journal of American Folklore* 44: 317–417.

Klein, Victor C. 1993. *New Orleans Ghosts.* Chapel Hill, NC: Lycanthrope Press.

————. 1999. *New Orleans Ghosts II.* Metairie, LA: Lycanthrope Press.

Long, Carolyn Morrow. 2012. *Madame Lalaurie: Mistress of the Haunted House.* Gainesville, FL: University Press of Florida.

Louisiana's Code Noir (1724). www.blackpast.org/primary/Louisianas-code-noir-1724, section XX.

Love, Victoria Cosner, and Lorelei Shannon. 2011. *Mad Madame Lalaurie: New Orleans' Most Famous Murderess Revealed.* Charleston, SC: The History Press.

Martineau, Harriet. 1838. *Retrospect of Western Travel,* vol. 2. London, UK: Sanders and Otley.

"New Orleans City Guide." 1938. Boston: Houghton Mifflin.

Northup, Solomon. [1853] 1991. *Twelve Years a Slave,* edited by Sue Eakin and Joseph Logsdon. Baton Rouge, LA: Louisiana State University Press.

Palmer, Vernon Valentine. 2009. "The Strange Science of Codifying Slavery—Moreau Lislet and the Louisiana Digest of 1808." *Tulane European and Civil Law Forum* 24: 83–113.

Saxon, Lyle. [1928] 1943. *Fabulous New Orleans,* illustrated by E. H. Suydam. New York: D. Appleton-Century.

————, Edward Dreyer, and Robert Tallant, eds. 1945. *Gumbo Ya-Ya: A Collection of Louisiana Folk Tales.* Boston: Houghton Mifflin.

Starr, S. Frederick, ed. 2001. *Inventing New Orleans: Writings of Lafcadio Hearn.* Jackson, MS: University Press of Mississippi.

Vella, Christina. 2004. *Intimate Enemies: The Two Worlds of the Baroness de Pontalba.* Baton Rouge, LA: Louisiana State University Press.

Which Witch is *Witch*?

Salem, Massachusetts

JEANNIE BANKS THOMAS

When the local high school proudly proclaims that it is the "Home of the Witches," you know you're not in just any small American town. You are in Salem, Massachusetts, where the supernatural can be both good business and also a conflicted aspect of local identity. Things certainly do get a little spooky/odd in the Witch City. For example, the mayor gets the same offbeat request from romantically inclined tourists every October: "Will you marry us? We want to be married in Salem. On Halloween. In the cemetery."

Kate Fox, executive director of Destination Salem—part of the Salem Office of Tourism and Cultural Affairs—told me that, for the benefit of an international television crew who wanted to do more than film a Wiccan in plainclothes, she once called a friend in the witch community and said, "I need a witch in full drag. C'mon down!" He did (personal interview 2009).

Erik Rodenhiser, a local businessman, worries that he won't be able to take his kids trick-or-treating because of Halloween demands on his theater business. The city council ponders whether theater companies can give tours in hearses and how close storefront haunted houses should be to each other.

Meanwhile, contemporary witches zip around on Segways, and college-student actors in 1692 garb arrest Bridget Bishop on the streets of Salem every weekday in the fall and try her as a witch in the Old Town Hall.

FIGURE 2.1. Sign at Salem High School. (Photo by Jeannie Banks Thomas)

In 2005, Salem hosted a Harry Potter conference, which included an all-day Quidditch tournament on the Salem Common. In 2009, a witch "school" in Illinois packed up and left town, seeking refuge in Salem because a "group of militant Christians had given them hell"—they hoped to find a more tolerant environment in Salem (Bartosik 2009). Salem was also the venue for GhoStock in 2012. GhoStock (2012) is a "hands-on, interactive . . . boutique" gathering for paranormal enthusiasts that advertised its Salem gathering by asking the question, "Tired of paranormal conferences where you sit in a dark lecture hall all day?"

INVASIVE NARRATIVES

This chapter takes as its subject the relationship between legend, place, tourism, and the supernatural. Specifically, the chapter outlines some of the complexities of Salem witch tourism, including how a particular type of narrative has shaped the place. It also considers the question: Why do the witch legends (and the resulting tourism) generate conflict in and critiques of the town? To explore these matters, this chapter draws on participant observation, several informal interviews, and four interviews conducted with Salem residents who make their living in the city's tourism industry.

The witch stories that are so common in Salem, and that shape its tourism, are what I call "invasive narratives." In this context, "invasive" draws its meaning from the straightforward dictionary definition of the term, not from the more specialized biological uses of the term. By "invasive" I simply mean "tending to spread."[1] An invasive narrative is not a story that locals live *by*; rather, it is a story that locals have to live *with*, whether they like it or not. These are the stories that threaten to take over a place—and sometimes they do. They are often homegrown; they spread to a notable and perhaps obnoxious degree. They can also move beyond local and regional boundaries.

Once they have a hold in an area, invasive narratives take root. They don't go away, they are not always easy to deal with, and they usually require that locals grapple with them in one way or another. For example, in Salem, the invasive and pervasive nature of the witch stories is recognized in the "Witch City" nickname, and the locals also say things such as, "We don't want to be known as *just* the Witch City" (Boston Globe 2014; emphasis added).

Invasive stories bear some resemblance to viral videos in that they spread rapidly and command people's attention. However, unlike viral videos, they tend to be more strongly rooted in a place, and they stay in an environment, often lasting longer in the local mind than viral videos last in the popular mind. The Internet can spread invasive legends, but the stories don't rely on the Internet for their existence. Invasive narratives were told before the Internet was created. Stories and legends associated with the witch trials and executions of 1692 have been a part of Salem's landscape for over 300 years.

These invasive witch narratives shape tourist events in Salem, including Haunted Happenings, which is the town's "family friendly" celebration of Halloween that runs for the entire month of October (Thomas 2011). In 2005, Haunted Happenings brought me to the door of a storefront museum, which was really a commercial haunted house. At that time, it was called the Museum of Hawthorne and Poe Soon after, the museum gave up on Hawthorne entirely, and then got rid of Poe. Ultimately, a new owner purchased the building, and it became "Count Orlok's Nightmare Gallery."[2] When I peered into the business on that particular fall day and realized that my museum experience would consist of struggling through a series of dark rooms punctuated by strobe lights and ear-melting screams, I decided I was just too old for this kind of high-decibel, low-budget scare factory, which I associated with the auditory carelessness of youth.

However, I later realized that, since this form of business was such an important part of Salem's autumnal landscape, I should experience it for the sake of folklore studies. So the next day, I summoned my courage and trudged back to Hawthorne and Poe through a sufficiently gloomy New England rain. I paid for my adult admission (what the current business calls the "Adult Creature" price; "Creature Spawn" under the age of five are free). As I did so, I imagined that I would be surrounded by tweens and teens ("Spawn") who'd be wondering who let the middle-aged mom ("Creature") out of suburbia and into the land of horror. Instead, I found something much more unexpected: middle-aged women like myself. We, instead of teenagers, were queued up for the museum that day. I hadn't imagined that I would have an age-appropriate cohort in the Scream-O-Rama. To the contrary, I expected goth kids to visit Salem in quiet but intense hearse-loads. I now realize that visitors of all kinds are often drawn to Salem due to the ability of its witch narrative to spread across the country via history books, Hawthorne's novels, television and movies, the Internet, and tourist promotions.

I asked the woman in line next to me why she came. She looked at my grim but game companion, who was still dripping from trekking through the hard October rain, sized me up, and finally said, "You *made* him come, didn't you?" I nodded. Then she told me that she thought it would be *fun* to be in Salem for Haunted Happenings, and fun is certainly what the festival promises.

SUPERNATURAL TOURISM

Fun. That is not the first word that comes to mind when one contemplates "hanging by the neck until dead," which is what happened to nineteen of Salem's accused witches in 1692—another victim was pressed to death. While this is the actual fate of the innocent people accused of witchcraft, sometimes the contemporary supernatural tourism industry does not demonstrate any fidelity to this story. My Museum of Hawthorne and Poe experience was my first and very obvious clue that local tourism can play fast and loose with Salem's ties to the supernatural. Sometimes the town's witch association operates as a gateway narrative to the larger category of horror stories—and any horror story will do, from Poe to vampires.

Some historians refer to the historical events that led to the construction of Salem's "Witch City" identity as the Essex County witch accusations of 1692. They are more accurately pointing out that many communities—not just Salem—in an entire Massachusetts county became involved in taking legal action against over 144 accused witches within the span of about four months (Norton 2004, 3–4). Despite this tragic history, today many people are drawn to Salem by fun—even if it's slightly dark fun with a somber historical basis.

Such ramblings are called dark tourism, which refers to the practice of traveling to sites of death, disaster, and even the macabre (Seaton 1996, 240–42; Stone 2006, 147). That some historical tourism sites are "dark" should not come as a surprise. As we well know, history is not sunshine, butterflies, and kittens. My daughter once made this point succinctly to me; she noted that she liked math more than history. Expressing surprise, I asked why, and she replied, "Nobody ever dies in math, but in history, it's just one horrible thing after another." The Western construction of history does place a strong emphasis on the massively bloody (battles, disasters) and the grimly tragic (witch trials).

Scholars John Lennon and Malcolm Foley posit that dark tourism emerges out of relatively contemporary places that shake our faith in our ability to humanely use the products of the modern world, including science, technology, industry, and mass communication. Their examples of dark tourist sites include concentration camps and other World War II sites, and you can see why: the creations of the modern world—science, technology, industry, and mass communication—all came together powerfully and heinously at these sites for the purpose of committing what was often state-sanctioned murder (2010, 11, 12, 27).

Lennon and Foley draw careful distinctions, and they are also interested in showing how dark tourism reflects our anxieties about modern life (2010, 21). Salient stuff. But their formulation also leaves us with a bit of a problem. Sites that are not modern, as in pre-twentieth-century locales, don't make their dark tourism list. Out go all battlefields and places like Salem, despite the fact that they, too, are examples of sites of state murder or

FIGURE 2.2. Dark tourism in Salem. (Photo by Jeannie Banks Thomas)

mayhem—which, like their twentieth-century variants, were also typically accomplished using the best technologies of the day that the locals could muster. So, how are we to refer to these sites and their accompanying traditions of visitation? Dark but dusty—and therefore less anxiety-producing—tourism? With apologies to Lennon and Foley, it can all be called dark tourism.

A. V. Seaton asserts that dark tourism is rooted in the traditions associated with the contemplation of death. He dates it to at least the Middle Ages and notes that it received a boost from nineteenth-century romanticism (1996, 240). Following Seaton and Philip R. Stone's work (2006, 151), I recognize that there are many shades of dark tourism, and varying levels of anxiety, sensitivity, insensitivity, education, and entertainment associated with such sites. Here, I return to one of the subjects of this chapter: What are the complexities of Salem tourism—particularly, how does tourism use Salem's invasive witch legends? Salem draws on dark tourism in its presentation of the local legends for profit, but some of the Salem stories are sometimes not so dark. Overall, Salem, I think, is a kind of threadbare, dark, tweedy,

New England grey—except in October, when it is a deliberate, bright, happy, Halloween orange.

I call much of what I see happening in Salem—especially Haunted Happenings—simply "supernatural tourism." This term is meant to be broad. I intend it to encompass a wide swath of sites that draw tourists primarily due to supernatural associations. Such places also prompt a variety of tourists, ranging from true believers (see Goldstein 2007a, 205) to those who trivialize, scoff at, or don't even consider belief in any fashion.

TOURIST THEMES

Despite the fact that it has very few extant structures and sites associated with the Essex County Witch Trials of 1692, Salem is most recognized by tourists for the trials, according to Kate Fox's market research. "Witch City" as a designation for Salem began appearing in the late-nineteenth century (Hill 2004, 284). Hawthorne's work in the mid-nineteenth century drew people's attention to Salem and, in 1856, what was in effect the city's first touring guide appeared, which included mention of Gallows Hill (Gencarella 2007, 273).

Entrepreneurs produced witch-related souvenirs in the 1860s and 1870s and published a "Visitor's Guide" to Salem in the 1880s (Gencarella 2007, 273–74). A film version of *The Scarlet Letter* appeared in 1926, and other movies followed, including *Maid of Salem* (1937), *The House of Seven Gables* (1940 and 1951), and *I Married a Witch* (1942), which was one of the movies that inspired the 1960-70s television series, *Bewitched*. In 2014, the WGN network launched a series called *Salem*, which is based loosely on Salem's witch history and involves much ahistorical smoldering, presumably to keep the ratings up.

The high school adopted its witch mascot in the late 1930s and early 1940s (McAllister 2000, 126; personal interview 2014). Also in the 1940s, a group of residents formed Historic Salem, Inc., a nonprofit dedicated to preserving historic buildings, including the only existing Salem building with a direct connection to the witch trials: the former home of trial judge Jonathan Corwin. Today, the city's tourism centers around the witch trials, maritime history, arts and culture, and Halloween.

The witch trials tourism theme emerged in the 1950s, when the family who owned the site of the old town jail built a replica of the dungeon where

FIGURE 2.3. Corwin home, Salem. Also known as "The Witch House," even though its owner was a judge and not one of the accused during the Salem trials. (Photo by Jeannie Banks Thomas)

the accused witches were held (Hill 2004, 284). The 1950s also brought Arthur Miller to town to do background research on what became one of his most famous plays, *The Crucible*, which is about the Salem witch persecutions and is also famously a commentary on McCarthyism and the communist witch hunts.

In the 1970s, Salem appeared in two episodes of the television show *Bewitched*, giving the city national television exposure. Also during this era, well-known neo-pagan Laurie Cabot moved to Salem and was dubbed "the official witch of Salem" by Massachusetts governor Michael Dukakis. Finally, in 1992, the town created an official memorial to the victims of the witch trials.

Nearby Danvers, Massachusetts, which was called "Salem Village" in 1692 (today's Salem was then known as "Salem Town"), has several structures and

FIGURE 2.4. Sign advertising a performance of *The Crucible*, Salem. (Photo by Jeannie Banks Thomas)

sites associated with the witch trials, including the stone foundations of the Reverend Parris' parsonage, where the first young girls, cousins Betty Parris and Abigail Williams, were pronounced bewitched by a local doctor (Roach 2002, 18). Tituba, one of the first women accused of being a witch, also lived in this household. Not too far from the parsonage is the restored farm of accused witch Rebecca Nurse. Despite these compelling sites and others, Danvers is not as heavily associated with witch tourism as Salem. According to Kate Fox (personal interview 2009), because Salem actively promotes tourism and Danvers has some of the big motels that Salem tourists stay in, it receives many benefits from Salem tourism—especially the motel tax— without having to hustle as overtly for tourists as Salem does.

Fox, who along with her tourism duties also serves on the "psychic licensing committee" for the town, says that Salem's market research makes it clear that the witch trials are the main reason that most tourists and hundreds of school children studying American history come to Salem, which speaks to the tenacity of this particular invasive narrative. Tourism officials in Salem don't have to try to generate an identity for the town as a tourist attraction. Nor do they need to create the desire within people to visit Salem. It's already there; Salem's witch story is firmly instilled in the public imagination. Fox says,

> If you're coming for the witch trials, I hope you leave knowing that they were innocent people, that it was a hysteria, and that we have hysterias today. Salem Witch Museum has a great wall that talks about the witch hunt, the ingredients of a witch hunt, and [it] makes the connections to contemporary time. So I hope people leave with those lessons of tolerance. . . . So, that's the lesson from the Salem witch trials: that this is human nature, and it's a society issue that we need to be aware of. (Personal interview 2009)

The city is also interested in being recognized for its maritime history and as an arts and culture destination.[3] Part of Fox's job is to try to raise the profile of the themes that are less well known than the witch trials, which is a kind of battle with (or a way of pruning back) Salem's invasive witch legends ("We don't want to be known as *just* the Witch City."). According to Fox, the maritime era in Salem was actually more historically significant than the trials because it lasted longer, had an important impact on America during the Revolutionary War, and also influenced the growth of the nation (see Goss 1999, 19–26): "We do have the working waterfronts and the Salem Maritime National Historic Site, which was the first national historic site in the country that was designated when everything—[such as] national parks—being designated were natural resources" (personal interview 2009).

While it has a significant collection of 1692 witch documents and artifacts in its Phillips Library, Salem's Peabody Essex Museum focuses on arts and culture from New England and around the world. Its mission includes celebrating "outstanding artistic and cultural creativity by collecting, stewarding and interpreting objects of art and culture" (Peabody Essex 2012). Salem is also the birthplace of Nathaniel Hawthorne and the home of the House of Seven Gables, which he made famous in his book by the same title. Today, the house operates as a tourist attraction. Salem is renowned for its First Period (homes built before 1725), Georgian Colonial (approximately 1726–1790), and Federal (1780–1820) architecture, as well as for its incorporation of Chinese motifs—the influence of its maritime history—into its architecture (Goff 2004, 185).

FIGURE 2.5. Costumed witch advertising a photo shop. (Photo by Jeannie Banks Thomas)

Finally, Halloween is one of the city's major tourism themes. As discussed earlier, during the month of October, Salem hosts Haunted Happenings. This event was started in 1982 (Hill 2004, 287), and it was in
part prompted by urban legends about tainted Halloween candy (see Ellis
1994, 28; Grider 1984) and parents' worries about their children trick or
treating. Kate Fox says, "Haunted Happenings was . . . a Saturday event
on Salem Common for children to come and have Halloween in a safe environment." The festival eventually took over the entire month. Fox believes
that American and international interest in celebrating Halloween (Rogers

2002, 6) drove the success of Haunted Happenings: "It's that business, it's that traveler [who is interested in Halloween] who created Haunted Happenings the way it is now. It's not Salem" (personal interview 2009).

Haunted Happenings doesn't derive solely from the historical tragedy of Salem, and that is the point. It does draw on the witch narrative, but it celebrates an entirely different aspect of the Salem witch: the supernatural, fun side of her as depicted in contemporary American consumer culture and lore (Santino 1996, 92). Salem's invasive witch legend allows passage to a kind of tourism that looks at the lighter side of witches and Halloween.

SIMULACRUM TRIPPING

Not surprisingly, when Salem's dark tourism collides with a spooky holiday like Halloween, things can get a little out of control. Consequently, Haunted Happenings has seen its share of controversy. Erik Rodenhiser notes that it makes parking in Salem during the month of October nearly impossible, much to the annoyance of the town's citizens. Locals complain about the misbehavior and crime that can accompany Haunted Happenings, and Kate Fox says that not all of Salem's mayors have supported the festival. Noting that Halloween falls right before Election Day, she says one mayor "lost the election because it was a really bad Halloween. There was crime, there was violence, there was public drinking; people were peeing on the mansions, and it was awful. He was pro-tourism. The common assumption is he lost that election because Halloween night was horrible." The mayor who won that election did not support Haunted Happenings, but Fox describes a mayor who did:

> We actually have planning meetings with police and public works and the MBTA to ensure that we have transportation, safety, and cleanup throughout the month. We provide the public toilets, you know, the portable toilets. We work with it . . . thus we actually document making money from it, so we can say to the residents, "This is a horrible inconvenience for four weekends of the year but it is generating money for the city, and we are doing the best with it that we can."
>
> And now we have also really focused on the marketing of Haunted Happenings as a family Halloween celebration. . . . We've seen a change in our audience on Halloween night and throughout

the month. You know, we've seen more day trippers coming in and bringing their kids in costume all the weekends of the month. So, embracing it has been very successful. . . . Prior to Destination Salem being involved with Haunted Happenings, it was run by private business people who did it to make their own money, which wasn't a great model because then you didn't have any communication between the marketing and the public safety and public works.

I think we've gotten caught up so that we have a good model. But, Haunted Happenings grew itself. It was the visitors and the customers that kept coming, and so the businesses kept expanding. . . . So, I hope when people come for Haunted Happenings, and they come for their ghost tours and the haunted houses and the costumes, that they do get a chance to learn about the witch trials, and that they're able to take off the mask to absorb some of the information from what happened here. And that they leave a little bit wiser. Haunted Happenings is not about 1692. (Personal interview 2009)

City officials addressed the chaos that emerged by making the holiday less dark and more orange, as befits Halloween. Fox says the city worked to make Haunted Happenings family friendly through the coordination of the groups involved. The festival is often successful, particularly if the weather is nice and Halloween falls on a weekend (Rice 2011); in previous years it has generated nearly nine million dollars for the local economy (Forman 2010). It has drawn as many as 250,000 revelers and tourists (Forman 2010). According to Fox, even during two years of economic downturn (2009–2010), it made money (Fox 2010).

It is not just that Haunted Happenings is seen as inappropriate and bothersome by some locals; other issues come up around Salem's painful history and its tourism. Stephen Olbrys Gencarella says, "The tension over tourism is as much a part of Salem's history as the Trials or Hawthorne or its maritime grandeur" (2007, 282).

The town's reliance on the witch figure in its tourist industry is controversial. For example, the 2005 dedication of a statue of Samantha from the *Bewitched* television series gave rise to commonly heard charges that the town sacrifices history on the altar of crass commercialism (Dalton and Burke 2005). Some locals approached the statue with the question that the locally sold t-shirts raise, "Are you a good witch or a bad witch?" Weighing in for the bad witch argument were residents who found the bronzed

FIGURE 2.6. *Bewitched* statue. (Photo by Jeannie Banks Thomas)

FIGURE 2.7. Salem t-shirts. (Photo by Jeannie Banks Thomas)

Samantha offensive and trivializing of those killed as witches. The *Salem News* captured their comments:

> The unveiling of the city's newest art work—and controversy—spurred an impromptu debate on Washington Street between local witches, dressed in black hats and robes, who love the statue, and residents of the city's historic neighborhoods, decked out in sport coats and bow ties, who hate it.
>
> A mass of media and TV cameras fled the press platform in an effort to catch every word.
>
> "We don't make fun of the Holocaust," said Bill Burns, who lives in the McIntire Historic District. "Why are we making fun of (the people who died in the Witch Trials)?". . .
>
> Sign-holder Meg Twohey . . . said, "There's a lot of wonderful history in Salem, and Samantha is not a part of that.". . . But Christian Day, a local witch, countered to an onlooker: "This is all about fun. People come to Salem to have a good time." (Dalton and Burke 2005)

The charge of crassness for cash and tourism is not, of course, limited to the statue. It has long been an issue in Salem, perhaps most notably seen in the film *Witch City* (1997), which critiques the insensitive ways the city turns its history into profit. Also, in a thoughtful essay, Bridget Marshall says that Salem "capitalizes on its haunted history at the same time that it distorts and evades that history" (2004, 244). However, Salem's story is complex, and it is much more than a simple account of dark tourism for cold cash.

One way of understanding Salem involves realizing that Salem doesn't only tell the stories of the accused witches' tragic deaths (which it does in abundance); it also holds an ongoing, messy, and commercialized wake for them. What is overlooked about Salem—but worthy of attention—is the manner in which it breaks down symbolic boundaries between solemnity and the festive (see Thomas 2011 for more on this topic). On Salem's streets, especially during Haunted Happenings, death meets lightheartedness. The city's tragic association with the witch trials and deaths exists cheek by jowl with the contemporary—and often playful—remaking and marketing of the figure of the witch.

So, a stroll on the downtown Salem mall will take you to the *Bewitched* statue, while a slight detour to the north will bring you to the Witch Trials Memorial. Such sites are liberally interspersed with the shops of various New Age practitioners, some of which are decorated with bumper stickers that say things such as, "In Goddess We Trust," "Eve was Framed," "Witches are Crafty People," "I'm Pagan and I Vote!" "Practice Safe Hex," and my favorite, "667, Neighbor of the Beast." Additionally, much farther away, in a suburban neighborhood, "Gallows Hill Road" meets "Witch Way" street and local children attend Witchcraft Heights Elementary School. Nearby is the officially recognized Gallows Hill, which boasts a park and a playground. In addition to such potentially jarring juxtapositions, Salem regularly castigates itself for its tasteless exploitation of its association with the Essex County witch trials (Hill 2004, 288; Marshall 2004, 244; *Witch City* 1997).

Have the town's economic hard times (Chomsky 2004, 240) led to a down-market, Disneyfication of death that draws middle-aged women like myself, teens, families, and a variety of demographic groups to its attractions? Possibly, but let's return to the Museum of Hawthorne and Poe to better understand tourist Salem. Despite all my reservations about it, I realized, just like the woman standing next to me in line had indicated, that the museum had, indeed, been a goofy kind of fun. This was due in large part to the interactions with the local teens who staffed it. They performed their

FIGURE 2.8. Street sign in Salem. (Photo by Jeannie Banks Thomas)

jobs with serious fidelity to the literary characters whom they were portraying. But they were flexible enough to break character or interact with their audience in entertaining, frank, and sometimes sweet ways. For example, they told me that, although Hawthorne was the native son and Poe was not, Poe's short stories just worked so much better for their enterprise than did Hawthorne's.

Toward the end of our journey, we had a fake stuffed cat thrust repeatedly into our faces, and we also encountered an earnest young woman swathed in yards and yards of an old-fashioned white nightdress. She was portraying the murdered wife in Poe's short story "The Black Cat," and she sadly noted my companion's arm around my shoulders by saying, in character, "Why won't someone put his arm around *me*?" My companion deadpanned a response that pointed to a time-honored rule of haunted houses and related sites (such as haunted corn mazes): "Because the guy who let us in gave us strict instructions not to touch *any* employees." To everyone's delight, the pallid, murdered wife cracked up in a very unPoe-like way. Still sharing that laugh, our group stumbled out of the final darkened corridor and into a very, very, very bright light—much as one does in the classic "near-death experience." Of course, this being Salem, the brilliant light was provided by the gift shop, which we all had to pass through in order to exit the building (see Gencarella 2003, 169).

Salem tourism encourages those who hear Salem's witch stories to engage in commodified legend tripping and legend questing—that is, visiting sites associated with the trials and other frightening things. Folklorist Bill Ellis says teens often hear a legend about uncanny events that occur in a particular spot and then decide to visit the spot (2004, 114). These trips have a three-part structure. First, the legends about the site are shared. Second, legend trippers travel to the site and interact with the legend and site in some way, which can be as simple as getting out of the car and walking to the site. And third, the group shares their perceptions and recapitulates what happened to them at the site (Ellis 1996, 440). Ellis notes that these practices are similar to historical pilgrimages to holy wells (440).

Pilgrimages, legend trips, and tourism can all be seen on a continuum; they are related to each other and overlap. Generally speaking, though, the pilgrimage part of the continuum pulls toward religious or spiritual motivations and experiences (Turner and Turner 1978, xiii). The tourism part leans more toward entertainment and commerce, though it may still share aspects with pilgrimages (Badone and Roseman 2004, 6). A descendant of pilgrimages and sometimes the basis of tourism, legend tripping is located in the most informal, spur-of-the-moment parts of the spectrum: its focus is on a legend and its related place, which is often an easy car ride away. Some folklorists also use the term *legend quest* to focus more specifically on the individual meaning sought in the trip. I use the broader term *legend trip* in this chapter in order to allow room to discuss more aspects of a legend trip than its meaning to a participant. And I use *legend trip* in this chapter instead of *pilgrimage* because, generally, the latter denotes the overtly sacred and religious. In Salem tourism, I see less of the sacred, or "extroverted mysticism," as Edith and Victor Turner call it (1978, 33), and more of the secular. The obvious exception is Salem's neo-pagan tourists who do visit Salem for overtly spiritual reasons (these neo-pagan pilgrimages are worthy of study in their own right but are beyond the scope of this chapter).

Salem makes it plain that legend tripping can provide the scaffolding from which tourism is built and encouraged. Salem tourism draws on its witch legends to encourage legend tripping that is commercialized in the form of various businesses, from "witch walks" to storefront haunted houses. It takes its invasive narrative and turns it into a commodified experience. Tourism also follows the same classic three-part structure, but with an additional fourth part: the purchase. That is, when tourists, like legend trippers, hear intriguing stories of sites, they then travel to the place and talk about their experiences after they return home. At various points along the way, they spend money in order to complete their legend trip, and they often buy souvenirs that somehow connect them to the site and help them recall their experience. In this way, the invasive narrative provides the town with both an identity and much-needed income. Like the women who travel to Lily Dale (chapter 6), some of these people seek the mystery and "re-enchantment" that legend-based tourism can offer adults (see Magliocco 2004, 120–21).

Most legend trips involve traveling to a site that has some *direct connection* to legend; however, this is typically *not* the case in Salem. The locales of visitation are rarely tangibly linked to the historical witches; instead, they are often entirely manufactured, commercial sites. Such sites in Salem are examples of what I call the "simulacrum trip." A simulacrum trip is a variant of a legend trip, but instead of traveling to a site with some sort of direct connection to legend or history, participants visit artificial sites, manufactured objects, and other obvious constructions that have no true, material connections to the story they tell. These simulated sites can become authoritative or "true" in their own right (Baudrillard 2002, 168), and perhaps even better liked and more heavily visited than places with closer links to the story (see Eco 1990). For example, the Salem Witch Museum is *the* place in Salem to visit, even though it doesn't house artifacts from the trials, nor is it located on a site associated with the trials. So, a tourist trekking to the museum is undertaking a simulacrum trip, whereas a visit to the site of the Parris home in Danvers, where the first two possessed girls twitched and contorted their way into history (Roach 2002, 18), is a legend trip.

Legend tripping is also described as ostension (Fine 1991, 179). Ostension comes in several forms. Pseudo-ostension is using a legend to perpetuate a hoax (Ellis 1989, 208). Quasi-ostension is misinterpreting events using a legend as a guide, and proto-ostension is when a person relates a legend but tells it as if it were a *memorate* (Ellis 2001, 163). Mass-mediated ostension is

FIGURE 2.9. Simulacrum tripping at the Salem Witch Museum. (Photo by Burt Feintuch)
FIGURE 2.10. The stone foundation of the Parris parsonage, where the first two young girls were "possessed," Danvers, Massachusetts. (Photo by Jeannie Banks Thomas)

the appearance of contemporary legends in film, television, and other media (Koven 208, 139). To these types of ostension I would add sim-ostension (think of "sim" as in "similar," "similize," and "simulacrum," meaning likeness or copy), which is when a legend is associated with a site that has no real or tangible connections to the content of the legend.[4] Following the paths of the witch in Salem demonstrates how tourism has commercialized the legend trip. It also suggests that the staple of tourism, the museum, can in some cases rely heavily on simulacrum tripping. Perhaps legend-related spending in gift shops could also be considered a form of sim-ostension.

A ONE-WITCH TOWN?

For folklorists, legends can be untrue or true (Dégh 1971, 66–67), so visits to historical sites—as long as they have legends told about them—can count as legend trips. Also, in some cases, the "guided tour" or visit to a gift shop is a form of commercialized legend tripping favored by adults. Legend scholar Linda Dégh reminds us that legends are not only about the supernatural and scary—they are often fun and funny. She says that "horror is pacified by humor," and that jokes have a symbiotic relationship with legends, often appearing alongside the conversational narration of legends (1969, 74; 1976). In its tourist attractions that emphasize fun (like the Museum of Haw-thorne and Poe), Salem enacts and makes material the relationship between the legend and humor.

Laughter and fun also exist in today's Salem because it is chronologically removed from the witch trials; thus, most visitors have emotional distance from the tragedy (Thomas 1997, 43). Places that have this kind of emotional distance are more conducive to attractions—such as haunted houses—that are intended to be pleasurable (Magliocco 1985, 25). Sites that are influenced by a large, emotional, or chronologically close tragedy, such as the 9/11 memorial, do not promote these kinds of "fun" attractions.

Halloween as a contemporary holiday is removed from the tragic histor-ical roots of its iconic figure, the witch. Rather, it renders her playfully and further opens up the "fun" side of the scary and supernatural. However, just because people can find this lighthearted side of Halloween and the witch figure in Salem doesn't mean that they ignore the serious and somber side of the Salem story when they are in different contexts, such as visiting the Salem Witch Trials Memorial.

FIGURE 2.11. Shop on the downtown Salem mall. (Photo by Jeannie Banks Thomas)

While I can pull out these different threads of Salem experience—such as scary fun or solemn remembrance—easily on the page, on the streets of Salem these same strands tangle together in a more chaotic way. This can be seen even in something as simple and overtly commercial as an ice cream shop. Dairy Witch Ice Cream provides a low-key example of the witch theme employed to promote profit, pleasure, and the consumption of extra calories. The shop has been a family business since the early 1950s, according to its owner Marietta Goodridge (personal interview 2014).

Dairy Witch Ice Cream might not only appeal to the average tourist in need of a sugar boost but also to nineteenth-century folklore scholar George Lyman Kittredge, who wrote a well-known study of witches that included a section on "dairy witches" (1972, 163–73; see also de Caro 1968, 18). For most Salem visitors, the dairy witch is simply another use of the town's most iconic figure. However, for the historically- or folklorically-minded, the dairy witch might also evoke some interesting, traditional connotations of the witch, including the fact that the everyday, historical witch has had a strong

association with dairy processes. For example, witches were often accused of such *maleficia* as causing cows to go dry or cursing milk so it couldn't be churned to butter. Dairy mischief was a big part of the historical witch's *modus operandi* (see, for example, Kramer and Sprenger 1971, 144–45).

In contemporary times, the witch has lost much of her specific associations with maleficent acts such as causing crop failure, impotence, or problems in the dairy. Instead, she is often associated with the festive because her image is used so much when celebrating Halloween. Kittredge might find it of interest—as I do—that the dairy witch has morphed and survived into the present day, becoming, in this case, literally associated with a sweet, fun thing: ice cream.

The Dairy Witch sign is meant to sell a treat, but, depending upon the viewer, it can also be seen to reference—whether intentionally or not—the complicated and variable history of the witch. And that is exactly what makes Salem so fascinating and maddening. The town embraces a cultural figure, the witch, whose meaning has changed dramatically over the centuries. And not only that, Salem has the temerity to allow many of history's *different* notions of the witch to exist on its streets and tourist sites in an anachronistic jumble for all visitors to see. For example, a basic sorting of the various witches manifested in Salem today reveals at least the following types:

1. The 1692 witches: people accused of witchcraft in the Essex County trials, who, most scholars agree, weren't witches at all
2. The Puritan ideal of the supernatural witch
3. The contemporary Halloween witch

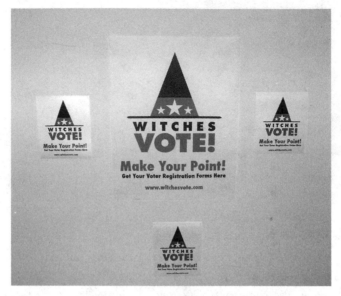

FIGURE 2.13. Signs urging members of the Salem witch community to vote. (Photo by Jeannie Banks Thomas)

4. The pagan and neo-pagan witch and other "modern witches"— as Kate Fox calls them (personal interview 2009)—of all kinds, such as contemporary witches who follow various traditions or even take their own idiosyncratic approach.[5]

When one is trying to understand the responses to witch tourism, such as the conflict that was visible at the unveiling of the *Bewitched* statue, the question "Which witch?" is relevant. The woman who stood in line next to me at the Museum of Hawthorne and Poe was seeking fun: the Halloween face of the witch, if you will. This is more likely to be found at the storefront haunted house than at the Salem Witch Trials Memorial, where one is much more apt to contemplate the somber, tragic, historical face of the witch.

Visitors to Salem can find the historical lessons and dark profundity offered by remembering those accused of witchcraft, *and* they can join in the fun of costuming as a contemporary witch during the town's Haunted Happenings, *and* they can find a religious, neo-pagan ritual on Gallows Hill during Samhain (Wicker 2006, 104–5). A visitor could see all of these differ-ent visages of the witch practically simultaneously or choose to engage only

FIGURE 2.14. Witches outside of a shop on the Salem mall. (Photo by Jeannie Banks Thomas)

one. If a tourist or local thinks that the only witch Salem should focus on is the tragic witch of 1692, then the varied guises of the witch that bombard those who walk the streets of Salem could easily cause dissonance. Some might find themselves offended by the *Bewitched* statue or the Halloween or neo-pagan witch who struts his or her stuff on the streets and in the town's shops. Conflict over how the witch is presented to the public and which witch should be presented is understandable. Sometimes tensions arise from perceptions of poor taste in the selling of the Salem witches. For example, the documentary *Witch City* depicts the selling of "Gallows Hill dirt" during the 300th anniversary of the trials (DeRosa 2009, 27). Other times, conflict comes from differing notions of which witch Salem should try to focus its still-protean local narrative around.

For those for whom Salem is a one-witch town (as in the witch of 1692), confronting a group of diverse, cackling, uproarious, fun, and even frivolous witch types could generate feelings of concern and give rise to conflict with those who think of Salem as a multiple-witch town. Add neo-pagan religious views to the mix, and then throw in other religious views (such as fundamentalist ones), and things get complicated. Rapidly. Those less concerned with privileging one definition of "witch" over another may find Salem's multitude of witches less troubling. Many people are used to sorting complicated meanings and know which witch to contemplate in which context, and they can easily shift between views of witches as the context changes, just as when they hear a homonym such as "hear" and "here" or "which" and "witch" and they know to rely on usage and context to determine whether "hear" means "listen" or "place."

Salem is the cauldron in which new and old notions of witches are thoroughly mixed together. As such, it offers a study of both the curses and benefits of the dynamic and variant nature of folklore—or, more specifically in this case, the changing lore of the witch. These diverse views of the witch also serve different functions. Some vie for tourists' dollars on the downtown mall, and some make us ponder the tragic timelessness of our inhumanity to each other. Some constructions of the witch function both to draw tourist dollars *and* direct us to sobering historical realities. Some witches are lighthearted, but at least one of these witches addresses real, urban problems. For example, city leaders were interested in having the *Bewitched* statue because the corporation that installed it, TV Land, also promised to pay for the maintenance of the small downtown park in which it was located, a move that some felt would help the area avoid decline (Wrong Witch, 2005).

The issues in Salem are also bigger and even more interesting than which iteration of the witch should be privileged. Currently, not only are visitors allowed to choose which witch with which to engage but they're also faced with a subtle, though much larger, issue and choice. Salem's native son Nathaniel Hawthorne alluded to this choice in his fiction in the nineteenth century. He used his famous short story, "The Maypole of Merry Mount," to ponder the influence of the Puritans both on his hometown and on New England in general.

FIGURE 2.15. Sign outside of Aphrodite Maternity store on the Salem mall. (Photo by Jeannie Banks Thomas)

In his story about May rites and their celebration in New England, Hawthorne writes, "Jollity and gloom were contending for an empire" (2012, 882). In Hawthorne's story of Puritan New England, of course, jollity goes the way of the maypole and gloom prevails on the landscape. The pagans and papists who introduced the maypole to both the Old and New Worlds may not be back in total control of the town of Salem, but many of the old elements of their religious festivals—which were also easily blended with the commercial—are strongly present in the town. In short, in contemporary

Salem, jollity exists right alongside gloom, and neither can yet be declared victor or vanquished.

DIDACTICISM AND COMMERCIALISM

What does the commercialization of the witch figure reveal about Salem as a place? The city's witch tourism practices indicate that the city acknowledges both its historical past *and* the much-changed witch of today's popular culture. Witch tourism demonstrates that Salem recalls the old and embraces the new. Salem's tourist presentations of the witch also show that it has hung onto and transmuted a key element of the historical witch accusations and trials: drama. Dramatic reenactments of the trials and other parts of Salem history are a mainstay in the town's tourist presentation of itself.

Theater-owner Erik Rodenhiser maintains that people enjoy fear when they know they are safe; he says that theater is a great medium through which this pleasure can be created (personal interview 2009). It's not surprising, then, that along with haunted houses—which can earn enough in October to support their owners for the rest of the year, according to Rodenhiser—several high-profile tourist attractions employ theatrical presentations related to the trials, including The Witch Dungeon Museum or Gordon College's *Cry Innocent*, which is an enactment of excerpts from the trial of accused witch Bridget Bishop (Gordon College, 2012). In his youth, Rodenhiser played Judge Hathorn, Nathaniel Hawthorne's infamous ancestor, in this production. Kate Fox says,

> I love the theater. I love all of the groups that are telling ghost stories
> in theatrical ways. They have professional actors. The Witch House
> [see Witch House, n.d.] does it where you go in, and you're hearing
> these incredible stories, and they're not all made up. You know some
> of them are just real stories from the seventeenth century that are
> very scary and really fun. The Salem Theater Company does it with
> their *Chilling Tales*, and this year [2009] they were Edgar Allen Poe
> inspired. (personal interview 2009)

Rodenhiser's own theater, The Griffen Theatre, was home to "The Witches Cottage," which hosted interactive, theatrical presentations. "The Witches Cottage" then became the "Gallows Hill Museum/Theatre,"

FIGURE 2.16. Erik Rodenhiser's theatre, Salem. (Photo by Jeannie Banks Thomas)

which includes a "mini-museum" in the lobby "with replica artifacts from the Salem Witch Trials" (Witches Cottage 2012). From January to September, Rodenhiser rents the theater out for other productions, such as Sam Shepherd's *True West* or Edward Albee's *The Zoo Story*.

Rodenhiser, who also does stand-up comedy, says he figured out how to turn what he loved into a career. "I loved growing up in Salem" he says as he fondly recalls childhood memories, such as swimming at the park. He lived in California for a while, but he moved back to Salem specifically because it is distinctive: "I can walk to work and it takes me an hour-and-a-half because I know everyone on the street, and they stop to say hi to me" (personal interview 2009).

While Rodenhiser talks about Salem as a cohesive community in a positive sense, he also paints a realistic picture of it. For example, he says, "The local attractions should work collectively more, but they don't." He is critical of local business owners who present outdated and incorrect information. He also says that seeing himself in the movie *Witch City* (1997) (he's a gravedigger in a haunted house), which critiques the commercialism that Salem brings to the witch trials, made him question himself and think about how exploitative he was being. He says, "Salem's identity keeps evolving; that's like people, too." It's also like Rodenhiser's own business: "I'm always changing and updating the productions. I want to scare the back row" (personal interview 2009). While he emphasizes fun and thrills in the production, he also wants to educate his audience, as can be seen from his description of the show as an "educational thrill ride" and the fact that October performances host question-and-answer sessions after the show that are designed to provide an "opportunity to ask questions about witches as they relate to history, myth and fact" (Witches Cottage 2012).

Along with Salem's perennial kitsch and commercialism is an irrepressible didacticism, which is seen in attractions like Rodenhiser's and in the goals of tourist organizations like Destination Salem. This is not a new phenomenon in Salem; Hawthorne is perhaps the most famous Salemite to employ local history to didactic ends. For example, in *The House of Seven Gables* Hawthorne presents the accused witches hanged on Gallows Hill as martyrs who can teach tolerance (Schulz and Morrison, 2004, 7). It is worth noting that commercialism doesn't drive this didacticism out, and sometimes it even amplifies it.

Salem's witch story has a clear moral along with a gripping, historically-based storyline about witches, fear, cruelty, and tolerance. Scholars Nancy Schulz and Dane Morrison argue that a place becomes "inextricably linked to tragedy when the loss of life is perceived as especially wasteful or unjust" (2004, 4). Of course, the witch trials fit that bill exceptionally well, so they've allowed the creation of a place that is about loss and includes a moral (Schulz and Morrison 2004, 7).

In another tragic chapter in its history, Salem lost thousands of its citizens to influenza in the early part of the twentieth century; however, this fact is not well known by outsiders because the flu deaths do not provide such a coherent narrative and a clear moral about human failings (Schulz and Morrison 2004, 4). Nor was this type of death unique to Salem. That the witch trial stories are remembered and staged didactically is due in large part to the lucid moral implicit in them from a modern-day perspective. The lack of justice at the time of the trials turned the victims into martyrs, so the miscarriage of justice made the witch story more enduring and memorable.

The witch narrative is so invasive that it has even spread outside the confines of Salem—simply saying "Salem" is enough to evoke "witches" in the minds of Americans. The dramatic historical events, implicit moral, and inherent injustice of the trials help perpetuate the story; however, so do its supernatural elements. Despite predictions of its demise, the supernatural in various guises remains firmly ensconced in narrative traditions around the world (Goldstein 2007b, 63–66). In the case of the Salem witch accusations, the supernatural aspects of the stories increase the drama and intrigue. Therefore, its supernatural qualities further ensure that this episode in Salem's history will be remembered. The didactic potential of Salem's witch story, along with the supernatural and fun elements that are connected to the figure of the witch, find the theater to be a perfect venue for the purposes of each. In sum, early American supernatural beliefs, the historical drama of the trials, and various cultural notions about witches—both historical and contemporary—have come to define Salem as a place today.

It's evident from his comments that Rodenhiser has thought about Salem's supernatural legacy and makes distinctions in that regard; he recognizes that Salem is home to a diversity of witches. He acknowledges the lighthearted aspects of today's Halloween by saying, simply, "Halloween is fun," and he distinguishes between witches and the witch trials:

> Today's witches aren't connected to the witch trials. . . . Real witches [today] are close to nature and very positive. They really take care of themselves physically. It's hard to be that positive all the time. I tried it while on vacation once and decided that it was fairly draining. . . . [In the presentations after the shows,] I make being a witch a more ordinary thing than a lot of people view it as. Really, if you want magic, go to Disney World. (Personal interview 2009)

Rodenhiser's perspective allows for the coexistence of multiple types of Salem witches.

Kate Fox also differentiates and is comfortable with the various types of witches found in Salem. She doesn't see the 1692 tragedy as the only witch story that can be told in Salem. For instance, she talks about some of its neo-pagan residents:

> The other piece is a modern witch. . . . We have . . . practicing witches and members of the Wiccan faith, which has nothing to do with 1692. . . . I work with the witch community to make sure in any marketing and promotion—because there are members of the witch community that find it exploitative that we put pictures of little girls

in pointy hats on the cover of our marketing materials for October.
That's perceived as negative. And so I work with members of the
community to ensure that that's not what we are doing. . . . We are
trying to market in a successful, family-friendly way to a mass audience that doesn't necessarily understand that there . . . is a religion
of witchcraft. We work with the museums and the attractions and
the educators in town to make sure that our marketing material . . .
is developed in a sensitive manner and is appropriate. But it's
hard and we will never, we'll never please everybody. . . . On one
hand, this is religion and this is history, and this is very sensitive.
And on the other hand, this is economic development. (Personal
interview 2009)

In its tourism industry, Salem witches are figures who embody local history,
religion, pleasure, popular culture, economics, and the supernatural. Scholar
Christopher White says of Salem, "The . . . irony . . . is that as powerfully
as Christians used the witch trials to limit, reduce, and expunge the men-
tality of the supernatural, in the end modern witches have brought it back"
(2004, 57).

Whichever Salem witch one focuses on, she or he will divulge something
about at least a part of Salem's identity as a place. One thing all of the incar-
nations of the witch share is that they generate drama—from the accused
witches in 1692 to the contemporary Wiccans fleeing Chicago for Salem—
whether they want to or not. The possessed girls of 1692 were so dramatic
that many today forget that adult men made most of the witchcraft accusations (Karlsen 1987, 183–84). Also, some of the courtroom exchanges
with the accused witches were poignant, riveting, and theatrical. Given the
inherently dramatic nature of the trials themselves, it's not surprising that
dramatic reenactments have become a key component of the contemporary
tourist trade in Salem.

SALEM'S INFLUENCE ON THE SUPERNATURAL

Take a tragic, dramatic historical event, mix it with moral overtones, and
you get the potential makings of an invasive narrative. Depending upon
the characteristics of the key event at the heart of the narrative (in this
case, a tragedy), sometimes just enough emotional distance can help the

narrative thrive. Distance from the actual supernatural drama of 1692 allows Salem to define itself as a tourist site. Fear, immediate and overpowering, of the supernatural, the unknown, and their neighbors seized Salem in 1692. Unlike Rodenhiser's theatrical presentations, the fear of 1692 was not generated in a context of safety. The passage of time allowed Salem to achieve distance from the all-too-real tragedy of 1692. Three hundred years after the trauma, the town officially took up its past by dedicating the Salem Witch Trials Memorial in 1992.

If the town tourism officials want visitors to leave with lessons of tolerance, well, then, to its credit, in many ways Salem practices what it preaches. It tolerates a certain amount of supernatural weirdness: stores proffering "custom fangs," Christian Day's Festival of the Dead, or a roomful of tired mediums plying their trade during Haunted Happenings.

In late nineteenth-century Salem, capitalism finally caught up with the witch, and some locals began using the phrase "Witch City." Today, if Austin, Texas, and Portland, Oregon, are known for "keeping it weird," Salem—whether all of its citizens like it or not—is known for keeping it witchy. Haunted Happenings is a manifestation of a sense of place that is shaped by owning, but being distant from, a historical tragedy with ties to

FIGURE 2.17. Sign on Salem's downtown mall during Haunted Happenings. (Photo by Jeannie Banks Thomas)

FIGURE 2.18. Advertisement for a witch-focused tour in downtown Salem. (Photo by Jeannie Banks Thomas)

the supernatural. Thus, contemporary Salem relies on drama—but, as Erik Rodenhiser says, it is drama from a safe distance.

The supernatural has shaped Salem as place; however, Salem has also shaped the supernatural. Halloween has shaped our view of witches and so has Salem. Both have helped to make the witch an iconic figure in American supernatural traditions. The multiple faces of the Salem witch have also become widely recognized ways of depicting the witch in larger supernatural traditions and mass-media forms, such as the television series *American Horror Story: Coven* or *Salem*. Also, from the nineteenth century onward, Salem has demonstrated the marketability of the witch.

Some of the commercial uses to which the 1692 witch legends are put can be crass. However, I don't think scholars and outsiders should castigate the city solely because it has commercialized the witch story. I do think it's healthy when Salemites themselves critique their own practices of witch-related commercialization, as Rodenhiser does earlier in this chapter. I think it's worth remembering that it's Salem's story, and Salemites have to live

FIGURE 2.19. Salem's "Witch City" identity is reflected on the local police cars. (Photo by Jeannie Banks Thomas)

with it. One way that some of them have found to live with this particular invasive narrative is to make a living from it.

I was thinking about the complexity and influence of Salem's many witches on that dank, grey October morning during my visit to Haunted Happenings that included my experience at Hawthorne and Poe. During that same trip, we stopped in at a Dominican café/bar for breakfast. At that time, the café was near yet another seasonal haunted house, "Dracula's Castle." A few strands of Christmas lights broke up the darkness in *Brisas del Caribe* and revealed some tables, chairs, and the presence of a sound system for late-night music. The café was a manifestation of Salem's contemporary Dominican culture, yet another part of the city's long history of immigrant tides (Chomsky 2004, 219).

The place was quiet and empty, and our breakfast took nearly two hours. At one point, we realized the kitchen staff was going out to buy the food to cook for our order. Since we had some time, and since I was thinking about the controversies generated by the figure of the witch during Haunted

FIGURE 2.20. Salem's "Witch City" identity is also reflected in the signage for a local business. (Photo by Jeannie Banks Thomas)

Happenings, I asked the waitress, "What do you think about Haunted Happenings?"

Her answer was influenced, I think, by her own culture, experiences, and distance from the witches of 1692. Her response came from a very different place than Kate Fox's, Erik Rodenhiser's, the teens staffing the haunted houses, or the tourists on the streets, yet it shared a resonant thread with some of their thoughts about Haunted Happenings and how Salem's witch narrative brings life, in terms of economics and human interactions, to the contemporary city.

Her comment also reminded me that, ironically, despite some of the negative qualities of invasive narratives, the powerful human-interest elements in these stories can draw people to the place associated with the narrative. They can also lend that place an identity, and sometimes that identity can help the local economy. Local tourism that draws on such narratives implicitly recognizes the allure and potential that invasive stories can possess.

Or, as the waitress shyly put it, "I think it's beautiful." Then she added, "The streets are filled with people."

NOTES

1. When combined with the word "species," "invasive" takes on a more specialized meaning than it does in general usage (or in my use of it): specifically, something (such as a kudzu), for example, that comes from the outside and takes over local plants. I use "invasive" in relation to narratives where the spreading can be internal to a region (like we talk about an invasive cancer spreading inside a body). At the same time, I recognize the much smaller possibility that the narrative may also come in from another place. In this chapter, I focus on stories with some sort of difficult or tough content matter (such as death) that spread well within a particular place. This doesn't mean that a story that spreads easily must always have challenging content, however. I am not using the term "dominant" narrative because these stories do not necessarily include an ideological component.

   I first began thinking about the concept of invasive narratives while legend tripping in the Happy Valley area in North Carolina to the historical sites associated with the Tom Dooley (Dula) legend (Fletcher 2003; West 2002). I realized the story had spread well within the region; for instance, it showed up miles away in Brushy Gap, where it lived in Doc Watson's family stories and musical traditions. Due to the popular Kingston Trio version of "The Ballad of Tom Dooley," it spread even further outside the community for a period of time in the mid-twentieth century, too. In Lily Dale, New York, the founding of spiritualism is another example of an invasive narrative.

   While this chapter uses interviews with those in the tourist industry to find out how they deal with Salem's invasive witch narrative, more work could be done in the future to explore how Salem's other resident populations deal with it.

2. Of course, "Count Orlock" here is a reference to the Dracula-like creature in the famed 1922 German film, which was an unauthorized adaptation of Bram Stoker's *Dracula*.

3. My formulation of the four major themes comes from Fox's interview and differs somewhat from the "four historic faces of Salem" (trials, maritime history, Hawthorne, and historic architecture) outlined in the 1995 pamphlet by William Story (Gencarella 2007, 282).

4. For a particularly lucid and more detailed overview of these forms of ostension, see de Vos (2012, 29–38).

5. The current owner of Dairy Witch Ice Cream is aware of the historical associations of witches with dairies, but she does not know if that association played a role in the original naming of the shop in the 1950s. Jim McAllister, a local historian and owner of Derby Square Tours, says that during the 1950s the city and its businesses really embraced the image of the witch: "People no longer ran

away from it" (personal interview 2014). Along with the publication of *The Crucible* in the 1950s, he notes that popular culture was really taking off, which also helped promote the witch–Salem association. Given this context, he said it's not surprising that the original owners came up with the name Dairy Witch. For more on various types of contemporary witches and their beliefs, see Adler (1986) and Magliocco (2004).

WORKS CITED

Adler, Margot. 1986. *Drawing Down the Moon*. Boston: Beacon Press.

Badone, Ellen, and Sharon R. Roseman, eds. 2004. "Approaches to the Anthropology of Pilgrimage and Tourism," 1–23. In *Intersecting Journeys: The Anthropology of Pilgrimage and Tourism*. Urbana, IL: University of Illinois Press.

Bartosik, Matt. 2009. "Witches Pack up Their Potions in Rossville." http://www .nbcchicago.com/news/local/Witches-Pack-Up-Their-Potions-in-Rossville -68587637.html.

Baudrillard, Jean. 2002. "Simulacra and Simulations." In *Selected Writings*, edited by Mark Foster and Jacques Mourrain, 169–87. Palo Alto, CA: Stanford University Press.

Boston Globe. 2014. "Salem." http://villageatvinninsquare.com/announcement.asp ?id=199.

Chomsky, Aviva. 2004. "Salem as Global City, 1850–2004." In *Salem: Place, Myth, and Memory*, edited by Dane Anthony Morrison and Nancy Lusignan Schultz, 219–47. Boston: Northeastern University Press.

Dalton, Tom, and Alan Burke. 2005. "City Bewitched by Statue." June 16. http://www .freerepublic.com/focus/f-chat/1424142/posts.

de Caro, Frank. 1968. "The Butter Witch." *Indiana Folklore* 1: 17–20.

de Vos, Gail. 2012. *What Happens Next? Contemporary Urban Legends and Popular Culture*. Santa Barbara, CA: Libraries Unlimited.

Dégh, Linda. 1969. "The Roommate's Death and Other Related Dormitory Stories in Formation." *Indiana Folklore* 2: 55–74.

———. 1971. "The 'Belief' Legend." In *American Folk Legend*, edited by Wayland Hand, 55–68. Berkeley, CA: University of California Press.

———. 1976. "Symbiosis of Joke and Legend: A Case of Conversational Folklore." In *Folklore Today: A Festschrift for Richard Dorson*, edited by Linda Dégh, Henry Glassie, and Felix Oinas, 81–91. Bloomington, IN: Indiana University Press.

DeRosa, Robin. 2009. *The Making of Salem: The Witch Trials in History, Fiction and Tourism*. Jefferson, NC: McFarland.

Dorson, Richard. 1974. *America in Legend*. New York: Pantheon.

Eco, Umberto. 1990 "The City of Robots." *Travels in Hyperreality*. Reproduced in relevant portion at http://www.acsu.buffalo.edu/~breslin/eco_robots.html.

Ellis, Bill. 1989. "Death by Folklore: Ostension, Contemporary Legend, and Murder." *Western Folklore* 48: 201–20.

———. 1994. "'Safe Spooks:' New Halloween Traditions in Response to Sadism Legends." In *Halloween and Other Festivals of Death and Life*, edited by Jack Santino, 24-44. Knoxville, TN: The University of Tennessee Press.

———. 1996. "Legend Trip." In *American Folkore: An Encyclopedia*, edited by Jan Brunvand, 439–40. New York: Garland.

———. 2001. *Aliens, Ghosts, and Cults: Legends We Live.* Jackson, MS: University Press of Mississippi.

———. 2004. *Lucifer Ascending: The Occult in Folklore and Popular Culture.* Lexington, KY: The University Press of Kentucky.

Fine, Gary Alan. 1991. "Redemption Rumors and the Power of Ostension." *Journal of American Folklore* 106: 179–81.

Fletcher, John Edward. 2003. *The True Story of Tom Dooley: From Western North Carolina Mystery to Folk Legend.* Charleston, SC: The History Press.

Forman, Ethan. 2010. "How Haunted Happenings Bewitched the City of Salem." *The Salem News*, October 25. http://www.salemnews.com/local/x356200542/How-Haunted-Happenings-bewitched-the-city-of-salem.

Fox, Kate. 2009. Personal Interview.

———. 2010. "Destination Salem with Host Mayor Kimberley Driscoll" (speech). December 20. http://www.youtube.com/watch?v=Rkn-q58Cv10.

Gallows Hill. 2013. http://gallowshillsalem.com/.

Gencarella, Stephen Olbrys. 2003. "More Weight: Social evil, civil rights and the commodification of the Salem Witch Trials." PhD diss., ProQuest, Dissertations & Theses (PQDT).

———. 2007. "Touring History: Guidebooks and the Commodification of the Salem Witch Trials." *Journal of American Culture* 30: 271–84.

GhoStock. 2012. Salem, MA. http://www.eventbrite.com/e/ghostock-salem-ma-tickets-2620245224?aff=eorg.

Godbeer, Richard. 2011. *The Salem Witch Hunt: A Brief History with Documents.* Boston: Bedford/St. Martin's.

Goff, John V. 2004. "Salem as Architectural Mecca." In *Salem: Place, Myth, and Memory*, edited by Dane Anthony Morrison and Nancy Lusignan Schultz, 185–216. Boston: Northeastern University Press.

Goldstein, Diane. 2007a. "The Commodification of Belief." In *Haunting Experiences: Ghosts in Contemporary Folklore,* edited by Diane E. Goldstein, Sylvia Ann Grider, and Jeannie Banks Thomas, 171–205. Logan, UT: Utah State University Press.

———. 2007b. "Scientific Rationalism and Supernatural Experience Narratives." In *Haunting Experiences: Ghosts in Contemporary Folklore,* edited by Diane E. Goldstein, Sylvia Ann Grider, and Jeannie Banks Thomas, 60–78. Logan, UT: Utah State University Press.

Goodridge, Marietta. 2014. Personal Interview.

Gordon College. 2012. "Fine Arts: History Alive!" http://www.gordon.edu/historyalive.

Goss, K. David. 1999. "The Maritime History of Salem." In *Salem: Cornerstones of a Historic City*, edited by Joseph Flibbert, K. David Goss, Jim McAllister, Bryant F. Tolles, Jr., and Richard B. Trask, 5–33. Beverly, MA: Commonwealth Editions.

Grider, Sylvia. 1984. "The Razor Blades in the Apples Syndrome." In *Perspectives on Contemporary Legend,* edited by Paul Smith, 129–40. Sheffield, UK: Centre for English Cultural Traditon and Language.

Hawthorne, Nathaniel. n.d. "Maypole of Merrymount." Electronic Text Center, University of Virginia Library. http://etext.lib.virginia.edu/etcbin/toccer-new2?id=HawMayp.sgm&images=images/modeng&data=/texts/english/modeng/parsed&tag=public&part=1&division=div1 (accessed March 16, 2012).

Hill, Frances. 2004. "Salem as Witch City." In *Salem: Place, Myth, and Memory*, edited by Dane Anthony Morrison and Nancy Lusignan Schultz, 283–96. Boston: Northeastern University Press.

Karlsen, Carol. 1987. *The Devil in the Shape of a Woman: Witchcraft in Colonial New England*. New York: W. W. Norton.

Kittredge, George Lyman. 1972. *Witchcraft in Old and New England*. New York: Atheneum.

Koven, Mikel J. 2008. *Film, Folklore, and Urban Legends*. Lanham, MD: Scarecrow Press.

Kramer, Heinrich, and James Sprenger. 1971. *The Malleus Maleficarum*. Translated by Montague Summers. New York: Dover.

Lennon, John, and Malcolm Foley. 2010. *Dark Tourism: The Attraction of Death and Disaster*. Andover, UK: Cengage Learning.

Magliocco, Sabine. 1985. "The Bloomington Jaycees' Haunted House." *Indiana Folklore and Oral History* 14: 19–28.

———. 2004. *Witching Culture: Folklore and Neo-Paganism in America*. Philadelphia: University of Pennsylvania Press.

Marshall, Bridget. 2004. "Salem's Ghosts and the Cultural Capital of Witches." In *Spectral America: Phantoms and the National Imagination*, edited by J. Weinstock, 244–63. Madison, WI: University of Wisconsin Press.

McAllister, Jim. 2000. *Salem: From Naumkeag to Witch City*. Beverly, MA: Commonwealth Editions.

———. 2014. Personal Interview.

Norton, Mary Beth. 2002. *In the Devil's Snare: The Salem Witchcraft Crisis of 1692*. New York: Vintage Books.

Peabody Essex Musem. n.d. http://www.pem.org/about/mission_vision (accessed January 6, 2012).

Rice, Justin A. 2011. "Haunted Happenings Net Revenues Down for Salem." December 5. http://articles.boston.com/2011-12-05/yourtown/30478483_1_halloween -net-revenues-salem.

Roach, Marilynne K. 2002. *The Salem Witch Trials: A Day-by-Day Chronicle of a Community under Siege*. New York: Taylor Trade Publishing.

Rodenhiser, Eric. 2009. Personal Interview.

Rogers, Nicholas. 2002. *Halloween: From Pagan Ritual to Party Night*. New York: Oxford University Press.

Santino, Jack. 1996. *New Old Fashioned Ways: Holidays in Popular Culture*. Knoxville, TN: University of Tennessee Press.

Schulz, Nancy Lusignan, and Dan Anthony Morrison. 2004. "Introduction: Salem Enshrined: Myth, Memory, and the Power of Place." In *Salem: Place, Myth, and Memory*, edited by Dane Anthony Morrison and Nancy Lusignan Schultz, 3–19. Boston: Northeastern University Press.

Seaton, A. V. 1996. "Guided by the Dark: From Thanatopsis to Thanatourism." *International Journal of Heritage Sites* 2.4: 234–44.

Stone, Philip R. 2006. "A Dark Tourism Spectrum: Towards a Typology of Death and Macabre Related Tourist Sites, Attractions, and Exhibitions." *Tourism* 54.2: 145–60.

Thomas, Jeannie Banks. 1997. *Featherless Chickens, Laughing Women, and Serious Stories*. Charlottesville, VA: University Press of Virginia.

————. 2011. "The Cemetery as Marketplace in Salem, Massachusetts." In *Fieldworking: Reading and Writing Research*, edited by Bonnie Stone Sunstein and Elizabeth Chiseri-Strater, 179–85. Boston: Bedford/St. Martin's.

Turner, Victor, and Edith Turner. 1978. *Image and Pilgrimage in Christian Culture*. New York: Columbia University Press.

West, John Foster. 2002. *The Ballad of Tom Dula: The Documented Story Behind the Murder of Laura Foster and the Trials and Execution of Tom Dula*. Durham, NC: Moore Publishing Company.

White, Christopher. 2004. "Salem as Religious Proving Ground." In *Salem: Place, Myth, and Memory*, edited by Dane Anthony Morrison and Nancy Lusignan Schultz, 43–61. Boston: Northeastern University Press.

Wicker, Christine. 2006. *Not in Kansas Anymore: Dark Arts, Sex Spells, Money Magic, and Other Things Your Neighbors Aren't Telling You*. New York: HarperOne.

Witch City. 1997. Directed by Joe Cultrera. Picture Business & Ferrini Productions.

"Witch Dungeon Museum." n.d. http://www.witchdungeon.com/schedules.html (accessed February 6, 2012).

"Witch House." n.d. http://www.witchhouse.info/ (accessed February 1, 2012).

Witches Cottage. 2012. "Frequently Asked Questions." http://www.witchescottagesalem.com/frequently-asked-questions.html.

"Wrong Witch in Salem." 2005. http://www.boston.com/news/globe/editorial_opinion/editorials/articles/2005/05/01/wrong_witch_in_salem/.

Tradition *and the* International Zombie Film

The Movies

MIKEL J. KOVEN

In the recent British horror-comedy, *Cockneys vs. Zombies*, Emma (Georgia King), a bank-robbery hostage, instructs the aptly named Mental Mickey (Ashley Thomas) to ensure the zombies attacking them are shot in the head. This information is treated as common sense; that is, "everyone" knows the only way to kill zombies is to shoot them in the head. Where does this knowledge come from? Why are movie characters supposed to know this? Of course, everyone knows that zombies can only be killed with a headshot; anyone who has even the smallest connection with popular culture should know this.

Zombies are also particularly partial to brains. Such "common sense" about zombies does not come from the folklore traditions of Haiti.[1] There is a historical build-up of "folk wisdom" situated less in Haiti than in the aggregate popular culture of zombie movies. Characterizing this kind of mass-mediated folk knowledge is not only the speed of dissemination but also how such ideas are responded to internationally and reinterpreted into local, cultural variant forms, *just like a traditional item of folklore*.

This chapter explores the diverse traditions of zombie movies: cinematic traditions that effectively create a film-based, neo-oral lore. Zombie films both draw on folklore and depart from it, creating new traditions in the process. My approach to the zombie film here is narratological; that is, my focus is on understanding the narrative of these films and exploring how that narrative reflects and inspires other filmmakers. In this regard, I position the filmmaker (i.e., producer, director, or screenwriter—sometimes these are different people, sometimes not) as storyteller.

Within Italian film studies, critics often speak of the *filone*,[2] which simply means vein or strand but is often used in place of *subgenre* or a short-lived cycle of films. However, the word *filone* has the idiomatic association of tradition, as in the expressions "*sullo stesso filone*" (literally "in the tradition of") or "*seguire il filone*" ("to follow the tradition of"). If we consider the filone to be a tradition of narrative expression (and this is different from the narrative expression being traditional), to see a genre or subgenre (in this case, the zombie movie) as a filone is therefore to identify distinct narrative units that persist in time and space and are subject to cultural variations.

I am arguing, therefore, for a modified historic-geographic approach to the zombie film: to trace the "life-history" of particular film traditions across a body of movies, and to demonstrate likely influences on other (zombie) film traditions. Unlike the historic-geographic method developed by Julius Krohn (in Kaarle Krohn [1926] 1971), my interest lies less in finding an "original" version of the narrative than in tracing the (often) transnational influences of these various films. My aim is to identify narrative tropes that demonstrate sufficient continuity as to be almost "narrative types" and to demonstrate how those types change over time.

In order to illustrate this dynamic, for the sake of argument in this chapter, I treat zombie movies as akin to traditional folktales. This is not to discuss zombie movies as folktale *adaptation* (see Koven 2008) but a hypothetical model in which film narratives circulate in a similar way as traditional folktales, at least in terms of the persistence of their narrative types and motifs. This discussion includes not only diachronic, historical developments of the genre but also, more significantly, the synchronic and international circulation of these narratives. It may, perhaps, be contentious to speak of "mass-mediated" texts as circulating like folk narratives.[3] However, at least in this case, the audiences for zombie movies—well beyond the mainstream Hollywood output and into what film scholar Jeffrey Sconce (1995) calls "paracinema," or film and film culture that lies beyond the mainstream and "official" film culture—have international awareness of the outputs from this genre. Put more succinctly, the zombie movie fan base in the United Kingdom and the United States is just as aware of zombie movies from around the world, both historical and contemporary (and not limited to English-language cinema either).

The zombie movie can be considered, for the sake of the following discussion, as a narrative category: films that feature resurrected dead bodies. Within that category are a (perhaps surprising) number of narrative types, which I will outline in due course. Furthermore, it is also possible to identify specific motifs within each type that suggest a further degree of continuity within a narrative-type tradition as well as across different narrative types. In other words, these motifs, like folktale motifs, are able to exist independently of their narrative type (Thompson [1946] 1977).[4]

Each film needs to be considered as a variant text in the larger zombie movie tradition. Some of these variants are highly conservative toward the narrative tradition—such as remakes and sequels, which depict little variation from one to another—while other texts attempt to be more "dynamic," as Barre Toelken (1996) would have it, which is to say they demonstrate substantial variation between them. Therefore, we must consider each film text, not as a definitive artistic creation, but merely as one variant text among many others.

In addition, I am taking a liberty here to discuss these films *like* folktales, as they are self-consciously fictional stories. While zombies are unlikely to actually crawl from the grave and begin eating people (although I could be wrong), the cultural discourses these narratives allegorically allude to fulfill a similar function as more traditional folktales. For their respective audiences, zombie movies entertain, validate the group's beliefs, educate others about the group's beliefs, and ensure conformity to the group's ideals (Bascom 1954); however, for this group of zombie movie audiences (and horror movie fans in general), those functions frequently challenge hegemonic norms as a form of cultural resistance—the group's norms are against the grain of the larger society's, as George A. Romero's anti-consumerist satire *Dawn of the Dead* demonstrates.

As in folktales, the setting in zombie films is often important to the narrative and its advancement. In these films, place (whether it's Afghanistan, a Caribbean island, or a suburban shopping center) helps convey the film's message, which is frequently political, as this chapter will illustrate. Not only are the filmmakers aware that these films are fictional, they embed clear markers to ensure the film's audience is also aware of this fictionality. Despite this appeal to the fictive, zombie movies occur in a recognizable world—regardless of being diegetically[5] contemporary or

near-futuristic—and are understood to be discursive to our own contemporary realities (Bascom 1965; see also Bacchilega 1997, Stone 2008, Tiffin
2009, Warner 1995, and Zipes 2006; 2011).

We understand these films to be fictions, despite their appeal to our
own experienced realism and the "realistic" make-up and digital effects they
employ. I also suggest that the use of digital special effects and monster
make-up in these films should be read "artificially" as discourse within the
film. It is because of these artificial and fictitious layers that I suggest these
films are best seen as ersatz folktales. It is for these reasons that I use a
modified historic-geographic approach to explore these films. In order to
most clearly demonstrate the various narrative traditions and types of zombie cinema across time and space, and to illustrate how these films influence
one another transnationally and within the spirit of the filone, this modified
historic-geographic approach seems the most illuminative.[6]

A quick note on the films examined in this chapter: while a substantial
number of films were studied for this analysis, at least as many (if not more)
were not. The post-2001 films are less represented here, even though more
zombie movies were produced in the dozen years after 9/11 than the sixty-
two years before. I focused as I did in order to develop as solid a historical
foundation as possible for this study. Also, some of the more vernacular films
I examined may be known by other titles, particularly with the Spanish and
Italian zombie movies. In the body of the essay, I have used the title on my
copy and have included the original title parenthetically in appendix B. In a
few cases, when the film is known by several different titles (for example,
Zombie is also known as *Zombie Flesh Eaters*, and *Hell of the Living Dead* is
known as *Zombie Creeping Flesh*), I have opted for the better-known title.

ZOMBIE SLAVES

The first narrative tradition in film is the "zombie slave," which is largely
characterized by Hollywood's (albeit, poverty-row Hollywood) stereotyping
of Caribbean Others. The Caribbean islands as sites for exotic adventure
and romance are constructed to also warn (assumedly) American film audiences about the dangers of these places, as a kind of cinematic *Warnmärchen*
(Bacchilega 1997, 55). *White Zombie* in 1932 began this narrative type, which
remained the dominant narrative form from the 1930s until the late 1960s
and early 1970s. The "zombie slave" narrative type is almost always situated

FIGURE 3.1. Movie poster from *White Zombie* (1932), which exemplifies the zombie slave narrative type. (Wikimedia Commons)

on a Caribbean island, and—with the exception of *The Serpent and the Rainbow*, which is "inspired" by true events (and the 1987 book by Wade Davis) and is therefore explicitly set in Haiti—the island in the film is either not named or given a fictional name, such as San Sebastian, which appears in RKO Pictures' *I Walked with a Zombie* and *Zombies on Broadway*.

The "zombie slave" film type is characterized by a central melodrama, often a love triangle, where one of those involved consults a *bokor*—a Vodou priest[7]—for help in turning the woman he loves into the ultimate passive wife. The 1930s advertisement for *White Zombie*, in fact, focuses on this aspect explicitly (see figure 3.1). The early films, where a woman is turned into a zombie, also contain a strong hint of necrophilia, although that is never made explicit. The bokor in these films tends to be white; a racial transposition to render the role safe and containable that suggests a fear of imbuing African, diasporic people with actual power over life and death. Black bokors appear in very few films: in *The Serpent and the Rainbow*, the bokor, Dargent Peytraud (Zakes Mokae), is black due to director Wes Craven's desire to maintain nominal verisimilitude with the cultural context of the narrative; in *Sugar Hill*, a blaxploitation film, the bokor is not only black but also a woman—Diana "Sugar" Hill (Marki Bey) consults with Mama Maitresse (Zara Cully) to raise a zombie "hit-squad" to take revenge on the mob boss who murdered her lover. While the actual agency that resurrects the dead is the god (or "loa") Baron Samedi (Don Pedro Colly), it is women of color who invoke and (to some extent) control the god. Both *Sugar Hill* and *The Serpent and the Rainbow* are conspicuous examples due to their relative rarity within this narrative type.

The main fear of the "zombie slave" narrative is not encountering a zombie and having one's brains eaten, but the fear of being turned into a zombie, of losing one's self and freewill. This fear is also found in traditional Haitian folklore (Davis 1988). The "zombie slave" film type is closer to traditional zombie lore than any other cinematic zombie narratives explored in this chapter. However, the other cinematic zombie types have created new traditions, some of which (such as the "zombie apocalypse") have also become contemporary oral traditions, as is discussed later in this chapter.

The "zombie slave" narrative also opens the discussion to postcolonial discourse. Some of the "zombie slave" films problematize the relationship between colonial hegemony and native compliance or rebellion. The white bokors, for example, problematize (or erase) the racial difference between control of the supernatural power and agency with the participants of the rituals themselves. The white bokor functions as a visual metaphor for colonialism: the white appropriation of black land and resources in order to civilize and control the island's African, diasporic populations (see Said [1978] 2003). Mrs. Rand (Edith Barrett), the white bokor in *I Walked with a Zombie*, demonstrates this complexity: as the matriarch at the Holland-Rand sugar plantation, she is the embodiment of colonial power, yet as the high priest(ess) of the local *hounfour*, she is (somewhat) native. As a white bokor, Mrs. Rand embodies the colonial appropriation of native belief traditions, but as a trained nurse she works with the local population to improve sanitation and health in the villages. In many of these films, the conclusion of the narrative involves some kind of rebellion; often, with the death of the bokor, the zombie slaves are released from servitude. They regain their selves and run riot, destroying all symbols of their servitude. These moments offer visual pleasure in the spectacle of the destruction of colonialism, and they seem to celebrate this chaos (Fanon [1961] 2001). Even the bizarre *The Incredibly Strange Creatures Who Stopped Living and Became Mixed-Up Zombies!!?* ends with the release of Madam Estrella's disfigured zombie slaves, who run amok through a skeevy funfair.

This first narrative type, the "zombie slave," features several facets: they usually have Caribbean settings and place is markedly inscribed within the film; and they often include love triangles gone wrong among the white lead characters and feature a white bokor who embodies the discourse of colonial control. The "fear" expressed in these films is not about encountering zombies, who are portrayed as victims rather than monsters, but of being turned into one by an evil bokor. Often films of this type use this narrative to call attention to, if not to fully problematize, the assumptions of colonial hegemony.

Zombie Vengeance Subtype

Within the "zombie slave" narrative type, a subtype can also be identified: using zombies for extracting some kind of revenge. In several of the zombie movies discussed so far, the zombies are raised in order to right some kind of wrong. Legende (Bela Lugosi) in *White Zombie*, for example, is protected by a small security force of zombies made from those who had been his enemies in life. The vengeance is doubled for Legende; not only does he get to dispose of his enemies, but now they work for him, presumably against their will. Even in *The Incredibly Strange Creatures Who Stopped Living and Became Mixed-Up Zombies!!?*, Jerry's skepticism toward Madame Estrella is what starts off a series of events that eventually brings Jerry completely under her spell. Both Estrella and Legende are protected by posses of zombies made up of former enemies, but, while Legende is a bokor-for-hire, Estrella uses her zombies for further revenge against those who slight her, thereby increasing her personal security force chained up in the basement.

Perhaps the strangest, or at least most incongruous, form of revenge appears in the appropriately titled *Vengeance of the Zombies*. Evil black magician Kantaka (Paul Naschy) raises a zombie "hit squad" to murder the descendants of the English colonialists, who he holds responsible for the deaths of his family in India (thereby making the postcolonial discourse explicit). Kantaka's twin brother, Krishna (also played by Naschy), is also controlled by Kantaka, despite being the "good twin." *Vengeance*'s combination of different traditions—Vodou, zombie slaves, Eastern mysticism, Western revenge, and Satanism—is a cocktail of exploitation motifs, not really for ideological purposes but simply to meet assumed genre expectations. The film's contribution isn't particularly successful, but the hodgepodge of motifs and narrative silliness is what this kind of exploitation cinema is about. The intention of many of these films is not to create a definitive or unique work of narrative art, but to contribute to the cine-storytelling tradition where narrative continuity and coherence are not the primary concerns as much as the play of motifs from previous films and traditions. The difference in *Vengeance* is that, within the "zombie slave" film type and the "zombie vengeance" subtype, enough narrative continuity and conservatism to film tradition is identifiable. But this film's project seems a bit pointless, particularly as this film type is on the wane. However, it is worth noting, at least parenthetically, that Kantaka's "zombie hit-squad" may have inspired *Sugar Hill*'s vengeance zombies two years later. Finally, it is apparent in *The Serpent and the Rainbow* that Peytraud uses Haitian's belief in zombies in order to exploit the peasantry via the "Tonton Macoute" secret police, but his particular focus on Alan (Bill Pullman) is motivated by revenge for drawing unnecessary attention to his (and Bébé Doc Duvalier's) abuses.[8]

ZOMBIE ARMY

While not the largest of the film narrative types, the "zombie army" holds a significant linking place between the "zombie slave" narrative and both the "zombie revenant" and "Nazi zombie" traditions. These films are connected to the "zombie slave" tradition insofar as the zombie armies serve dual purposes: as invincible soldiers that cannot be readily stopped by bullets and as slave labor at the front. Significantly, an important innovation occurs in these films: the fear is less about being turned into a zombie than encountering one, but here the encounter would be on the battlefield and reflects anxiety about meeting an invincible foe in combat. Specifically with wartime-produced films, such as *King* and *Revenge*, wherein the zombie armies are at the service of the Third Reich, this anxiety is palpable. Wartime films feed into a Hollywood propaganda context, but this motif appears to run out with the Second World War—at least, the zombie army does not reappear again during the Korean War, the Cold War, or Vietnam. Even in Cold War-era *Teenage Zombies*, the ersatz Communist plot is about zombie enslavement, not militarization.

ZOMBIE REVENANTS

A revenant is kin to the ghost and vampire in supernatural lore (and is frequently used interchangeably). Revenants are returning spirits that take on an identifiable human form (as they were in life), often for a specific task. Although a revenant is a type of ghost, it takes on a more corporeal form—with a more physical shape to it—than the ethereal ghost and, within English oral traditions, it physically interacts with the environment. While zombies are dead bodies without spirits (and, in Haitian tradition, the souls of zombies are horded by the evil bokors who created them), there is a zombie film tradition that draws heavily on the role folklore has traditionally assigned to revenants (Buchan 1986, 145-146; see also Thompson [1946] 1977, 256). More significantly, unlike the other zombie traditions discussed here, these narratives cluster around ideas of a hidden (or repressed) past that literally comes back to life. While revenants are not really zombies, neither are the monsters in the Spanish series of *Blind Dead* movies by Amando de Ossorio or the *Outpost* films by Steve Barker. The creatures in these movies, however, demonstrate very strong, zombie-like behaviors and function along similar lines to the living dead.[9] The "revenant zombie" narrative holds a significant place within this history: George A. Romero's *Night of the Living Dead* (1968) more or less ended the "zombie slave" tradition, but, although the "zombie apocalypse" narratives do not begin to dominate cinema screens until after Romero's *Dawn of the Dead* (1978), the interim decade between these two films saw the "revenant zombie" narrative flourished alongside the last of the "zombie slave" films. And, while "revenant zombie" movies persist until today, they do so in their modified form of the "Nazi zombie" subgroup, which I'll discuss below.

Revenants are strongly linked with ghosts, and, while these films utilize zombies as their monsters, they fulfill a role and function more akin to earlier folkloric ghost traditions. For example, in de Ossorio's Spanish *Blind Dead* series of horror films, the "blind dead" are the resurrected skeletal remains of the Knights Templar. But their resurrection is dependent on different factors in various films. In the first of these films, *Tombs of the Blind Dead*, young backpackers attempt to spend the night in the haunted abbey ruins at Bouzano, a village on the border with Portugal. Here place is inscribed as liminal—neither Spain nor Portugal—and Bouzano is a village literally haunted by its liminal status. It is suggested that the "blind dead" ride out every night, so locals live in fear and avoidance of the old abbey ruins. But in *Return of the Evil Dead*, the Knights Templar need to be summoned by witchcraft. In *The Ghost Galleon*, they sail the Atlantic aboard a ghost ship, and, in *Night of the Seagulls*, every seven years seven maidens are sacrificed on seven nights to appease these revenants. In each of these examples, the "blind dead" suggest polysemic interpretations: while the films are easily dismissed, the fact that they emerged out of the last few years of Generalissimo Franco's Fascist Spanish state suggests a slightly more serious interpretation is warranted, which further inscribes the specifics of place within these narratives.

Franco's regime was deeply dependent on the Vatican for legitimacy; what was good for Roman Catholicism was good for all of Spain. While the backstory of de Ossorio's Templar Knights isn't historically accurate, they function significantly in the film to suggest the history of Catholic atrocities—from the Crusades to the Inquisition to the Vatican's role during the Holocaust to their support of European fascism in the guise of Franco's regime. De Ossorio's Knights Templar are discredited as Satanists within the films, probably to avoid state censorship, but their historical role as Christian envoys during the Crusades cannot be escaped. The "blind dead" represent the persistence of Catholic abuse within local communities, especially their hegemonic control over everyday activities. It is no accident that, in several of these films, the abbey's ruins is the focus for much of the action. A similar evocation occurs in the Italian film *Burial Ground*, where Etruscan zombies are released due to archaeological digs around a stately home. The suggestion here is that digging into the local history and uncovering the past can release forces that were hidden for a reason. The inscription and repression of place again is central to the film as gentrification of the film's villa assumes ownership of the land; the Etruscan zombies prove otherwise. The characters in these films function like Pandora in the myth: by opening the box/tomb, they release the evil. The local peasantry know not to do this, which is why they avoid Bouzano Abbey and don't go about digging up Etruscan graveyards.

Nazi Zombie Subtype

The Nazi "revenant zombies" are a bit different from the Spanish and Italian ones. In the Norwegian *Dead Snow* and the Spanish/French co-production *Oasis of the Zombies,* the undead protect stolen gold, which is a variant on a motif from oral tradition (motif V67.3 "Treasure buried with the dead" [Thompson 1958, 810]). In *Oasis,* the promise of Nazi gold is the impetus for searching out these zombies in the Sahara (a vestige of Rommel's occupation of that land); in *Dead Snow,* a group of medical students happen upon the cache with the Nazi zombies returning to reclaim the gold, strongly echoing the Nazi occupation of Norway. *Dead Snow* in particular plays on familiar imagery from both the zombie and World War II movie traditions as comic pastiche (see figure 3.2). And place is even more significant in *Dead Snow 2: Red vs. Dead.* Nazi general Herzog's original mission was to liquidate a Norwegian village in retribution for their helping the Allies. Now that the

FIGURE 3.2. Nazi zombies in *Dead Snow* (2009; screen capture). (Tommy Wirkola)

zombie army is awake, zombie-Herzog wants to finish his mission, but physically blocking him is the resurrected platoon of Soviet zombies he fought back during the war. Place, history, and ideology clash on this northern fjord coast. In the three British *Outpost* films, instead of gold, everyone is after Nazi science via the uncovering of an abandoned bunker in the Balkans that contains a device that creates an electro-magnetic field, rendering those inside the field invincible. *Outpost* and its first sequel fuse both the "revenant zombie" film narrative with the "zombie army" tradition.[10] While the Nazi zombies in *Oasis* and *Dead Snow* are cursed to be zombies, the revenants of the *Outpost* films persist due to the electro-magnetic field that protects them.

In the "revenant zombie" tradition generally and the "Nazi zombie" narratives specifically (including the earlier *King* and *Revenge*, both of which are set in the Caribbean), there is no opportunity to join the zombie horde. Unlike the "zombie apocalypse" films, being bitten or eaten is not a way of becoming like them. So, like the "zombie army" narrative, these film types reflect the fear of encounter rather than the fear of assimilation. But those fears are directly about the spaces of encounter: European sites of historical atrocities.

ZOMBIE APOCALYPSE

When people think about zombie cinema, most often the movies they are referring to are the "zombie apocalypse" films, not just in terms of overall number of variant films within this narrative classification but also in the centrality of those films to most discussions of zombie movies as a whole.

These films inform new oral traditions, such as the lighthearted discussions of individual plans to withstand the zombie apocalypse that are mentioned in the introduction of this volume. George A. Romero's *Night of the Living Dead* was a game changer for zombie storytelling; never before had such an unrelentingly intense horror film been produced. Romero introduced the visceral resurrected corpse, not as a hypnotized unfortunate or a corporeal revenant, but as very human cadavers, as if they just sat up on the slab, wearing (or not) whatever they had on when they died (see figure 3.3). The true impact of Romero's vision wouldn't be noticeable for another ten years, until his sequel, *Dawn of the Dead*. While Romero's *Night* more or less stopped the "zombie slave" narrative tradition, the "zombie revenant"

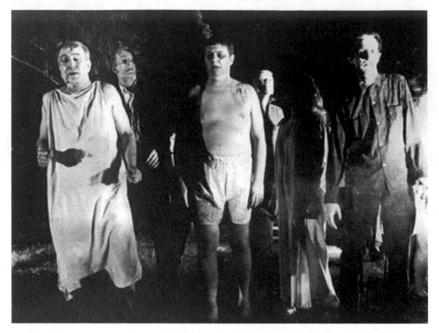

FIGURE 3.3. Zombies from the influential *Night of the Living Dead* (1968), which introduced the "zombie apocalypse" narrative. (Public domain, Wikimedia Commons)

tradition flourished at the same time, at least for a little while. The "zombie
apocalypse" narrative type is highly consistent across these films: the dead
rise and, as they shamble along slowly (though the zombies in Snyder's
Dawn of the Dead remake are fast runners and jumpers), they eat the living,
right down to the bones. While much diegetic speculation happens regarding why the dead are rising to eat the living—radiation, disease, virus, or,
as is suggested in Romero's *Dawn of the Dead,* "When there's no more room
in Hell, the dead will walk the Earth"—the actual cause of the "zombie
apocalypse" always remains unconfirmed within this narrative type. When a
definitive cause for the apocalypse is given within the film, it is categorized
as a subtype (discussed below).

In the Italian *Zombie 5: Killing Birds* and the American *Porn of the Dead,*
while no explanation of the "zombie apocalypse" is given, the reasons are
different. *Killing Birds* was not made initially as a zombie film, but it was
marketed as such (with a zombie tacked on to the end of the film). In the
case of *Porn* however, without the pre-existing film narrative type of the

"zombie apocalypse," some kind of backstory would likely be needed (how-ever redundant to its purpose). The "zombie apocalypse" narrative cluster gave license for other zombie movies to avoid specifying the causes of the apocalypse. The cause is irrelevant—we don't need to know *why* the apoca-lypse has happened; we just need to know that it has.

Romero's influence on zombie movies, while undeniable, needs contex-tualizing. The first of his trilogies (1968–1985) changed the nature of the zombie forever. Those films produced after 1978 still required some kind of explanation for the "zombie apocalypse." The international success of both the remake of *Dawn of the Dead* and the British fan-boy homage of *Shaun of the Dead*, while they maintain the ambiguous cause of the zombies, kicked off a wave of post-2004 zombie films, including Romero's second zombie trilogy (2005–2009). In the Cuban zombie movie, *Juan of the Dead*, the Cuban media keep insisting that the zombies are political dissidents sent by Washington. Part of Romero's legacy is that it became more acceptable to avoid a concrete explanation of what caused the apocalypse, evidenced by the French *La Horde*, the American *Zombieland*, or the British *Cockneys vs. Zombies*.

The "zombie apocalypse" narrative type enables us to see how each film can be considered a variant text within a set of localized story traditions. Under this category, we have two cycles of sequels by the same filmmaker—the George A. Romero trilogies—and a partial set of separately produced remakes. The Romero films offer us a consistent narrative trajectory within a coherent story world, despite not making any references to the other films.[11] The remakes however, were idiosyncratic productions based on the original film, not the previous remake—i.e., the *Dawn of the Dead* remake is unrelated to the 1990 *Night of the Living Dead* remake or even the origi-nal 1968 film. It is a partial remake of the 1978 *Dawn of the Dead*. The *Day of the Dead* remake is not coherent with either Snyder's *Dawn of the Dead* or Romero's original *Day of the Dead*, which is why it is discussed elsewhere. Romero is credited with the screenplay in the 1990 remake of *Night of the Living Dead*, despite not directing it himself. Conventional wisdom would recognize the screenplay and the direction of the film as being sufficiently different products, which of course they are, but on occasion (like with the 1990 remake of *Night*) Romero appears to have worked closely with the film's director, Tom Savini,[12] developing the ideas initially expressed in 1968.

Romero's 1990 script deviates slightly, but tellingly, from his original film: both versions follow the same narrative path, but Romero is able to adapt the racial and gender politics to reflect the different temporal contexts (1990 instead of 1968). These revisions are relatively minor and have as much to do with the different cast as with the different script. The themes of the original are brought into more relief as Romero developed, and is more confident, as a screenwriter in the twenty-two years since the original. In this regard, we can see the two versions of *Night of the Living Dead* as alternative performances of the same narrative at different points in the same storyteller's career, and then account for those differences. In the final act of the 1990 production, however, Romero shifts the narrative considerably. Romero and Savini, working together, assume familiarity with the 1968 film and play with their audience's expectations. The (sometimes quite subtle) changes Romero introduced work to unsettle our assumptions while watching it. The 1990 variant also concludes very differently than the 1968 film.

The 2004 partial remake of *Dawn of the Dead* is also divergent. While the unexplained zombie apocalypse occurs and the film follows a group of survivors as they hole up in a suburban shopping mall, these are the only two motifs that connect the 2004 film with the 1978 one. From the very beginning of Synder's 2004 film, depicting a serene American suburbia with The Sterophonics' "Have a Nice Day" playing on the soundtrack, we see the world before the apocalypse. In Romero's 1978 film, the action opens *in media res*, with a television broadcast trying to keep up-to-date with all the continually changing information. The first zombies we see in Snyder's film move with great speed and agility rather than the shuffling dead of Romero's. The remake offers up so much variance at the beginning of the film that it becomes entirely about Snyder's variations, rather than about demonstrating continuity with Romero. And, as we've seen before, this apocalyptic vision is rooted within an ideologically conservative American place—the suburban shopping mall.

Each of the films considered in this narrative category are stand-alone stories; none of them depend on knowledge of the previous films for understanding the current one, including Romero's sequels. The narrative rules most consistently adhered to include the unexplained source and the shuffling, cannibalistic living corpses who can only be killed/stopped with severe head trauma. Bites from these zombies pass on the infection (like rabies), and the bitten die only to come back to life. The zombie rules Romero developed lend a poignant texture to these films, such as having central characters fall victim to the zombie virus—like Stephen (David Emge) in the original *Dawn* (see figure 3.4). As variant texts, there is a certain sameness about each one, even when they are telling different stories. Some "zombie apoca-lypse" films demonstrate little variation from one to the next, while others demonstrate substantial change. But the core clusters of motifs remain con-stant throughout. It is significant that, of all the narrative clusters, it is this one in particular that reflects a strongly conservative discourse about place; most of these films are about the idyllic American suburbia. However, this idyll appears to be difficult (but not impossible) to export.

Despite Romero eschewing a concrete explanation for the "zombie apoc-alypse" in his films, most zombie movies post-1978 have been inspired by Romeo's storytelling in one way or another. Significantly, later filmmakers have often felt the need to explain the origin of the zombies.

Pollution/Chemical Spill Zombie Subtype (Accidental)

Zombies in this category signify the end of the world as per the "zom-bie apocalypse" tradition, but they are created accidentally via pollution (in the case of *Let Sleeping Corpses Lie*) or through an accidental chemical spill (in *Hell of the Living Dead*). While the former reflects early 1970s anti-pollution fears, the latter reflects post–Three Mile Island anxieties about the safety of modern industrial manufacturing. Two components are essential here: that the cause of the zombies is explained, and that their creation was accidental. This is what distinguishes these films from the "zombie apoca-lypse" and "chemical/biological weapon zombie" traditions. Significantly, both of the above films are Spanish/Italian coproductions and reflect a not-unreasonable concern about an American Other destroying the planet. These films situate their discourses in a southern European perspective on ecological issues.

Chemical/Biological Weapon Zombie Subtype

Probably in terms of the sheer number of films within this category, the "chemical/biological weapon zombie" (CBW) is the largest narrative tradition. This narrative cluster also reflects the greatest diversity of international collab-oration and local variants. In addition to many stand-alone films, this category includes two (possibly three)[13] different franchises. These films, despite differ-ent story worlds, all posit that the "zombie apocalypse" narrative occurred due to a failure in the development of some kind of biological or chemical weapon (usually the failure of *American* weapons of mass destruction and its impact on other countries around the world). The establishment of backstory to explain the "zombie apocalypse" is central to this particular narrative subtype. The number of films within this category suggests that explaining the apocalypse by way of a security or safety failure, usually within an American military context, is often the simplest explanation. Even *not* offering an explanation—like the "zombie apocalypse" category—requires a confidence in the story being told that many of these films do not demonstrate.

There are several key issues with this particular narrative tradition: first, it is not a coincidence that most of these films are produced during Republican administrations in the United States. Whether it is the Reagan–Bush years (1981–1993) or the George W. Bush years (2001–2009), these films reveal a cynicism toward the American military's experimentation and transparency. And this is particularly acute in non-American films. The military in these films, while they may also be the saviors of humanity by the end of the film, are the ones experimenting with chemical and biological weapons. This cynicism is perhaps best illustrated by the American comedy-horror movie *Return of the Living Dead*, wherein the military's solution to the zombie outbreak is to nuke Kansas City, the site of the outbreak. This solution is too myopic to be effective; the zombie chemical is vaporized but then carried away by rain clouds that distribute the chemical all over the country every time it rains, compounding the problem exponentially. Such is, the film argues, military logic.

Within the military-industrial context of the "CBW zombie," particularly in the post-2001 films, the zombie horde takes on a videogame disposability. The "CBW zombie" narrative does not individualize the zombies in the way some of the "zombie apocalypse" narratives do (specifically Romero's). If we compare the two, the difference becomes clear. One of the strengths of the Romero films, *all* the Romero films, is the sense that the zombies are us. Each zombie is given a character and a backstory based on what she or he was wearing at death. This device creates nostalgia for a lost America in these films. In Romero's *Dawn of the Dead*, a zombie wearing a baseball uniform seems captivated by Fran's (Gaylen Ross) beauty. He stares at her longingly (although it may be just because she looks edible), and she returns his look. Elsewhere in the Romero saga, there are those zombies who demonstrate residual memory: Bub (Howard Sherman) in *Day of the Dead*, Big Daddy (Eugene Clark) in *Land of the Dead*, and Jane (Kathleen Munroe) in *Survival of the Dead*. In contrast, the zombies of the *Resident Evil* films have little backstory. They are undifferentiated targets for the protagonists

FIGURE 3.4. "Zombies are us," from *Dawn of the Dead* (1978; screen capture). (George A. Romero)

to shoot at, reflecting the narrative's origin as a popular video game. In any combat film, when the enemy is presented as an undifferentiated mass of evil, no sympathy or understanding of the Other is possible. Due to the differentiation in the Romero films, we are aware that those zombies were once us, and we may become them in time—the chief anxiety of these films. The "CBW zombie" is more an extension of the "zombie army" tradition, wherein the fear is encounter, not assimilation. With such an undifferentiated mass of enemy, the zombies can be shot at without empathy.

In perhaps the most offensive of these films, *Osombie*, an Allied platoon (one British soldier is included to avoid suggesting an American bias) behind enemy lines in Afghanistan has two enemies to contend with: the insurgents and the zombies. The backstory here is "Operation Godsmack," a bio-chemical weapon initiative that turns the Afghanis into zombies who destroy each other. Then in come the Allies to mop up the mess. The Taliban (somehow) gets their hands on this weapon and uses it on themselves, in particular to turn Osama Bin Laden into an unstoppable monster. Both the Taliban and the zombies are effectively faceless combatants; the Taliban have their faces covered throughout, making any empathy for them impossible. These are the enemies we all love to hate.

While it is Umberto Lenzi's *Nightmare City* that really begins the "CBW zombie" film tradition, the narrative is an extension of the "pollution/

FIGURE 3.5. "Send more paramedics," from *Return of the Living Dead* (1985; screen capture). (Dan O'Bannon)

chemical spill zombie" type. What we see in a comparison of these two narrative subtypes is how a (relatively) simple change to a motif—in this case intentional contamination rather than accidental—takes on its own life and evolves quickly into its own narrative category. The key film here is O'Bannon's *Return of the Living Dead*. It modifies earlier motifs and establishes, through the film's success, the "CBW zombie" tradition.

Return of the Living Dead works on the premise that Romero's *Night of the Living Dead* was based on a true story that was covered up. A chemical designed to combat marijuana growing has the unfortunate side effect of resurrecting the dead. The "zombie apocalypse" narrative (*Night*) is modified into a "CBW zombie" narrative (*Return*) by this inclusion. Steve Miner's in the *Day of the Dead* remake does the same thing; by making the zombies "CBW zombies" he severs any connection with Romero's original film. Miner's *Day* has even less in common with the original than Snyder's *Dawn*; by changing the narrative into a "CBW zombie" subtype, the only connection appears to be the title. This suggests—rather cynically, but I think accurately—that Miner's *Day* uses the title for "brand-name recognition" on a completely different product. Such is life in the filone.

Return of the Living Dead is also noteworthy for introducing the popular motif that zombies eat brains and are sufficiently loquacious to moan the request for "Braaaaiiinns." From the corpus of films selected for this study, the specificity of the brain-eating motif is exclusive to the *Return of the Living Dead* series, at least in zombie films (the zombie computer game *Plants vs. Zombies* also use this motif). My point is that common sense suggests this motif is more ubiquitous (and global) than it actually is.[14] However, (perhaps because it was cool to make the noise) it became a popular motif in contemporary, oral lore about zombies.

Another motif introduced in the "CBW zombie" narrative also seemingly originates in *Return of the Dead*; the only way to stop the zombies in this film is to burn them (cremate them)—they seem to be immune to the severe head trauma of the Romero zombies. However, such cremation only compounds the problem because the chemical that caused the reanimation in the first place is further distributed via the rainclouds across a greater area, as I noted above. This motif is picked up in Lucio Fulci's *Zombi 3* (an Italian film made in the Philippines). *Zombi 3* also suggests that ecological disasters are easy to ignore, but that doesn't make the problem disappear. And *Zombi 3* ends in a pollution-created zombie apocalypse scenario to underline that point.

Medical Experiment Zombie Subtype

The "medical experiment" zombie narrative is obviously linked to the "CBW zombie" in that zombies are created, but it is a different subtype since these films' mad scientists are not intentionally developing weaponry. Instead, the "medical experiment" zombie narrative attempts to yoke the "zombie apocalypse" narrative back to the "zombie slave" tradition. In the "medical experiment" films, zombies themselves are often the focus of medical research. These films' doctors are trying to understand the science behind the "superstitions," which motivates the narratives in the Italian produced *Zombie, Zombie 4: After Death* and, of course, the American *The Serpent and the Rainbow*. The balance between life and death and whether it was scientifically possible to reactivate a corpse after it has died is also the focus of the *Re-Animator* films and Pupi Avati's *Zeder*.

With the exception of the *Re-Animator* series (which is set in the United States) and *Zeder* (which is set in Italy), these "medical experiment" films are set on various Caribbean islands and directly engage with issues of colonialism. In *I Eat Your Skin*,[15] for example, Dr. Biladeau (Robert Stanton) creates zombies as a byproduct of his main research, trying to develop a cure for cancer. But this discovery is taken over by Charles Bentley (Walter Coy) to develop his own personal "zombie army." In *I Eat Your Skin*, we see native populations experimented on for the benefit of Western (that is, white) civilization, as well as the notion that any quasi-benevolent attempt to introduce modern health care on these islands will be exploited by the wealthy for their own personal gain.

Perhaps Lucio Fulci's *Zombie* best illustrates not only this narrative subtype but also how categories like the zombie film can be cross-pollinated by other—quite different—genres. While the film starts off as a traditional "zombie apocalypse" movie, the zombies themselves are traced back to a mysterious Caribbean island (the fictional Matul), thereby fusing the zombie movie with the jungle adventure film. *Zombie* ignited the Italian zombie movie craze in the early 1980s. Despite the film's Italian marketing team trying to cash in on the success of Romero's *Dawn of the Dead* (released in Italy as *Zombi*, thereby making Fulci's *Zombi 2* an unofficial sequel), it owes more than a little to H. G. Wells' anti-vivisection novel, *The Island of Dr. Moreau* (1896), and Don Taylor's 1977 film version starring Burt Lancaster and Michael York specifically. *Zombie*'s Dr. Menard (Richard Johnson) is cut from the same cloth as Wells' Moreau, who attempts to discover the science behind the walking dead and refuses to believe in "native superstitions."

Despite Menard's self-congratulatory, "superior" knowledge, the postcolonial literally rises out of the ground to prove the good doctor wrong by way of a zombie epidemic he is unable to control. Like the characters in the "zombie apocalypse" films, Menard tries any number of scientific theories to explain the phenomena, but none work. The film's postcolonial discourse centers on the impotence of Menard's experiments, of the rejected attempt to impose Western culture on the island. The zombies descending on the village hospital, on a converted church, instantly suggests images of the postcolonial from earlier films like *Revolt of the Zombies* or even *Incredibly Strange Creatures*. The building represents both the imposition of Christianity and of Western science on the island, and, as such, it is a fit symbol of colonial repression for the zombies to attack. The film ends with the zombie outbreak reaching New York City, and we see the Brooklyn Bridge filled with the shambling undead on their way to take America by storm—it is this image that suggests its tenuous link with Romero's "zombie" (i.e., *Dawn of the Dead*) as almost a prequel (see figure 3.6).

In *Zombie 4: After Death*, the postcolonial discourse is made explicit: white mercenaries blame the Vodou priest for awakening the zombies, but the priest blames the mercenaries for the colonial invasion of their island.

FIGURE 3.6. "Crossing the Brooklyn Bridge." The zombie horde immigrates to take over the United States in *Zombie* (1979; screen capture). (Lucio Fulci)

What characterizes these films as postcolonial is the display of the social and cultural mechanisms of oppression—the church, science, and so forth—even if the story is told from the perspective of colonial invaders. White, European control of, for example, the Caribbean Islands, is held up for scrutiny and open critique, and the "unnaturalness" of that control is exploited (this critique is better explored in *Zombie* than in *After Death*).

While the "medical experiment" zombie subtype derives much of its identity and form from the "zombie apocalypse" narrative—and films like Fulci's underline that connection—the difference is in the story's attempt to understand the zombie scientifically. Central to the narratives in this tradition is the "mad scientist," and each of these films feature one: Dr. Biladeau in *I Eat Your Skin*, Dr. Menard in *Zombie*, the unseen Paolo Zeder in *Zeder*, and—most explicitly—Dr. Herbert West in the *Re-Animator* films. Even among the "zombie apocalypse" films, only Romero's *Day of the Dead* attempts this narrative approach of trying to study the zombies scientifically, with a character jokingly referred to as Dr. Frankenstein (Richard Liberty).

DEMONIC POSSESSION ZOMBIES

Zombies raised by "demonic possession" are not common across zombie cinema, but in certain clusters—specifically, the Spanish *[REC]* series—they suggest cultural differences that cause these narratological mutations to occur. Lucio Fulci followed up his international success of *Zombie* with two more zombie movies that were very different. Both *City of the Living Dead* and *The Beyond* are much more metaphysical horrors; the gates of hell are opened and the living dead spew forth. Together, with *Zombie*, these three films form a kind of "zombie trilogy" in Fulci's work. Demons also wreak havoc in Sam Raimi's *Evil Dead* series of films, although these are raised by reading (aloud) from the *Necromonicon*, the Book of the Dead, rather than opening one of the gates of hell.

But it is the *[REC]* series that particularly interests me here. The first *[REC]* film is a "found footage" film; a recent film style that presents (fictional) unedited footage shot by one of the characters in an extreme situation. In this case, we follow a late night television host, Angela (Manuela Velasco), and her cameraman as they follow a fire service crew to a crisis in a Barcelona apartment building. Once they arrive, they discover they are locked in the building in an attempt by the public health department, supported by the police, to isolate a zombie outbreak. Toward the end of *[REC]* and throughout *[REC]2*, the zombie outbreak narrative conforms to none of the previously discussed types: the zombie virus is a demonic presence within that building. While the zombies in *[REC]* more or less act like the zombies we've come to know—only killed with a headshot, virus contracted by bites, resurrected dead bodies—*[REC]2* and *[REC]3: Genesis* explore more of the demon/zombie connection.[16] These zombies, for example, can be pacified by the powers of prayer, they cannot cross onto hallowed ground, and they are hurt by holy water. While the films end with a "zombie apocalypse" scenario, this apocalypse is demonic rather than traditional.

The possession scenario the *[REC]* films present is predicated on an assumption of Christian (Roman Catholic) belief traditions. In Spain and Italy (to include Fulci's films in the discussion), the zombie takes on specific, religious worldview interpretations, while American zombie traditions seem to be relatively free from religious particularism.[17] We have seen the connection between zombies and the Catholic Church in the Spanish *Blind Dead* films also. Although Raimi is American (and Jewish), his adoption of the "demonic possession" narrative for his *Evil Dead* films is more to create continuity with *Grindhouse*-style horror films, like Fulci's, that were produced in the late 1970s/early 1980s than to comply with the Christian worldview.

It is debatable whether or not the "demonic possession" films qualify as proper zombie movies. I would not have included the *Evil Dead* films, for example, but I would have included the Fulci films. When I first saw the *[REC]* movies, particularly the second one, my initial thought was that, by playing the demon card, *[REC]2* removed the entire series from consideration as zombie movies. But the fact that such discussions are possible, and occur on a regular basis when fans of these films get together, suggests that these divisions and classification systems are important to those for whom these films are made.

CONCLUSION

Since 1932 and Victor Halperin's production of *White Zombie,* quite literally hundreds of zombie movies have been made around the world. These films, at least from the point of view of their narratives, cluster into distinct textual types. These narrative types demonstrate sufficient variance and continuity, and I have approached them in a modified historic-geographic way. Treating these narrative clusters as *types* enables us to examine how and why key trends emerge at specific times and in certain locations. Furthermore, we can begin to map out the life history of particular film narrative types across time and space, including seeing how these types cross-pollinate. Motifs, too, can be identified in many of these clusters: the white bokor in the "zombie slave" narrative or the undifferentiated zombie mob in the "CBW zombie" tradition, for example.

In order to do this kind of analysis, we must avoid seeing certain kinds of films as summary texts of artistic achievement. That is to say, we need to discuss each new zombie film as a variant narrative of the type, and not attempt to analyze a specific film as in any way definitive. As narrative storytelling traditions, each storyteller (the filmmaker) is (usually) aware of the tradition he or she is working in—of the other films that precede and compete with theirs. These storytellers also attempt certain kinds of innovations, or they modify the narrative in order to give the audience some kind of variety. Some of these films offer tremendous variety, others not so much.

By way of a conclusion, I will discuss one last film, *Zombie Holocaust* (1980) because it demonstrates many of the dynamics I've been discussing so far. It also demonstrates how these narrative traditions—or the filone to further embed that word in English-language film studies—operate within the Italian horror/American *Grindhouse* traditions. *Zombie Holocaust* is an intriguing crossroads film: it was produced at the point within Italian exploitation cinema when the cannibal *filone* was replaced by the zombie film. Apparently, what occurred was, while the Italian exploitation filmmakers were making pseudo-anthropological jungle adventures about cannibals, along comes George Romero's *Dawn of the Dead*. That film's success had the international exploitation market salivating. Lucio Fulci was the first to see if Romero's film was just a flash in the pan with his first zombie movie, *Zombie* (along with a healthy borrowing from *The Island of Dr. Moreau*). The international success of *that* film sent everyone scattering to make zombie pictures.[18]

Most of the action in *Zombie Holocaust* occurs on the actual jungle island of Kito (part of the Tonga archipelago) and involves a savage cannibalistic tribe. In the film's final third, zombies appear and scare off the cannibals. The zombies are the slaves of Dr. Obrero (Donald O'Brien), the result of his experiments on the island, which involved removing the brains of captured natives and putting them in the bodies of the recently dead. We effectively have the "zombie slave" tradition fused with the "medical experiment" zombie type. And Dr. Obrero himself, despite being the typical "mad-scientist" (like Dr. Menard in Fulci's *Zombie* or Dr. Moreau before that), also functions as something akin to the white bokor figure of the earlier type. *Zombie Holocaust* appears to be a casualty of this changeover of filone: while production was underway on a cannibal film, the call came through to somehow change everything to a zombie picture. The visual similarities between the two films are extraordinary, not the least of which being that they share leading man Ian McCulloch, and *Zombie Holocaust* was filmed on the same sets as *Zombie* (in Italy). More to the point, the extended gory sequences of cannibals pulling out entrails and fresh flesh from their victims owe more to the imagery from zombie movies than the cannibal filone.

The centrality of the "zombie apocalypse" cannot be minimized. To summarize the evolution of the various zombie movie traditions: 1968's *Night of the Living Dead* changed the narrative for everyone, but it wasn't until 1978's *Dawn of the Dead* that the momentum was felt throughout the filone. The success of Romero's *Dawn of the Dead* was responsible for most of the later zombie traditions. Despite *I Eat Your Skin*'s inclusion, the "medical experiment" tradition properly began in 1979 with *Zombie*. The "demonic possession" and the "CBW zombie" traditions both began in 1980 (after *Dawn* and *Zombie*) with *City of the Living Dead* and *Nightmare City*, respectively. Significantly, in their impact on world horror cinema, it was the Italians who got the zombie ball rolling. The rest, as they say, is history.

I began this chapter by evoking the explicit question asked in *Cockneys vs. Zombies*: how do we know how to kill a zombie? Like any popular culture matrix, the zombie's appearance in locales that include video games, books, television series, and—of course—mainstream and vernacular cinemas suggests that we share a good deal of knowledge about these monsters of fantasy. We know zombies are resurrected dead bodies. We know they eat people. We know they particularly like to eat brains. And we are familiar with the groaning noises they sometimes make. We know all these things simply because of the proliferation of these ideas throughout popular culture, regardless of whether one engages with these movies or not. Those who do not like gory zombie movies may still have the game *Plants vs. Zombies* on their iPhones, or they may hear about these motifs through conversations with their friends (the oral tradition). Thus, zombie popular culture motifs proliferate, much like the zombie horde itself.

APPENDIX A: LISTS OF FILMS BY COUNTRY OF PRODUCTION

The following breakdown illustrates the various countries that have produced, or contributed to the production of, zombie movies over the years. This is a small sample and should not be read as exhaustive.

Australia (AU)
Resident Evil: Extinction (US/GB/FR/DE/AU, Russell Mulcahy, 2007)

Canada (CA)
Diary of the Dead (US/CA, George A. Romero, 2007)
Land of the Dead (US/CA/FR, George A. Romero, 2005)
Resident Evil: Afterlife (DE/FR/US/CA, Paul W. S. Anderson, 2010)
Resident Evil: Apocalypse (US/GB/FR/DE/CA, Alexander Witt, 2004)
Resident Evil: Retribution (DE/FR/US/CA, Paul W. S. Anderson, 2012)
Survival of the Dead (US/CA, George A. Romero, 2009)

Cuba (CU)
Juan of the Dead (CU, Alejandro Brugues, 2011)

France (FR)
La Horde (FR, Yannick Dahan and Benjamin Rocher, 2009)

Land of the Dead (US/CA/FR, George A. Romero, 2005)
Oasis of the Zombies (FR/ES, Jesus Franco, 1982)
Resident Evil (US/GB/FR/DE, Paul W. S. Anderson, 2002)
Resident Evil: Afterlife (DE/FR/US/CA, Paul W. S. Anderson, 2010)
Resident Evil: Apocalypse (US/GB/FR/DE/CA, Alexander Witt, 2004)
Resident Evil: Extinction (US/GB/FR/DE/AU, Russell Mulcahy, 2007)
Resident Evil: Retribution (DE/FR/US/CA, Paul W. S. Anderson, 2012)
Zombie Lake (FR/ES, Jean Rollin, 1981)

Germany (DE)
Resident Evil (US/GB/FR/DE, Paul W. S. Anderson, 2002)
Resident Evil: Afterlife (DE/FR/US/CA, Paul W. S. Anderson, 2010)
Resident Evil: Apocalypse (US/GB/FR/DE/CA, Alexander Witt, 2004)
Resident Evil: Extinction (US/GB/FR/DE/AU, Russell Mulcahy, 2007)
Resident Evil: Retribution (DE/FR/US/CA, Paul W. S. Anderson, 2012)

Hong Kong (HK)
Bio Zombie (HK, Wilson Yip, 1998)

Italy (IT)
The Beyond (IT, Lucio Fulci, 1981)
Burial Ground (IT, Andrea Bianchi, 1981)
City of the Living Dead (IT, Lucio Fulci, 1980)
Hell of the Living Dead (IT/ES, Bruno Mattei, 1980)
Let Sleeping Corpses Lie (IT/ES, Jorge Grau, 1974)
Nightmare City (IT/ES/MX, Umberto Lenzi, 1980)
Zeder (IT, Pupi Avati, 1983)
Zombie (IT, Lucio Fulci, 1979)
Zombi 3 (IT, Lucio Fulci, 1988)
Zombie 4: After Death (IT, Claudio Fragasso, 1989)
Zombie 5: Killing Birds (IT, Claudio Lattanzi, 1987)
Zombie Holocaust (IT, Marino Girolami, 1980)

Japan (JP)
Return of the Living Dead 3 (US/JP, Brian Yuzna, 1993)

Mexico (MX)
Nightmare City (IT/ES/MX, Umberto Lenzi, 1980)

Norway (NO)

Dead Snow (NO, Tommy Wirkola, 2009)

Dead Snow 2: Red vs Dead (NO, Tommy Wirkola, 2014)

Spain (ES)

Beyond Re-Animator (ES, Brian Yuzna, 2003)

The Ghost Galleon (ES, Amando de Ossorino, 1974)

Hell of the Living Dead (IT/ES, Bruno Mattei, 1980)

Let Sleeping Corpses Lie (IT/ES, Jorge Grau, 1974)

Night of the Seagulls (ES, Amando de Ossorino, 1975)

Nightmare City (IT/ES/MX, Umberto Lenzi, 1980)

Oasis of the Zombies (FR/ES, Jesus Franco, 1982)

[REC] (ES, Jaume Balaguero and Paco Plaza, 2007)

[REC]2 (ES, Jaume Balaguero and Paco Plaza, 2009)

[REC]3: Genesis (ES, Paco Plaza, 2012)

[REC]4: Apocalypse (ES, Jaume Balagueró, 2014)

Return of the Evil Dead (ES, Amando de Ossorino, 1973)

Tombs of the Blind Dead (ES, Amando de Ossorino, 1972)

Vengeance of the Zombies (ES, Leon Klimovsky, 1973)

Zombie Lake (FR/ES, Jean Rollin, 1981)

United Kingdom (GB)

Cockneys vs. Zombies (GB, Matthias Hoene, 2012)

Outpost (GB, Steve Barker, 2007)

Outpost: Black Sun (GB, Steve Barker, 2012)

Outpost III: Rise of the Spetsnaz (GB, Kieran Parker, 2013)

The Plague of the Zombies (GB, John Gilling, 1966)

Resident Evil (US/GB/FR/DE, Paul W. S. Anderson, 2002)

Resident Evil: Apocalypse (US/GB/FR/DE/CA, Alexander Witt, 2004)

Resident Evil: Extinction (US/GB/FR/DE/AU, Russell Mulcahy, 2007)

Shaun of the Dead (GB, Edgar Wright, 2004)

United States of America (US)

Army of Darkness: The Medieval Dead (US, Sam Raimi, 1992)

The Astro-Zombies (US, Ted V. Mikels, 1968)

Bride of Re-Animator (US, Brian Yuzna, 1989)

Dawn of the Dead (US, George A. Romero, 1978)

Dawn of the Dead (US, Zack Snyder, 2004)

Day of the Dead (US, George A. Romero, 1985)

Day of the Dead (US, Steve Miner, 2008)

Diary of the Dead (US/CA, George A. Romero, 2007)

I Eat Your Skin (US, Del Tenney, 1964)

The Evil Dead (US, Sam Raimi, 1981)

Evil Dead (US, Fede Alvarez, 2013)

Evil Dead 2: Dead by Dawn (US, Sam Raimi, 1987)

I Walked with a Zombie (US, Jacques Tourneur, 1943)

The Incredibly Strange Creatures Who Stopped Living and Became Mixed-Up Zombies!!? (US, Ray Dennis Steckler, 1964)

King of the Zombies (US, Jean Yarborough, 1941)

Land of the Dead (US/CA/FR, George A. Romero, 2005)

Night of the Living Dead (US, George A. Romero, 1968)

Night of the Living Dead (US, Tom Savini, 1990)

Osombie (US, John Lyde, 2012)

Porn of the Dead (US, Rob Rotten, 2006)

Quarantine (US, John Erick Dowdle, 2008)

Quarantine 2: Terminal (US, John Pogue, 2011)

The Re-Animator (US, Stuart Gordon, 1985)

Resident Evil (US/GB/FR/DE, Paul W. S. Anderson, 2002)

Resident Evil: Afterlife (DE/FR/US/CA, Paul W. S. Anderson, 2010)

Resident Evil: Apocalypse (US/GB/FR/DE/CA, Alexander Witt, 2004)

Resident Evil: Extinction (US/GB/FR/DE/AU, Russell Mulcahy, 2007)

Resident Evil: Retribution (DE/FR/US/CA, Paul W. S. Anderson, 2012)

Return of the Living Dead (US, Dan O'Bannon, 1985)

Return of the Living Dead Part II (US, Ken Wiederhorn, 1988)

Return of the Living Dead 3 (US/JP, Brian Yuzna, 1993)

Return of the Living Dead: Necropolis (US, Ellory Elkayen, 2005)

Return of the Living Dead: Rave to the Grave (US, Ellory Elkayen, 2005)

Revenge of the Zombies (US, Steve Sekely, 1943)

Revolt of the Zombies (US, Victor Halperin, 1936)

The Serpent and the Rainbow (US, Wes Craven, 1988)

Sugar Hill (US, Paul Maslansky, 1974)

Survival of the Dead (US/CA, George A. Romero, 2009)

Teenage Zombies (US, Jerry Warren, 1959)

The Walking Dead (US, AMC, 2010-present)

White Zombie (US, Victor Halperin, 1932)

Zombie Strippers! (US, Jay Lee, 2008)

Zombieland (US, Ruben Fleischer, 2009)
Zombies on Broadway (US, Gordon Douglas, 1945)
Zombies vs. Strippers (US, Alex Nicolaou, 2012)

APPENDIX B: LISTS OF CATEGORIZED ZOMBIE MOVIES

The following lists and breakdowns are meant to be illustrative only; they should not be read as comprehensive.

Zombie Slaves (1932–1988)
White Zombie (US, Victor Halperin, 1932)
I Walked with a Zombie (US, Jacques Tourneur, 1943)
Zombies on Broadway (US, Gordon Douglas, 1945)
Teenage Zombies (US, Jerry Warren, 1959)
The Incredibly Strange Creatures Who Stopped Living and Became Mixed-Up Zombies!!? (US, Ray Dennis Steckler, 1964)
The Plague of the Zombies (GB, John Gilling, 1966)
The Astro-Zombies (US, Ted V. Mikels, 1968)
Vengeance of the Zombies (ES, Leon Klimovsky, 1973; originally titled *La rebelión de las muertas*)
Sugar Hill (US, Paul Maslansky, 1974)
The Serpent and the Rainbow (US, Wes Craven, 1988)

Zombie Vengeance Subtype (1932–1988)
White Zombie (US, Victor Halperin, 1932)
The Incredibly Strange Creatures Who Stopped Living and Became Mixed-Up Zombies!!? (US, Ray Dennis Steckler, 1964)
Vengeance of the Zombies (ES, Leon Klimovsky, 1973)
Sugar Hill (US, Paul Maslansky, 1974)
The Serpent and the Rainbow (US, Wes Craven, 1988)

Zombie Army (1936–1964)
Revolt of the Zombies (US, Victor Halperin, 1936)
King of the Zombies (US, Jean Yarborough, 1941)
Revenge of the Zombies (US, Steve Sekely, 1943)
I Eat Your Skin (US, Del Tenney, 1964; originally titled *Zombies*)
Outpost III: Rise of the Spetsnaz (GB, Kieran Parker, 2013)

Dead Snow 2: Red vs Dead (NO, Tommy Wirkola, 2014; originally titled
    Død Snø 2)

Zombie Revenants (1972–2012)
The *Blind Dead* Series:
Tombs of the Blind Dead (ES, Amando de Ossorino, 1972; originally titled
    La noche del terror ciego)
Return of the Evil Dead (ES, Amando de Ossorino, 1973; originally titled
    El atarque de los muertos sin ojos)
The Ghost Galleon (ES, Amando de Ossorino, 1974; originally titled *El buque
    maldito*; also known as *Horror of the Zombies*)
Night of the Seagulls (ES, Amando de Ossorino, 1975; originally titled
    La noche de las gaviotas)
Burial Ground (IT, Andrea Bianchi, 1981; originally titled *Le notti del terrore*;
    also known as *The Nights of Terror*)
Zombie Lake (FR/ES, Jean Rollin, 1981; originally titled *Le lac des morts
    vivants*)
Oasis of the Zombies (FR/ES, Jesus Franco, 1982; originally titled *La tumba de
    los muertos vivientes*; also known as *The Treasure of the Living Dead*)
Outpost (GB, Steve Barker, 2007)
Dead Snow (NO, Tommy Wirkola, 2009; originally titled *Død Snø*)
Outpost: Black Sun (GB, Steve Barker, 2012)

Nazi Zombies Subtype (1941–2012)
King of the Zombies (US, Jean Yarborough, 1941)
Revenge of the Zombies (US, Steve Sekely, 1943)
Zombie Lake (FR/ES, Jean Rollin, 1981)
Oasis of the Zombies (FR/ES, Jesus Franco, 1982)
Outpost (GB, Steve Barker, 2007)
Dead Snow (NO, Tommy Wirkola, 2009)
Outpost: Black Sun (US, Steve Barker, 2012)
Outpost III: Rise of the Spetsnaz (GB, Kieran Parker, 2013)
Dead Snow 2: Red vs Dead (NO, Tommy Wirkola, 2014)

Zombie Apocalypse (1968–present)
The Original Romero Trilogy:
Night of the Living Dead (US, George A. Romero, 1968)
Dawn of the Dead (US, George A. Romero, 1978)

Day of the Dead (US, George A. Romero, 1985)

Zombie 5: Killing Birds (IT, Claudio Lattanzi, 1987; also known as *Killing Birds: Raptors*)

Night of the Living Dead (US, Tom Savini, 1990)

Dawn of the Dead (US, Zack Snyder, 2004)

Shaun of the Dead (GB, Edgar Wright, 2004)

Porn of the Dead (US, Rob Rotten, 2006)

The Second Romero Trilogy:

Land of the Dead (US/CA/FR, George A. Romero, 2005)

Diary of the Dead (US/CA, George A. Romero, 2007)

Survival of the Dead (US/CA, George A. Romero, 2009)

La Horde (FR, Yannick Dahan and Benjamin Rocher, 2009)

Zombieland (US, Ruben Fleischer, 2009)

The Walking Dead (US, AMC, 2010-present)

Juan of the Dead (CU, Alejandro Brugues, 2011; originally titled *Juan de los Muertos*)

Cockneys vs. Zombies (GB, Matthias Hoene, 2012)

Zombies vs. Strippers (US, Alex Nicolaou, 2012)

Pollution/Chemical Spill Zombie Subtype (Accidental) (1974–1980)

Let Sleeping Corpses Lie (IT/ES, Jorge Grau, 1974; originally titled *Non si deve profanare il sonno dei morti*; also known as *The Living Dead at the Manchester Morgue*)

Hell of the Living Dead (IT/ES, Bruno Mattei, 1980; originally titled *Virus*; also known as *Zombie Creeping Flesh*)

Chemical/Biological Weapon Zombie Subtype (1980–present)

Nightmare City (IT/ES/MX, Umberto Lenzi, 1980; originally titled *Incubo sulla città contaminata*; also known as *City of the Walking Dead*)

Return of the Living Dead series:

Return of the Living Dead (US, Dan O'Bannon, 1985)

Return of the Living Dead Part II (US, Ken Wiederhorn, 1988)

Return of the Living Dead 3 (US/JP, Brian Yuzna, 1993)

Return of the Living Dead: Necropolis (US, Ellory Elkayen, 2005)

Return of the Living Dead: Rave to the Grave (US, Ellory Elkayen, 2005)

Zombi 3 (IT, Lucio Fulci, 1988; also known as *Zombie Flesh Eaters 2*)

Bio-Zombie (HK, Wilson Yip, 1998; originally titled *Sun faa sau si*)

Resident Evil series:

Resident Evil (US/GB/FR/DE, Paul W. S. Anderson, 2002)

Resident Evil: Apocalypse (US/GB/FR/DE/CA, Alexander Witt, 2004)

Resident Evil: Extinction (US/GB/FR/DE/AU, Russell Mulcahy, 2007)

Resident Evil: Afterlife (DE/FR/US/CA, Paul W. S. Anderson, 2010)

Resident Evil: Retribution (DE/FR/US/CA, Paul W. S. Anderson, 2012)

Day of the Dead (US, Steve Miner, 2008)

Quarantine (US, John Erick Dowdle, 2008)

Zombie Strippers! (US, Jay Lee, 2008)

Quarantine 2: Terminal (US, John Pogue, 2011)

Osombie (US, John Lyde, 2012)

Medical Experiment Zombie Subtype (1964–2003)

I Eat Your Skin (US, Del Tenney, 1964)

[REC]4: Apocalypse (ES, Jaume Balagueró, 2014)

Zombie (IT, Lucio Fulci, 1979; originally titled *Zombi 2*; also known as *Zombie Flesh Eaters*)

Zombie Holocaust (IT, Marino Girolami, 1980; originally titled *Zombi Holocaust*; also known as *Dr. Butcher, M. D. [Medical Deviant]*)

Zeder (IT, Pupi Avati, 1983; also known as *Revenge of the Dead*)

The *Re-Animator* series:

The Re-Animator (US, Stuart Gordon, 1985)

Bride of Re-Animator (US, Brian Yuzna, 1989)

Beyond Re-Animator (ES, Brian Yuzna, 2003)

The Serpent and the Rainbow (US, Wes Craven, 1988)

Zombie 4: After Death (US, Claudio Fragasso, 1989; originally titled *Oltre la morte*; also known as *After Death*)

Demonic Possession Zombies (1980–present)

City of the Living Dead (IT, Lucio Fulci, 1980); originally titled *Paura nella città dei morti viventi*; also known as *The Gates of Hell*)

The Beyond (IT, Lucio Fulci, 1981; originally titled *E tu vivrai nel terrore! L'aldinà*)

The *Evil Dead* series:

The Evil Dead (US, Sam Raimi, 1981)

Evil Dead 2: Dead by Dawn (US, Sam Raimi, 1987)

Army of Darkness: The Medieval Dead (US, Sam Raimi, 1992)

Evil Dead (US, Fede Alvarez, 2013)

Zombie 4: After Death (IT, Claudio Fragasso, 1989)

The *[REC]* series:

[REC] (ES, Jaume Balaguero and Paco Plaza, 2007)

[REC]2 (ES, Jaume Balaguero and Paco Plaza, 2009)

[REC]3: Genesis (ES, Paco Plaza, 2012)

[REC]4: Apocalypse (ES, Jaume Balagueró, 2014)

NOTES

1. The history of the Haitian zombie figure can be found in a variety of ethnographic (and sensationalist) books (see Brown 1989; Davis [1987] 1994; Hurston [1938] 1990; Russell 2005; Seabrook [1929] 1999).
2. Pronounced "phil-ony."
3. The complexity of the repercussions of such an understanding cannot be fully expressed in a chapter. One is either prepared to grant the benefit of the doubt to see where this analysis leads, or one is not.
4. Appendix B gives a list of these narrative types and a selective list of films that would be included under each. Needless to say, some films can appear in more than two categories, although that is rare. This list also functions as this chapter's filmography.
5. Diegetic refers to the "story world" of the film as a self-contained space separate from the audience's "real world."
6. Appendix A lists the films discussed in this chapter categorized by their producing countries; some films were the product of several countries' contributions (usually financial) and are therefore listed multiple times. This list is intended to illustrate the international diversity of these movies, and should not be assumed to be comprehensive nor exhaustive.
7. While the *bokor* is often highly respected within Haitian village life, legend narratives abound that tell of *bokors* going bad and using "black magic" for their own gain, or who are paid by those who wish to gain (see Davis [1987] 1994).
8. The Tonton Macoute was the secret police force set up to support dictator Francois "Papa Doc" Duvalier after his coup d'état in 1957. The force was named after a figure from Haitian folklore, one of the "loa" (gods) who would kidnap children in gunnysacks and take them to be eaten. The Macoute were used to spread a reign of terror throughout the island nation; their atrocities included unknown numbers of rapes, murders, public stonings, and burning people alive. After his death in 1971, "Papa Doc" was succeeded by his son, Jean-Claude (known as "Bebe Doc"), until his exile in 1986, but the Tonton Macoute were active into the 1990s.

9. Horror films about Egyptian mummies coming back to life also fit into this category.

10. The third film, *Outpost III: Rise of the Spetsnaz*, is a World War II-set backstory to the other *Outpost* films.

11. This isn't strictly true, as the National Guard patrol members who stop the young filmmakers in *Diary of the Dead* become the central characters in *Survival of the Dead*. But this is the exception that proves the rule.

12. Savini, of course, is the special effects makeup guru (who also worked on Romero's *Dawn of the Dead*); with *Night of the Living Dead*, he was making his directorial debut.

13. The *Quarantine* series is not yet a franchise; at the time of this writing, only two films have been produced. Should a third be produced, it would become a franchise.

14. The only exception I've come across to date that proves this rule is the low-budget *Zombies vs. Strippers*. In this film, the zombies are also brain hungry.

15. Despite the wonderfully exploitive title, *I Eat Your Skin* was filmed as "Zombies" but was bought out in 1970 to act as a double bill with *I Drink Your Blood*. This illustrates exploitation marketing and how distributors are able to recycle older films.

16. *[REC]4: Apocalypse* more or less abandons the demonic elements of the zombie virus but recontextualizes within a more medical experimentation narrative.

17. While the American *Quarantine* is almost a shot-for-shot remake of *[REC]*, it does away completely with the "demonic possession" motif from the Spanish film. And it's sequel, *Quarantine 2: Terminal*, does not attempt to remake *[REC]2* at all, thereby avoiding the demonic/religious elements that might be a more difficult "sell" at American multiplex cinemas.

18. This is, of course, a crude oversimplification to make a point.

WORKS CITED

Bacchilega, Cristina. 1997. *Postmodern Fairy Tales: Gender and Narrative Strategies*. Philadelphia: University of Pennsylvania Press.

Bascom, William. 1954. "Four Functions of Folklore." *Journal of American Folklore* 67: 333–49.

———. 1965. "The Forms of Folklore: Prose Narratives." *Journal of American Folklore* 78: 3–20.

Brown, Karen McCarthy. 1989. "Voodoo." In *Magic, Witchcraft, and Religion: An Anthropological Study of the Supernatural*, edited by Arthur Lehmann and James Myers, 321-26. Mountain View, CA: Mayfield.

Buchan, David. 1986. "Tale Roles and Revenants: A Morphology of Ghosts." *Western Folklore* 45.2: 143–60.

Davis, Wade. [1987] 1994. *The Serpent and the Rainbow*. London: Time Warner.

Fanon, Frantz. [1961] 2001. *The Wretched of the Earth*. London: Penguin.

Hurston, Zora Neale. [1938] 1990. *Tell My Horse: Voodoo and Life in Haiti and Jamaica*. London: Harper and Row.

Koven, Mikel. 2008. *Film, Folklore, and Urban Legends*. Lanham, MD: Scarecrow Press.

Krohn, Kaarle. [1926] 1971. *Folklore Methodology*. Formulated by Julius Krohn and expanded by Nordic Researchers; translated by Roger L. Welsch. Austin, TX: University of Texas Press.

Russell, Jamie. 2005. *Book of the Dead: The Complete History of Zombie Cinema*. Godalming, UK: FAB Press.

Said, Edward. [1978] 2003. *Orientalism*. London: Penguin Books.

Sconce, Jeffrey. 1995. "'Trashing' the Academy: Taste, Excess, and an Emerging Politics of Cinematic Style." *Screen* 36(4): 371–93.

Seabrook, William. [1929] 1966. *Voodoo Island*. London: Four Square Books.

Stone, Kay. 2008. *Some Day Your Witch Will Come*. Detroit, MI: Wayne State University Press.

Thompson, Stith. [1946] 1977. *The Folktale*. Berkeley, CA: University of California Press.

Tiffin, Jessica. 2009. *Marvelous Geometry: Narrative and Metafiction in Modern Fairy Tale*. Detroit, MI: Wayne State University Press.

Toelken, Barre. 1996. *The Dynamics of Folklore*. Logan, UT: Utah State University Press.

Warner, Marina. 1995. *From the Beast to the Blonde: On Fairy Tales and Their Tellers*. New York: Vintage.

Zipes, Jack. [1983] 2006. *Fairy Tales and the Art of Subversion*. London, UK: Routledge.

———. 2011. *The Enchanted Screen: The Unknown History of the Fairy-Tale Film*. London: Routledge.

4

Twihards, Buffistas, *and* Vampire Fanlore

The Internet

LYNNE S. MCNEILL

If there is in this world a well-attested account, it is that of vampires. Nothing is lacking: official reports, affidavits of well-known people, of surgeons, of priests, of magistrates; the judicial proof is most complete. And with all that, who is there who believes in vampires?

—Jean-Jacques Rousseau, quoted in Barber (1998)

Because I would tell people that I watch the show and people would go, "Buffy the Vampire Slayer?" and then I'd feel silly. And it was a place to go where I didn't feel silly. It made me feel like it was okay for me to watch the show and like it as much as I did. A place that I felt like I belonged 2 and I could go anytime I wanted and I didn't have to worry about being mocked or judged . . . unless it was in a fun way.

—amberlynne, quoted in Tuszynski (2006)

Even the most cursory consideration of where vampire folklore exists leads to some rather obvious locales: Transylvania and Eastern Europe for a start, though perhaps more commonly nowadays we'd find Sunnydale, California, and Forks, Washington, on the list, too.[1] But there's another place that we find a different type of vampire folklore: the Internet. This chapter examines vampire folk culture online and considers why the digital setting is an ideal place for certain kinds of vampire folklore.

When Rousseau posed the question, "Who is there who believes in vampires?" to the archbishop of Paris, he was making a rhetorical point about the potential hazards of the easy interpretation of evidence. The fact that the same rhetorical scenario seems equally plausible almost 300 years later—vampires could hardly be more pervasive in the popular landscape and yet, as will be discussed, their ubiquity rarely takes the form of actual belief—makes his question perhaps a bit more pointed. While genuine, traditional vampire folk beliefs, beliefs in a supernatural undead creature that preys on the living, do still exist in some places, the majority of vampire interest in contemporary American culture today falls outside the realm of literal, or even potential, belief.

As saturated as our contemporary culture is with vampires, there's a clear awareness that vampires are a literary creation. In a brief online survey of just over 100 people,[2] 78% answered "No" to the question "Do you believe in vampires?" An additional 14% replied "It's complicated," and offered such elaborations as "[Only] as a metaphor," or "I believe in people that practice vampirism," or "[I] know people drink blood or feed off energy but they are not living dead or immortal," or "I believe in psychic vampires, and I have no problem with vampire lifestylers wanting to be referred to as Vampires. But I'd have to be bitten by an immortal with a cape before I believe in Dracula."[3]

When asked about their general awareness of traditional beliefs about vampires, most of the respondents listed the common information provided in literary and popular depictions of the vampire: aversion to garlic and sunlight, sleeping in coffins, no reflection, harmed by religious imagery and consecrated objects. Some respondents even pointedly ascribed their understandings of the vampire to popular media: "Vampires used to be ugly until *Interview With a Vampire* and then people started thinking they were shmexy. Vampires sleep in coffins, can't be in daylight, can only be killed by a stake to the heart, find garlic aversive, feed on blood (preferably human) . . . that's about all I can remember. I'm sure everything I learned was from pop culture (buffy the vampire [sic] and all the newer shitty vampire movies)."

The most popular source of "legitimate" information (as perceived by respondents) was, unsurprisingly, Bram Stoker's *Dracula*, which has had inordinate influence over perceptions of vampires (not to mention perceptions of the entire country of Transylvania, a place Stoker himself never visited).[4] Other mass-media sources cited are LeFanu's *Carmilla*, Anne Rice's *Interview with the Vampire*, and the popular television shows *Buffy the Vampire Slayer* and *True Blood*. Stephenie Meyer's *Twilight Saga*, both the books and the films, received a lot of attention but were generally considered a corruption of the "traditional" vampire. The concept of a "traditional" vampire was ambiguous for many respondents; older works of fiction are considered more traditional than the more modern creations. As one respondent put it: "I get confused between what I've read in fictional works vs. what I've read about folklore." It's interesting to note, however, that, as illustrated in this comment, both literature and folklore are treated as external cultural productions; the folklore mentioned is not the participant's *own* folk beliefs, but the traditional beliefs of others about which he or she has read. The awareness of a folk tradition separate from the more literary works still doesn't place the vampire firmly in the realms of possibility for the respondents themselves.

Respondents who did know of the more folkloric model of vampire belief cited it mainly from an exoteric perspective, listing off other cultures' beliefs and past misunderstandings of death, burial, and decomposition. In almost no cases were vampires treated as a legitimate subject for possible belief. Some respondents said something along the lines of "I don't really believe, but I can't say for sure, as I have no true evidence either way," but most responses revealed a surprising lack of the additional information that typically accompanies such ambivalent statements about other supernatural phenomena: *memorates*. While personal encounters with ghosts, aliens, guardian angels, and Bigfoot are fairly commonly reported, there are very few memorates dealing with vampires. For example, the holdings of the Fife Folklore Archives at Utah State University offer a meager three instances of vampire belief, all of which attribute the belief to past foreign cultures or feature literary tropes. In contrast, the archives has over fifty stories of Bigfoot sightings and several hundred personal accounts of ghosts.

This contrast is common; several respondents volunteered ghosts and aliens as possible realities, despite being asked specifically about vampires. The prevalence of genuine belief (or potential belief) in ghosts and aliens casts the non-viability of vampires into stark relief; not only in folklore but also in popular culture, ghost and aliens receive a consideration that vampires do not. Television shows that feature technological ghost hunting and historical alien seeking abound, but no reality shows exist about searching for literal, undead vampires. Some popular shows even consider the possibility of blatantly supernatural realities when it comes to ghosts—Britain's *Most Haunted* has employed a psychic along with the technophiles to help apprehend any errant spirits. But even with the apparent willingness of popular media to allow for the consideration of ghosts as a real phenomenon, we have yet to see the same treatment for vampires, further evidence that they are widely regarded as fiction.

PARTICIPATORY CULTURE

The fact that vampires are generally regarded as a fictional concept does not, interestingly, prevent the formation of a contemporary folk culture about vampires; it simply means that we shouldn't be looking at the genres of belief in order to find it. If we turn instead to the realms of fandom, we find a thriving folk culture centered on vampires. Most people don't automatically think of fan culture when they think of vampire folklore, but, given the current state of popular attention, fandom far outweighs supernatural belief when it comes to actual folk circulation of vampire-themed lore. Television shows such as *Buffy the Vampire Slayer* and *True Blood*, along with books and films like *Interview with the Vampire,* Bram Stoker's *Dracula,* and *The Twilight Saga,* all provide audience members with rich grounds on which to build an intense fandom.

The understanding of fandom as a folk culture is not new, and, with the rise of new media studies, the consideration of fandom as a subject worthy of academic study has been taken to new heights. Henry Jenkins, an early scholar of fan cultures, notes in 1998 that this was not always the case:

> The fan constitutes a scandalous category in contemporary American culture, one that calls into question the logic by which others order their aesthetic experiences, one that provokes an excessive response from those committed to the interests of textual producers. Fans appear to be frighteningly "out of control," undisciplined and unrepentant, rogue readers. Rejecting "aesthetic distance," fans passionately embrace favored texts and attempt to integrate media representations within their own social experience. (39)

This integration of media representations into fans' own cultural endeavors is at the root of the concept of "participatory culture." Rather than simply remaining as passive consumers of mass media, fans now have the technological capabilities to engage with the media they receive. They become active agents in the further evolution of that media. Not only in the writing of fanfiction (which took place long before the Internet was in popular use, but which found a much broader mode of distribution there) but also in the creation of high quality fan art, movie trailers, cross-title mash-ups (e.g., *Twilight* meets *Buffy*), and role playing games[5] can we see a new level of personalization and engagement with popular culture.

This level of engagement and participation has always been a quality of folk culture. When people hear legends, tales, folksongs, and jokes, or when they observe the enactment of customs or the making of crafts, they are able—and often expected—to turn around and recreate them in new contexts and with new audiences, perpetuating both the conservative and dynamic elements of the folk transmission process.[6] This level of personal engagement and creation simply wasn't possible with many forms of popular culture before technological advances made easy-to-use audio-, video-, and image-editing tools available on a wide scale. When moviegoers first saw *Star Wars* in theaters in 1977, they didn't have the skills or technology to recreate and build upon that material. They could see the film again, knowing it would be identically reproduced each time, and they could certainly discuss it with fellow moviegoers (and, in many cases, engage in imaginative play based on the material), but they couldn't utilize the forms and tools of film production to add their iterations to the film, nor could they widely broadcast any imaginative engagement they did pursue.

Personal computing technology has changed that. When Canadian teenager Ghyslain Raza filmed himself fighting with a golf ball retriever as though it were a double-sided lightsaber in 2002, he was engaging in a common form of fan play. When that video went viral online in 2003, it spawned an amazing, ongoing fan response.[7] Just over a week after its initial upload, the first CGI-enhanced version debuted.[8] Subsequent viewers added sound effects and visual effects; some even added official frames such as the Lucasfilm Ltd. and 20th Century Fox logos to turn Raza into the star of impressively edited, faux movie trailers. In an increasingly common response from the mass media, several television programs made reference to the "*Star Wars* Kid," as Raza is now known, swinging the content back into the realm of mass-mediated production.

This fan-generated process of creation simply would not have been possible before contemporary communications and design technology, but the process isn't new. People have always taken the expressive culture around them—as skill and access have allowed—and regenerated it into new forms of their own. Participatory culture is basically the folk process enacted with the stuff of popular culture.

In fact, the distinction between a regular audience member and a true "fan" of a given popular franchise seems to speak to the familiar folkloristic distinction between passive and active bearers. Some audience members simply listen or observe and know and even enjoy the content, but others take that reception as a launching point for re-creation and production. As Jenkins explains, "One becomes a 'fan' not by being a regular viewer of a particular program but by translating that viewing into some kind of cultural activity, by sharing feelings and thoughts about the program content with friends, by joining a 'community' of other fans who share common interests. For fans, consumption naturally sparks production, reading generates writing, until the terms seem logically inseparable" (2006, 41).

In this sense, fandom is comprised of active engagement with the traditional (re)creation of popular media materials. Others may define "fan" less stringently, allowing for a more passive interest to qualify, but it's evident that the folk process is most clearly represented by an engaged participatory culture (which, by definition, needs to be participatory). The greater attention this process has received—due to more people taking part in it—has gone a long way to legitimize both fandom and the academic study of it.

VAMPIRE FAN CULTURE ONLINE

For the sake of containment, this chapter is going to focus on two main sources of vampire fan culture: *Buffy the Vampire Slayer* and *Twilight*.[9] As fandoms go, these two franchises have seen enormous success in generating active and committed fan cultures. *Buffy the Vampire Slayer* is a television show (initially a stand-alone film) created by writer/director Joss Whedon that aired from 1997 to 2003. It recounts the story of a young woman, Buffy Summers, who, despite her appearance as a cute and friendly high school student, is in fact the latest in a long history of young women called to protect the world from evil supernatural forces. The academic consideration of *Buffy* as a pop culture phenomenon is not new (Ulaby 2003); from the start, many "aca-fans" (academics who are also fans) found the series ripe for scholarly consideration. Non-academic fans apparently felt similarly, as Buffy fans (sometimes self-labeled as "Buffistas" or denizens of "Buffonia" or "the Buffyverse") have gone to great lengths to construct opportunities to engage in their fandom, creating online and offline fan clubs, organizing conventions and conferences, and generating an insider culture unique to their fandom.

Stephenie Meyer's *Twilight Saga*, first a series of books and then a movie franchise, came on the scene much later, in 2005, after new episodes of *Buffy* had stopped airing. The book series was spectacularly popular, and—while it received mixed criticism for its quality of writing and its seemingly anti-feminist message—it was an immediate hit with readers. The saga tells the story of Isabella Swan, a high school student who has moved to the tiny town of Forks, Washington, where she meets and falls in love with Edward Cullen, a vampire. Fans of the books and films often identify as "Twihards" or affiliate with a sub-group such as "Team Edward" or "Team Jacob," depending on which of the two male romantic leads they feel Bella (or they themselves) should choose. The *Twilight* fandom has received a lot of attention in the press, especially once the extent to which the fandom had spread beyond the target audience of young adult female readers was realized.

These two franchises are similar in placing a vampire story in a typical American high school setting (a strong commentary on the nature of the high school experience, if nothing else) and giving the audience a female lead. Both involve romantic relationships between humans and vampires, and both portray vampires as powerful, appealing, and attractive, at least most of the time. While vampires in the Buffyverse transform into frightening monsters when they feed on humans, they are able to pass as human at other times. *Twilight*'s vampires go a step further, becoming *more* beautiful as vampires than they were as mortals in order to better attract their prey (humans). This is a motif that has grown increasingly common since Anne Rice's *Interview with the Vampire* was published in 1976. Rice situated the vampire as the protagonist of the story, rather than the antagonist. During this "tectonic shift" in the vampire mythos, as gothic literature scholar Victoria Nelson puts it (2011, 143), vampires not only went from object to subject but also from "undead" to "immortal," casting them almost as gods rather than monsters.

This is a far cry from the earliest folkloric accounts of vampires, which much more closely resemble today's cinematic zombies than Robert Pattinson's handsome, glittering Edward Cullen. Vampires and zombies, at least as they are popularly understood, share many traits: they are the living dead, walking corpses that pass on their affliction through bites and feed on living humans. The themes brought out by both these supernatural creatures are very similar—contagion, bodily decay, the questionable value of life after death—with the key difference being physical repugnancy. It seems that as a society we have a psychological need to confront the horror of the decomposing body and the dangers of contagion; as our vampires have grown more sanitized and beautiful (to the point where we would perhaps *want* to become one), we have increasingly turned our cultural attention toward the zombie apocalypse.

Despite the growing attention to zombies, fans still find the vampires emerging from this tectonic shift incredibly appealing, and fan culture reflects their interest. As Jenkins's (2006) focus on "textual" poaching suggests, an enormous amount of shared fan culture online centers on the creation of fanfiction (commonly known as "fanfic," or, in the context of *Twilight* specifically, "twific"). This is one of the most significant ways that fans can engage with a fictional world: creating relationships,[10] plotlines, and related scenarios that they'd always hoped to see in the source material. Almost all fanfiction sites clearly state that they do not own any of the characters and are not intending to infringe on copyright. However, there is still a clear sense of ownership over the material:

!! ATTENTION !!
Twilight and its characters belong to Stephenie Meyer, kay?
No copyright infringement is intended with the writing and distribution of this story.
BUT . . .
Http://angstgoddess003.livejournal.com
Http://www.FanFiction.net/~angstgoddess003
Http://www.Twitter.com/angstgoddess003
Credit is awesome, you know? Like . . . baked goods. Like even if I baked you cookies from a recipe that's not mine, you still say, "Hey, dude, look! AG made us cookies from Stephenie Meyer's recipe!"
Then you omnomnom them, and I'm all smiley happy,
because you gave me credit for the baking of the cookies.
It's totally like that.
Except I don't make cookies.
I make FanFiction. (AngstGoddess003 2009)

This is an interesting illustration of the question of ownership in participatory culture. Borrowing and copying have always been regular methods of re-creation in folk transmission. No one who retells a joke or an urban legend feels the slightest sense that they owe royalties to the person they heard it from. In fact, Rebecca Tushnet's (1997) consideration of copyright

law and fanfiction opens with a typical folk-play situation: a young girl
playing with Barbie dolls and making up her own story about them. Is that
little girl violating the law? What if she sends the stories, or a video of her
dramatic play with the dolls, to her friends via email or posts them online?
These are typical forms of play, and it's with this same instinctive folk spirit
that much participatory culture happens, but the Internet has introduced an
opportunity for everyday people to achieve mass broadcast, so the copyright
holders may see infringement over creativity. As Tushnet says, "Most readily
available and widely known characters are now corporate creatures" (1997,
652); our easy integration of corporate property into our own creative works
shouldn't always be taken lightly.

Fanfiction proliferates nonetheless, and its subjects range from mundane
and true to the source material to wildly inventive and contradictory to the
canon. Despite popular perception, not all fanfiction contains adult content,
and often authors simply create short vignettes that flesh out a situation
suggested in the source. A detailed and complex vernacular has cropped up
within the fanfiction realm that helps readers identify stories they might be
interested in. While the specifics are unique to various web forums, one can
typically find rating systems, content markers, relationship indicators, and
theme designations. Some fan communities sponsor challenges or contests
designed to get writers focused on a specific topic, relationship, or theme.

Some writers prefer to create more complex types of fanfiction, stories
that address, riff on, or question the very nature of the source material as a
fictional universe. The freedom of fanfiction allows for the breaking of the
fourth wall at any time, and it's not uncommon to find Stephenie Meyer's
characters talking about Meyer herself:

> "We've been through this before." I pout, chewing my lip as if it's a
> particularly tough piece of steak.
>
> "We haven't," Edward assures me. "Please, Bella, I have so much
> regret. I've been a fool."
>
> "No doubt!" I snort, unbuttoning my hospital gown. "It's not
> your fault, buddy. Stephenie Meyer wrote you as an emo douchebag.
> I suppose it's part of your appeal. Although for reasons I'll never
> understand, you're sometimes portrayed as a wealthy CEO in fanfic-
> tion who's into sado masochistic sex."
>
> "That's preposterous."
>
> "I certainly thought so. But the unwashed masses seem to dig it."

"What exactly are we talking about here, Bella?"
"Nothing. I'm lost in a tangent."
"And who is Stephenie Meyer?" (BellaFlan 2009)

This particular scene comes from an intense, fifty-one-chapter story of a young woman who suffers from an identity crisis due to, among other things, her love for the *Twilight* book series. While still participating in the fictional world of the source material, the author demonstrates an awareness of the externality of the real world. She is able to criticize Edward Cullen as a fan might (acknowledging that his flaws are simply how he was written) as well as reference other works of fanfiction (the wealthy CEO is Christian Grey from the book *Fifty Shades of Grey*, which originally began as *Twilight* fanfiction).[11]

The creation of fanfiction aside, other shared practices among most online fan groups clearly highlight a shared folk culture.[12] Folkspeech is a common identity-reinforcing element of virtual communities; Nancy Baym notes that shared "terms and genres are markers of insider status and hence help to forge group identity" (2010, 78). The unconscious nature of this language patterning emphasizes how these online communities form and evolve quite naturally—"they guide one's communication without having to be considered" (79)—and the skill in using the language and norms of a group is one way in which internal hierarchies are observed and maintained. Only truly committed group members will acquire true skill in communicating successfully, despite the fact that often a glossary of insider terms is provided. Buffistas.org's FAQ page provides a sample:

Q. TT?
A. Table Talk. The discussion forum at Salon.com.
Q. WX?
A. World Crossing. (X = Cross. Geddit?)
Q. Why do you call yourselves the Buffistas?
A. It comes from a tagline "Do not startle the Buffistas."
(2008)

It's clear that the delineation of insider vs. outsider is a key element to the knowledgeable use of these terms. There is even sometimes a confusing use of insider terminology while explaining other terminology, and group-specific vernacular often plays off of an understanding of other groups' vernaculars, such as in the following examples from the same FAQ page:

FIGURE 4.1. *Twilight* Moms. (Tycho124, motifake.com)

Q. What's the deal with BuffyNAngle4Evah!!!?
A. BuffiNAngle4Evah!!! is a parody of the sort of thing people Not
Like Us say. It's a way of saying "Yes, I am unalterably committed to
the Buffy/Angel relationship being Eternal, and yes, I am well aware of
how silly this makes me look." In a compact fashion. It saves us all an
argument. And, you know, everybody on the Internet is a bad speller.

Or

Q. Hey, who or what is a DH, SO, GF, BF?
A. Dear husband, significant other, girlfriend and boyfriend,
respectively.
Q. What's with the exclamation points in stuff like ShitTogether!-
Xander and Mopey!Buffy?
A. According to Dana D., it's something originated in other fandoms,
especially those that have a lot of fanfic. It's used to describe a commonly seen variety of a character; we usually apply it to a particular
trait or dimension of a character, such as Catty!Willow.

While most of this folkspeech is both generated and perpetuated by
insiders to the fandom, there is also a good deal of exoteric folklore, often

FIGURE 4.2. Buffy versus Edward. (deviantart.com)

bordering on *blason populaire*: folk culture about fans from other fans or from non-fans. This divides not only vampire fans from non-fans but also certain types of vampire fans from other types. The label "Twimom," self-applied by many adult women who are fans of *Twilight* (and the name of a large online fan community), is often etically applied with a derogatory tone, as exemplified in the popular "Twilight Moms" Internet meme (figure 4.1).

There are also folk creations within the fandoms that highlight in- and out-group preferences. The "Buffy vs. Edward" memes are a common example (see, for example, figures 4.2 and 4.3). Blurring the lines between source materials allows fans to break the confines of commercial designations and make statements about the comparative validity of those sources.

FIGURE 4.3. Buffy versus Edward. (WeirdNutDaily.com)

In figure 4.4, which contrasts *Buffy* and *Twilight* (though it never explicitly mentions the latter), we see fans placing both an awareness of and opinions about *Twilight* into the minds of Buffy and Angel. Here, it's not the Buffistas who are critical of *Twilight*'s depiction of a vampire/human relationship, but Buffy and Angel themselves.[13]

THE INTERNET AS A "PLACE"

Internet ethnographer Christine Hine (2000) has noted that, for many years now, ethnographers have derived authority over a specific culture by means of travel to a particular place. Especially in times when global travel wasn't typical or readily accessible, simply having been to a particular place made one something of an expert on that place. Even today, when travel is accessible to many people and the line between ethnographer and thoughtful tourist is quite blurred, physical travel still stands as something of a prerequisite for quality ethnographic study. This concept is understandably thrown into disarray when the "place" under ethnographic consideration is the

FIGURE 4.4. *Buffy* contrasted with *Twilight*. (rattlesnakeroot, photobucket.com)

Internet. The concept of "travel," if it still applies at all, can only be used in a metaphorical way. This, of course, is because the Internet isn't a "place" in the way a city or country or region of the world is. But to hear Internet users speak of it, it *is* a kind of place—a place to go to meet people, pursue hobbies, find information, go shopping, pay bills, watch movies, argue points, and catch up with friends. In fact, given the diversity of activities that happen there, the Internet appears to be several places all at once.

Conceiving the Internet as a place might be instinctual for those who spend time there, but it clearly requires rethinking the basic concept of "location" or "geography." Hine discusses this and concludes that "visiting the Internet focuses on *experiential* rather than *physical* displacement" (2000, 45; emphasis added). This more open understanding of the concept of place isn't new; in 1977 cultural geographer Yi-Fu Tuan conceived of place as a "concretion of value" more than a specific location, as "an object in which one can dwell" (Tuan 1977, 12). John A. Jakle's (1987) concept of place as "a setting that, because it contains a distinctive range of social interactions, may be thought of as inviting or inducing the continuation of those inter-actions" (4) suits the Internet quite well, as technology has come to be used for social, cultural, and commercial interaction on a regular basis. For fans, interaction with and about their chosen subject takes place consistently and regularly in a variety of web forums, thus making those sites places that they consistently visit.

With regard to Internet fandom, technology has provided people with a way to have interactive access within a fictional universe that would other-wise exclude them. Speaking about The Bronze, a longstanding Buffy fan forum named after one of Buffy's favorite hangouts in Sunnydale, one mem-ber explains:

> I don't think I ever even said "I'm going to go look at the Bronze."
> I would say "I'm going to the Bronze." I remember the first time I
> said it to my father, and I was literally in the living room and my
> home office was down the hall and he said, "What are you getting
> ready to do?" And I said, "Oh, I'm going [to] the Bronze." And he
> said, "Oh okay, see you later." And I was going into another room!
> And we both kind of stopped and went, "Yeah, okay, this is weird."
> (Tuszynski 2006)

While Buffy fans can't physically visit The Bronze in Sunnydale, California, they can indeed visit it online.

VIRTUAL OSTENSION

The ability to interact with fictional places personally and socially opens the door for a particular kind of activity in which belief scholars have long been interested: ostension. Ostension comes from the Latin word *ostendere* ("to show"), and in the context of legend and belief studies it refers to the acting out of legend themes, plots, and concepts. Legend tripping, where people visit locations associated with particular legends—haunted houses, creepy tunnels, abandoned buildings—in order to test the veracity of the story (or, at least, to "see what happens" or "find out what's really there"), is a common form of ostension. Michael Kinsella, writing about legend tripping online, has pointed out that the virtual realm lends itself quite well to ostensive activities, augmenting "participants' efforts toward creating a shared ritual environment constructed from temporally or spatially distant real environments, or even from entirely mediated environments, which can provide an overall sense of presence" (2011, 40). In other words, when dealing with a fictional reality (which exists, by necessity, in a mediated state if it is expected to have an objective existence),[14] the Internet opens the door for ostensive behavior.

The connections between the ideas of ostention and participatory culture are clear: both involve the active participation of an individual with a body of cultural expression, and both also lead to the deepening of the connection between the individual and the subject of the cultural production. Kinsella describes the Internet as a "world-making [venue] that invites participants to search for and share experiential knowledge that pertains to specific imaginary content—to perform belief in worlds of plausibility to which the community gives breadth, coherence, and a sense of the real" (2011, 63). Like the "simulacrum trips" that Jeannie Thomas discusses in chapter 2, the Internet allows for the creation, *ex nihilo*, of a "site" to visit, one that is based in popular source material and yet expands, through participation, far beyond that origin. The fact that the site of the legend trip is known to be fictional is beside the point; it's made temporarily real for those visiting and experiencing it.

Ostension within a fictional world can be achieved without technology, of course; Milspaw and Wesley describe how LARPing (live action role playing) allows for participation in a world that exists "alongside the everyday," a world "the players imagine as dangerous, unpredictable, and crying out for exploration" (2010, 215). Engagement with this world can be quite serious; fictional does not equal unimportant: "These players see themselves as living both in the regular daylight world of jobs, family, and study, and as inhabitants in their character selves of a parallel dark, inverted, 'shadowing' version of the visible world" (2010, 217). The Internet, however, provides this opportunity even for those who may not have an offline community of fans with whom to engage, or for those whose only free time is at odd hours. It also provides the opportunity to escape the possibly confining realities of one's own physical body and appearance. To paraphrase the popular "on-the-Internet-nobody-knows-you're-a-dog" *New Yorker* cartoon: On the Internet, no one knows you're not a vampire.[15]

Interaction with a cherished fictional reality is made more widely available through technology, which also brings together a much broader population to share the experience. Much as visiting a haunted house leads to a deeper connection with the legends about the place, visiting a *Twilight*- or *Buffy*-themed web forum and engaging deeply with other fans there leads to a deeper connection with that show's, film's, or book's content, while still allowing that content to be fictional.

CONCLUSION

This brings us to the question of why the realm of Internet fandom is such a popular place for vampire folk culture. Supernatural folk beliefs, as a genre, rely heavily on the idea of possibility—this leads to variations in belief, to debates over belief, and to ostensive acts of legend tripping. As noted earlier, for most people today, vampires—at least the literary and filmic vampires that people are interested in—are not perceived as literally possible. Thus, we don't see ostensive vampire hunting like we see ghost hunting; vampires are almost entirely characters of fiction. When vampires are acknowledged as fiction, engaging them ostensively requires that a shift in reality be made, a space created where fiction can become truth. This shift in the interpretive frame regularly takes place online, where users can slip the confines of their mundane lives[16] and allow not only the supernatural but also the literary or filmic to be the shared reality for a time: "Wearing fiction suits or engaging in deliberate ostensive role-play not only allows people to embody a fictional character or personify part of a legend narrative, but also permits them to *actually exist within fictional realities*" (Kinsella 2011, 109; emphasis added). Literal truth, or the real possibility of belief, becomes a side issue; a temporary and inconsistent, yet participatory and shared, truth becomes the goal.

The real world doesn't offer daily opportunities for ostensive engagement with fictional characters, but the Internet does. Thanks to the possibility of interpretive drift, the lack of possible belief isn't a hindrance to immersion in the subject of vampires. As Lev Grossman observed in his *TIME* article on the popularity of Stephenie Meyer's work (comparing her to J. K. Rowling), "People do not want to just read Meyer's books; they want to climb inside them and live there. . . . There's no literary term for the quality *Twilight* and *Harry Potter* (and *The Lord of the Rings*) share, but you know it when you see it: their worlds have a freestanding internal integrity that makes you feel as if you should be able to buy real estate there" (2008). The current popularity of vampires in mass culture creates in people a number of ostensive desires, especially given the readily available opportunities for participatory culture. By shifting the frame of ostension online to a widely accessible fictional world, belief can be readily performed and perceived, even when none exists. The Internet can provide an ostensive outlet that targets the type of vampire culture that most interests the most people—not the folkloric vampire of the past, but the more mass-mediated vampire of the present.

NOTES

1. These are the hometowns of Buffy Summers and Bella Swan of *Buffy the Vampire Slayer* and *Twilight*, respectively.
2. I designed a ten-question survey with SurveyMonkey.com and conducted it via snowball sampling using a variety of social networking outlets. The various initial calls for participation indicated only that the survey subject was "vampire folklore and fandom"; participants were those who self-identified as interested and/or opinionated.
3. Awareness of psychic vampires was fairly high in the survey. This is a non-supernatural (or at least non-undead) perception of vampires that attributes the ability to drain energy from certain individuals.
4. It is also a place that, worryingly, many people believe to be fictional.
5. See Milspaw and Evans (2010) for examples.
6. The informal process of person-to-person folk transmission introduces both variation and repetition into a given form. This "no-one-right-version" quality distinguishes it as a form of cultural expression.
7. This was not necessarily a positive experience for Raza. As one of the early viral Internet stars, Raza suffered from bullying (both online and offline) and had very few resources to assist him. Raza explains that he lost many friends and even had to change schools. Now in his mid-twenties, he is speaking out against cyberbullying (Trudel 2013).
8. http://knowyourmeme.com/memes/star-wars-kid.
9. Interestingly, this will likely annoy *Buffy* fans, who often create fanlore than decries the arrival of *Twilight* on the vampire fan scene.
10. This is often known as "slash" fiction, a reference to the punctuation used when designating the story's characters: for example, Buffy/Angel, Bella/Edward, and Angel/Edward.
11. *Fifty Shades of Grey* is a testament to the power of fanfiction. While it has been roundly criticized for its poor writing and obvious storytelling, it is a prime

example of the power that writers (especially female writers, which Jenkins's [2006] work addresses) can gain from these folk levels of engagement.

12. It is not my intention to exhaustively catalog all the forms of fan folklore that exist for *Twilight* and *Buffy*—that would take much more space than this chapter allows. My intent is mainly to illustrate that there is a clear and active folk culture of vampire fandom that exists online.

13. It's interesting to note that most *Twilight/Buffy* crossover lore has *Buffy* coming out on top. For a video version, check out Jonathan McIntire's mash-up: http://www.youtube.com/watch?v=RZwM3GvaTRM.

14. This is as opposed to, say, an imaginary realm of offline play that ceases to be accessible to others when the initial creators of the realm are currently not playing.

15. The original cartoon, created by Peter Steiner and published in the *New Yorker* in 1993, depicts a dog seated at a computer, explaining to another dog that, "on the Internet, nobody knows you're a dog."

16. If slipping out of real life into a fictional world is desired, that is; many fan forums become friendly settings for typical, comfortable, daily interactions about offline selves, too.

WORKS CITED

AngstGoddess003. 2009. "Wide Awake." http://www.angstyg.com/fic/Wide%20Awake%20by%20AngstGoddess003.pdf.

Barber, Paul. 1998. "Forensic Pathology and the European Vampire." In *The Vampire: A Casebook,* edited by Alan Dundes, 109–42. Madison, WI: The University of Wisconsin Press.

Baym, Nancy K. 2010. *Personal Connections in the Digital Age.* Cambridge, UK: Polity Press.

BellaFlan. 2009. "Becoming Bella Swan." *FanFiction.net.* http://www.fanfiction.net/s/5452501/1/Becoming-Bella-Swan.

Buffistas.org. 2008. "FAQ." http://www.buffistas.org/faq/#whitefont.

Grossman, Lev. 2008. "Stephenie Meyer: A New J.K. Rowling?" *Time.* http://www.time.com/time/magazine/article/0,9171,1734838,00.html.

Hine, Christine M. 2000. *Virtual Ethnography.* London: Sage Publications.

Jakle, John. 1987. *The Visual Elements of Landscape.* Amherst, MA: University of Massachusetts Press.

Jenkins, Henry. 2006. *Fans, Bloggers, and Gamers.* New York: New York University Press.

Kinsella, Michael. 2011. *Legend Tripping Online.* Jackson, MS: University Press of Mississippi.

McIntosh, Jonathan. 2009. "Buffy vs. Edward: Twilight Remixed." http://www.youtube.com/watch?v=RZwM3GvaTRM.

Milspaw, Yvonne, and Wesley Evans. 2010. "Variations on Vampires: Live Action Role Playing, Fantasy and the Revival of Traditional Beliefs." *Western Folklore* 69.2:211–50.

Nelson, Victoria. 2012. *Gothicka: Vampire Heroes, Human Gods, and the New Supernatural*. Cambridge, MA: Harvard University Press.

Trudel, Jonathan. 2013. "10 Years Later, 'Star Wars Kid' Speaks Out." *Maclean's*. http://www2.macleans.ca/2013/05/09/10-years-later-the-star-wars-kid-speaks -out/.

Tuan, Yi Fu. 1977. *Space and Place*. Minneapolis, MN: University of Minnesota Press.

Tushnet, Rebecca. 1997. "Legal Fictions: Copyright, Fan Fiction, and a New Common Law." *Loyola of Los Angeles Entertainment Law Review* 17.3:651.

Tuszynski, Stephanie. 2006. "IRL (In Real Life): Breaking Down the Binary of Online vs. Offline Social Interaction." PhD dissertation, Bowling Green State University.

Ulaby, Neda. 2003. "'Buffy Studies': End of TV Series Clouds Future of Odd Academic Discipline." NPR. http://www.npr.org/templates/story/story.php?storyId= 1262180.

5

Legend Quests *and the* Curious Case *of* St. Ann's Retreat

The Performative Landscape

LISA GABBERT

Physical, tangible places are important elements of the supernatural. The practice of legend tripping or legend questing (Tucker 2007), for example, involves traveling to an extraordinary (usually supernatural) location in order to see if anything might happen; that is, to discover for oneself whether or not, in Bruce Jackson's phrasing, "the story is 'true'" (2008). For a legend quest to occur, there must be a legend—that is, a narrative about an extraordinary event purported to be true—and there must be a specific locale where the event allegedly took place. Legend questing behavior could not exist without the element of landscape, yet—with the exception of scholars studying Native American materials (e.g., Basso 1996; Nabokov 2007; Wehmeyer 1993), to which applying the category "legend" can be problematic (see Ben Amos 1969; Toelken 1976)—the role of landscape or place in legend formation remains somewhat underexamined by legend scholars, perhaps because in folklore studies legends are generally considered either as a species of narrative (Georges 1971; Nicolaisen 1996) and/or a postulate of belief, neither of which are necessarily associated with physical realms.[1]

Yet the sites of legend quests are places already pre-inscribed with narrative, and the stories that circulate are inextricable from the locations in which they occurred. The narrative makes the landscape mean, and the landscape gives evidence to the story. An object, house, railroad track, or cemetery statue holds the narrative, grounding it in place, while human behavior brings it to life. Such landscapes can be considered performative, meaning that they "gather together" people, narratives, memories, and events to produce an emergent and synergistic reality (Casey 1997). The more a landscape gathers to itself, the more a reality is created that is greater than the sum of its parts; the site develops into an event that is ever "becoming." It is this becoming that can be difficult to control and, in some instances, can be quite dangerous.

Here I want to think about the role of supernatural landscapes as performative spheres by examining the curious case of St. Ann's Retreat. Located approximately eight miles from the mouth of Logan Canyon in Mormon-dominated Cache County, Utah, St. Ann's is a former private summer home and Catholic spiritual retreat center. For years it has been the object of horror stories that include rumors of pregnant nuns, infanticide, ghostly cries, witches, and demon hounds. The following text, collected in 2001, is a typical example that emphasizes illegitimate pregnancy, the murder of infants, and ghosts:

> The only thing I remember about St. Anne's [sic] Retreat is that when we were kids, we were always told that you don't want to go [to] St. Anne's because it was haunted, cause all these nuns were sent to the retreat cause they had gotten pregnant by the [C]atholic priest. They would go there and then they would have their babies and drown them in the pool there. After they would drown them, they would just bury the babies there and the place became haunted." (Fife Folklore Archives[2])

Teenagers, drawn largely from the Latter-Day Saint community and naturally attracted by the stories they themselves likely generated, have been legend questing to St. Ann's for at least fifty or sixty years. The property has been subject to much vandalism and destruction as a result, adding mystery to the now-neglected site. In 1997, St. Ann's was the location of actual violence and horror as thirty-eight legend-questing teens were physically assaulted on the premise, held at gunpoint, and shackled by the neck by the property's caretaker and his companions. This event caused a political scandal and moral uproar in the local community, resulting in prosecution and jail time for the gun-wielding men. Clearly, something strange is going on.

What can we learn about the relationship between landscape, performativity, and the supernatural from this bizarre case study?

One definition for *landscape* is "a picture representing natural inland scenery, as distinguished from a sea picture, a portrait," while another definition is "a view or prospect of natural inland scenery, such as can be taken in at a glance from one point of view; a piece of country scenery" (*Oxford English Dictionary*). Both of these definitions emphasize the accepted connotation of landscape as the serene object of a contemplative gaze. The landscape is a passive, aesthetic object, viewed from a distanced, omniscient perspective and divorced from any human interaction. These ideas are still commonly held at least tacitly when the term *landscape* is used.

But places that are the sites for legend quests such as St. Ann's are decidedly *not* quiet, still places of aesthetic contemplation, but rather what geographer Yi-Fu Tuan calls "landscapes of fear," or manifestations of the forces of chaos and death ([1979] 2013, 6). Legend-tripping landscapes are ruptured landscapes in which past and present mingle; a horrible or supernatural event not only allegedly occurred there once, but remnants of the event preternaturally continue to occur in the present. Geographer Kenneth E. Foote (2003) classifies landscapes upon which violence has occurred according to what happens to them afterward. In his schema, some sites of violence become sanctified, designated, or rectified while others become obliterated, meaning they are abandoned and forgotten, and are never returned to normal use unless the entire site is razed or demolished.[3] Performative landscapes such as St. Ann's go one step further: while they are frequently abandoned, forgotten, or neglected by property owners and civic officials, as Foote suggests, they also invite attention and command participation at the folk level because their rupture is supernatural and ongoing. Legend-questing participants go to a specific spot not only as a matter of interest or as a tourist activity (Goldstein, Grider, and Thomas 2007), but they also go to see if anything might happen and ultimately end up as active participants. Legend questing therefore is akin to visiting a holy place, as there is potential for supernatural intervention and lasting effects afterward. Teens in southern Indiana, for example, visit the Tunnelton Tunnel, where a night watchman is rumored to have been decapitated after the Civil War, his head found hanging from the tunnel's roof (Hall 1980). Those who visit the tunnel today report a mysterious floating light and eerie noises; the floating light is thought to be the night watchman's lantern as he looks for his head. There is an "interanimation" (Basso 2007) between people and place that emerges here, belying the *Oxford English Dictionary*'s definition that landscapes are simply passive vehicles for the containment of meaning—instead, meaning emerges from them (Gabbert and Jordan-Smith 2007). To see how this works, let us turn now more specifically to the case at hand.

A BRIEF HISTORY OF ST. ANN'S RETREAT

St. Ann's was originally developed in the first decade of the twentieth century in a portion of the Wasatch-Cache National Forest (in northern Utah) that was specifically designated for summer homes. First known as "Hatch's Camp" and "Pine Glenn Grove," the site was owned by the well-to-do Hatch and Odlum families for several generations. They built and developed the site from approximately 1915 to the 1930s and used it as a summer vacation home away from the heat of their permanent home in New York City.

At its peak, Hatch's Camp was an amazing place, representing the opulence of early to mid-twentieth-century wealth. The site originated as a single cabin adjacent to the Logan River but was expanded over time to

FIGURE 5.1. Odlum main cabin at Hatch's Camp/St. Ann's Retreat, near Logan, Utah. (Photo by Korral Broschinsky, National Register of Historic Places, Utah State Historic Preservation Office)

FIGURE 5.2. The interior of the lodge at Hatch's Camp/St. Ann's Retreat. (Photo courtesy of the archives of the Catholic Diocese of Salt Lake City)

include two main lodges, numerous guest cottages, several maid's houses, stables, a theater with seating for twenty-four persons, a ticket booth, a swimming pool and pool house, a life-size children's playhouse, a badminton court, and an amphitheater; it also had lawns, outdoor fireplaces, retaining walls, stone steps, a picnic area, and a pond (Broschinsky 2006). The Hatches and the Odlums, originally from Utah, formed the investment company that today is known as the Atlas Corporation and made their wealth in the 1920s and 1930s in investments that included Kodak, Greyhound, Universal Studios, Madison Square Garden, and the Hilton hotel chain. In 1933, property owner Floyd B. Odlum was considered one of the ten wealthiest people in the country, and the families entertained Hollywood movie directors, actors, political figures, and company presidents at the camp (Broschinsky 2006).[4] Today, the site is listed on the National Register of Historic Places because the buildings that remain typify important early twentieth-century architectural movements, including bungalow, arts and crafts, and national park rustic styles (Broschinsky 2006).

The use of the site by the Hatch and Odlum families declined by midcentury, so the Hatch family donated their portion of the camp to the Catholic

FIGURE 5.3. Sisters of the Holy Cross at St. Ann's Retreat. (Photo courtesy of the archives of the Catholic Diocese of Salt Lake City)

Diocese of Salt Lake City in 1951–1952, and the Odlum family donated their share in 1953. The Catholic Church changed the name from Hatch's Camp to St. Ann's Retreat. As a diocesan project, the camp was not owned by any particular parish or order, but was intended to serve the needs of sisters throughout the diocese for a spiritual retreat, although diocesan priests could have access if the sisters were not using it. Many orders enjoyed the site over the years, such as the Sisters of the Holy Cross and the Benedictines, a monastic order whose members include both men and women. The sisters converted one of the cottages into a chapel and erected a statue of Mary as part of the site's transformation into a place of contemplation, rest, and prayer. Beginning in 1971, the diocese also began using St. Ann's as a nondenominational youth camp, partnering with, for example, the Boys' Club of Weber and the Salt Lake City Central City Community Center.[5]

It was after this transfer of property to the diocese that the ghost and horror legends that continue today likely first arose. It is difficult to document precisely when stories about pregnant nuns and murdered babies began to circulate. Some of the earliest evidence from the Fife Folklore Archives is a murdered baby tale collected in 1974. This tale locates the murdered baby in a nearby scouting camp in Logan Canyon called Camp Lomia, but it still associates the murder with Catholic nuns; it also intimates the ancient idea of

foundation sacrifice. According to this tale, a baby had been walled up inside
the main lodge's fireplace, and its body was found when a stone was removed:

> Many years ago, before cabins were built at Camp Lomia, the girls
> used to sleep in bunk beds in the upper story of the lodge. One night
> the girls were awakened by the sound of a baby's cry. They couldn't
> tell where the sounds were coming from, but every night they heard
> the same cries. Finally, the girls became so terrified that they had to
> leave camp early. Even after the girls were home, however, they were
> still very frightened and many of them started having nightmares.
> The families of these girls decided to conduct a search of the lodge
> to see if they could locate the source of the cries. A group of men
> went up one night and waited in the top floor of the lodge. Just after
> midnight, the cries of a small baby could be heard clearly by every-
> one present. It seemed to fill the entire room. The men finally deter-
> mined that the cries were coming from the fireplace at one end of the
> room. Upon close inspection, they found that one of the stones was
> loose. They removed the stone and found the skeletal remains of a
> newborn baby. It was later learned that the lodge had once been used
> as a retreat for Catholic nuns. Apparently, one of the nuns had been
> pregnant and had gone to the lodge to have her baby. Unable to face
> the humiliation of her situation, she buried the newborn alive in the
> fireplace. (Fife Folklore Archives[6])

Sister Agnes Reichlin of St. Gertrude's monastery in Cottonwood, Idaho,
is a female Benedictine monk who retreated at St. Ann's in the mid 1950s.
Sister Reichlin trained as a nurse at St. Benedict's Hospital (now Ogden
Regional Medical Center) in Ogden, Utah, between 1954 and 1957 and recalls
a very pleasant stay, organized by Father Jerome Stoffel of St. Thomas Aqui-
nas church in Logan, who was responsible for overseeing St. Ann's as an
outing for the Catholic student nurses. In particular, Sister Reichlin recalls
her fondness of the swimming pool, since it was one of the few times in her
life she had had access to one.[7] She did not recall any kind of specific intru-
sions by teenagers during her stay, but she did note in conversation that
there was anti-Catholic sentiment in Utah during that period—religious
tensions between Mormons and Catholics still occasionally arise.[8] It is likely,
therefore, that the presence of various orders of nuns and female monks in a
small, rural, largely Latter-Day Saint (Mormon) region piqued local curiosity

FIGURE 5.4. The swimming pool at St. Ann's Retreat. (Photo courtesy of the archives of the Catholic Diocese of Salt Lake City)

and drew unwanted attention. Indeed, a note to an undated letter from the 1950s in the diocese archives about St. Ann's reads "gate on bridge is not padlocked. It is wise, however, to keep it closed to avoid curious visitors."

Yi-Fu Tuan notes that one way in which ordinary landscapes transform into landscapes of fear is when they become associated with human evil of a supernatural order, such as witches or ghosts ([1979] 2013, 105), which is exactly what happened at St. Ann's. The stories and rumors that started circulating about St. Ann's included the notion that the retreat was actually a nunnery (it continues to be known incorrectly today as "the nunnery"); that pregnant nuns were using St. Ann's to secretly have their babies; that they had become pregnant by priests; that they were secretly having abortions or drowning their illegitimate babies in the swimming pool; that one could hear the cry of the murdered babies at night; and that demonic dogs guarded the grounds. In some variants, the nuns themselves had been murdered and the nunnery burned to the ground. Over time, these stories

amalgamated with other stories from Logan Canyon, including one about
the existence of the witch Hecate, who in local legend is sometimes characterized as the mother superior of the nunnery who murdered babies and/or
the nuns herself. A typical example, collected in 1981, follows:

> It (St. Anne's [sic]) used to be an old nunnery. It was a sin for nuns to
> have kids. Well there was a camp up there and there was a couple of
> nuns that did have kids. The mother nun, I don't know what they call
> them, found out about the babies so she stole the kids one night and
> threw them in the swimming pool and drown them [sic].
>
> There is a big swimming pool up there and a bunch of old build-
> ings. The main nunnery where they used to hold their meetings
> burned down and all that's left is an old building place. The cement
> foundation is still there and that is about all.
>
> She threw the babies in the pool and they drown [sic] and that
> same night the whole place burned down. It all happened in one day
> and one night. From what I hear, the nuns aren't permitted up there
> any more. They aren't suppose [sic] to go up there and they closed
> it all down. I don't know if they (the nuns) all left or if they are still
> here in the valley.
>
> The original name of that mother nun was Saint Hecida [or Hec-
> ate]. There is suppose to be some dogs sitting there watching the
> place for Witch Hecida. When ever [sic] you go up there you are
> suppose [sic] to be able to hear their chains or hear them bark." (Fife
> Folklore Archives[9])

Hecate, a Greek goddess, is often associated with witchcraft, ghosts, the
crossroads, and magic. Many other variants have circulated as well.[10]

At least some aspects of the legend/belief complex surrounding St. Ann's
have deep historical roots. The concept of sexually active and pregnant
nuns is certainly not original to the region; references to nuns having sex
and becoming pregnant—both actual and fictional—can be traced back
at least one thousand years. One well-known story, recorded by St. Ailred
of Rievaulx (1110–67) is about the "Nun of Watton," who was born in the
1140s and allegedly entered the convent as a toddler. As a teen, she became
pregnant and had a child. Another story, dating from the thirteenth century, tells of the alleged "Pope Joan," a woman masquerading as a man who,
as Pope, had a child. Classical literature is also rife with ribald stories of

FIGURE 5.5. Girls cabin at Hatch's Camp/St. Ann's Retreat. (Photo by Korral Broschinsky, National Register of Historic Places, Utah State Historic Preservation Office)

nuns, sex, and pregnancies resulting from untoward behavior. Boccaccio's *Decameron, Day 3 Tale 1*, (2004, 186) from the fourteenth century, tells of a man who pretends to be mute, enters a convent, and eventually services all of the nuns, including the abbess. He fathers many children and leaves only after a long and pleasurable life.[11] This story finds its modern-day equivalent in some stories about St. Ann's that tell of various men (miners, sheepherders, traders) sneaking into the "convent" and raping and/or murdering the nuns (Fife Folklore Archives[12]).

The concept of nuns having sexual relations and/or having babies also is found in the *Motif-Index of Folk-Literature*, including motif H509.1, "Guest of convent is given choice of nuns"; motif J1264.6, "Nun claims child is by Holy Ghost. Accepted as Defense"; motif J1264.4, "When asked why she did not cry out during rape, nun claims it was during the Silent Period"; motif K1321.4, "Men disguised enter convent, seduce impious nuns"; motif T640.1, "illegitimate child of nun"; and motif V465.1.2.2, "Nun tempted into sinning with man who says God can't see things that happen in the dark."

Finally, according to Barbara Yorke, author of *Nunneries and the Anglo-Saxon Royal Houses*, actual sexual assault on nuns was a common problem, enough so that the bishop was concerned that nuns might fall further into sin by killing the illegitimate child (2003, 153, note 69). Today, the idea of pregnant nuns remains popular. One can buy a pregnant nun Halloween costume in nearly any commercial costume store, and such costumes are prevalent in Mardi Gras and Carnival celebrations, where rites of inversion encourage carnivalesque behavior. In addition, a plethora of pregnant nun jokes abound, as well as a brand of "pregnant nun" ice cream recently for sale in the United Kingdom that caused much uproar.

It is possible that the traditional dress of nuns—which includes robes designed to cover the body and sometimes a wimple to cover the hair and frame the face—have generated mystery and questions about the body of the nun hidden underneath. Nuns also take vows of celibacy and sometimes live in communal seclusion, thus adding to their mysterious nature, particularly to outsiders unfamiliar with Catholic practices. Nuns generally are associated with childbirth and the care of children; some orders are primarily dedicated to Mary, the mother of Christ, who is the consummate mother. Also, until the miraculous nature of her conception was revealed, Mary was thought to be illegitimately pregnant. As her followers, nuns abstain from sex or having babies themselves, but their traditional work is in schools, orphanages, and hospitals. Additionally, unwed, pregnant women have historically been sent to nunneries and, hence, ideas about nunneries, celibacy, illegitimate pregnancy, children, and mothering have become linked over time.

Finally, the notion of mothers (though not necessarily nuns) drowning their children also has historical roots, as well as the idea that murdered people (including babies) return to haunt the place of their untimely demise. Hatch's Camp/St. Ann's was closely associated with water because of the swimming pool on the premises and the site's proximity to the Logan River. One thinks immediately of the story of *La Llorona*, a mother sometimes characterized as a whore or the mistress of the Spanish conquistador Cortéz, who drowns her children, kills herself, and then haunts the water's edge crying and looking for her little ones. Traditional folksongs also frequently feature the murder or death of innocent babes, such as the song "Twa Babes." Ghostly water babies, which are sometimes murdered children, are thought to exist along the banks of waterways and make sounds like crying (Fife Folklore Archives[13]).

Local teenagers therefore were drawing on these already-established ideational complexes when they presumably started the rumors about the allegedly unholy use of St. Ann's by various Catholic orders. And yet, as Jeannie Thomas (1991) points out in her study of St. Ann's, these ideational complexes also closely articulate LDS belief systems. Latter-Day Saints value large families, both socially and religiously, and so telling stories about pregnant, murderous nuns speaks to a violation of local norms. The nuns' traditional value of celibacy goes against Mormon religious dictates to marry and have many children. To then violate this "foreign" vow by illicitly having sex and murdering illegitimate children is therefore double wickedness; this is why the legend is appealing. The excerpted comment above, which frames vows of celibacy as "a *sin* for nuns to have kids" (emphasis added), exemplifies this point. In essence, the St. Ann's legend cycle frames Catholic nuns as witches—people who are not quite people, who are both lustful and murderous, who cavort with the devil, and who "subvert society's most deeply held beliefs" (Tuan [1979] 2013, 107). The identification of the mother superior with Hecate supports this idea. Thomas also points out that legend tripping to St. Ann's allows LDS teens to physically confront (and presumably conquer) powerful, evil, childless female figures (i.e., witches) in the form of demonic nuns, thus suggesting an ambivalence about Catholicism and reconfirming traditional LDS beliefs about the proper role of women.

Such belief complexes and actions, however, are not without consequence. Jack Santino (1996; 2004) notes that what is interpreted as "fun" by one group may be perceived as threatening by another. Wynne L. Summers (2000) writes that, whether intended or not, the practice of legend questing can grow into a form of harassment. The activities of the Cache Valley teenagers—which included nocturnal visits and frequent incidents of vandalism—frightened the sisters, who eventually acquired guard dogs to warn them of intruders and help them feel safe at night (Arnlkóts 2000, 1). In a clear example of how "facts become legends and legends become facts" (Ellis 1996), the sister's dogs were then reinterpreted back into the legend cycle as visible evidence of "hounds of hell." (Hecate is also associated with dogs.) Legend questers described seeing ferocious black mastiffs (or sometimes white Dobermans) with glowing red or green eyes and hearing horrible baying sounds—dogs clearly sent by the devil himself.[14] These stories clearly "connect an evil and frightening supernatural world to the world of Catholicism" (Thomas 1991, 16).

The ongoing harassment and vandalism by local teens were part of a wider array of property management and financial issues facing the Catholic

Dioceses of Salt Lake City, which was forced to stop offering St. Ann's as a spiritual retreat and summer youth camp. By 1980 the property was in need of major repair, which the Catholic Dioceses of Salt Lake City undertook with great financial difficulty; caretakers sometimes mismanaged the property, and it was too expensive to maintain a much-needed, year-round property manager. The minutes of the 1984 St. Ann's Camp Advisory Board refer to problems of "keggers" during the end of the school year, while the minutes from a 1986 board meeting mention $500.00 worth of property damage from vandalism.[15]

By 1987, the Catholic Dioceses of Salt Lake City decided that, although the need for a camp continued, St. Ann's was not the place for it and began to make arrangements for its sale. The property was sold to a private owner in 1993, but the site remained unused and continued to fall into decay. Legend-questing teens never stopped visiting, adding to the circulation of stories by telling stories of nuns engaging in devil worship and satanic rituals—stories that coincided with a national panic about satanic rituals in the 1980s (Ellis 1996)—and further reinforcing the idea of St. Ann's nuns as local witches. Stories about demonic guard dogs continued as well, alongside stories about a watchman with a gun who owned the dogs to keep trespassers out.

VIOLENCE AT ST. ANN'S

St. Ann's was already a performative site "play[ing] an active role in [its] own interpretation" when it was thrust dramatically into the public sphere in October 1997 (Foote 2003, 5). According to newspaper reports and local testimony, two different groups totaling thirty-eight teenagers were legend questing at St. Ann's when they were attacked and held hostage at gunpoint by three men beginning around ten o'clock at night. One of the men, John Jeppson, worked unpaid as the property's caretaker in exchange for use of the place. Jeppson and two friends took it upon themselves to protect the property from the continuous stream of young legend questers, who had caused approximately $100,000 worth of damage over the past few years, according to the owner. Armed with shotguns mounted with flashlights, plastic handcuffs, and the element of surprise, Jeppson and his friends captured the teens by jumping from the bushes, ordering them to "Hit the ground!" and firing the guns over their heads. The teens were searched, handcuffed

FIGURE 5.6. Abandoned pool and pool house at Hatch's Camp/St. Ann's Retreat, where teenagers were held against their will in October 1997. (Photo by Korral Broschinsky, National Register of Historic Places, Utah State Historic Preservation Office)

with plastic ties, and led to the bottom of the empty swimming pool. The men then tied a continuous nylon rope around the neck of the teens, which was apparently a prisoner of war trick so that when one person moved, the rope tightened around the necks of the other prisoners. The teens were told that the ropes were tied to explosives and they would be blown up if they moved. The men also told the teens they would shoot their legs off if they tried to run. Additionally, the men allegedly took pictures of the captured kids while they waited for the sheriff's department to arrive. One of the men put a pistol to the head of an Asian American boy, called him a "gook" and threatened to shoot, and then discharged the pistol into the ground.

When members of the sheriff's department arrived, they congratulated the men for their accomplishment in catching the trespassers. They removed the plastic handcuffs from the teens' hands, replaced them with real handcuffs, arrested them, and cited them for trespassing. Their cars were impounded and the men apparently continued to take pictures of the teens even after the police arrived. Eventually the teens were released, and the police department hailed the caretaker and his companions as local heroes.

One boy was treated at the local hospital for a concussion and head wound received from a blow to the head.

The incident led to outcry throughout Cache Valley and the Logan community. In a flurry of op-eds and letters to the editor, the public debated not only issues of trespassing and the proper reach of law enforcement but also moral values. Supporters of private property rights saw the teens as trespassers and the property's caretaker and his friends as defending private property. According to this view, the teens "deserved what they got," and people expressed hope that the teens had learned their lesson about breaking the law and trespassing. Some people were quite upset that the teens were not prosecuted.

Many parents of the traumatized teens and others saw things differently, vehemently protesting their treatment. They felt that what the teens were doing was essentially harmless, and that the actions of the men and the complicity of the police/sheriff's department far outweighed any wrongdoing on the part of the kids. Jeppson and the other two men were eventually charged with six counts of aggravated assault, a third-degree felony. In a plea deal, Jeppson pled guilty to two felony counts and spent time in jail. The trespassing charges against the teens were dropped. In a guest commentary for the *Herald Journal*, Cache County attorney Scott Wyatt explained that his reason for dropping the trespassing charges was because the property owners themselves had requested it, while the newspaper reported that the teens technically could not be charged with trespassing since the property was located on Forest Service land.[16]

The outrage and debate over the appropriateness of the men's actions and whether or not the teenagers "got what they deserved" was a community conversation about property rights, justice, and local tradition (see Arnlkóts 2000). It was also a fundamentally *moral* debate, which is why the flurry of letters were frequently so emotional. The St. Ann's legend cycle is a moral debate as well. Part of the allure of the idea of nuns becoming pregnant and murdering babies is that such ideas are moral comments—society's imagining of wrongdoing by people who are supposed to be holy and close to God. As benevolent, motherly figures, nuns are supposed to love and protect children, not murder them, so the actions of the nuns in the legend cycle somewhat parallel the real-life actions of the men in 1997, since many of the teens reported in the newspaper that they feared for their lives (although these men were certainly not motherly). And the correlation between the imagined drowning of babies in the swimming pool and the actual holding of teenagers at gunpoint, bound by a single rope around the neck at the bottom of the abandoned pool, comes a little too close for comfort, illustrating that the caretaker and his friends may have been acting in an ostensive manner, playing out roles and sequences of actions predetermined in legendry.

A PERFORMATIVE LANDSCAPE

Jack Santino (2004) is one scholar in the field of folklore who has applied the idea of performance to physical locations. Drawing on J. L. Austin's notion of performative utterances—words that get things done—Santino uses the term *performative commemoratives* to describe the action accomplished by certain public commemorations of untimely death. Santino argues that spontaneous shrines and other folk forms of memorialization not only commemorate the deceased but are forms of "doing" in the Austinian sense: they draw attention to and change public attitude toward the social and political conditions that caused the untimely death in the first place.

Austin (1975) developed the notion of performative utterances partly to counter the prevailing notion among philosophers that language (or, more specifically, an utterance) was primarily utilitarian, used to describe some external reality such as a state of affairs or a fact. Austin argued that certain kinds of utterances, said under specific conditions, did not simply describe an external state of affairs but actually accomplished that state of affairs in the act of its utterance (such as saying "I do" within the context of a wedding ceremony).

Along with Santino, I think that Austin's notion of performative utterances can be applied to certain landscapes. Crouch (2012) recently sought recourse for the term *performative* with respect to landscapes as way of building upon scholarship that conceptualizes space as open to change and becoming, as "spacing."[17] His formulation focuses on the overlap of art and life as a way of connecting landscape to modern mobility; in this formulation, landscape becomes a performance of the poetics of spacing. Here I propose a somewhat different formulation, suggesting the term *performative landscape* as a way of identifying certain landscapes that "do."

As the previous discussion of the definition of landscape from the *Oxford English Dictionary* reveals, landscapes are frequently considered passive, representational, or as containers for meaning. Conceptions about land-scape are similar to the philosophical misconception that language is simply a passive means with which to describe an objective, external reality. Austin contributed to the understanding that language is its own reality and can sometimes create reality if conditions are "felicitous." Similarly, landscapes, such as the types of landscapes visited by legend trippers (but certainly other kinds of landscapes as well, such as holy sites), are not simply passive receptacles into which meaning is put, but may actively create or shape the reality in which they participate.

Like places that spawn folk commemoration of untimely deaths, St. Ann's also has a set of horrific events attached to it, although none of the "events"—illicit sex, pregnant nuns, infanticide, and the like—have any basis in reality. In the case of St. Ann's, the alien presence of Catholic sisters spurred the re-emergence and circulation of ancient, traditional belief com-plexes that became attached to the camp in a kind of folk "remembering" or "commemoration" of allegedly unholy, sinful nuns. Once this set of beliefs and ideas became anchored to St. Ann's—aided by the presence of actual nuns, water, and dogs, as well as the articulation of these ideas with local religious values—the site became a nexus of landscape and narrative that invited people to participate.

Local teens eagerly accepted the invitation. How could they refuse such a heady offer? They participated by visiting, climbing fences, telling stories, vandalizing property, encountering the supernatural, and sharing their experiences afterward. Their actions contributed to the ongoing, ever-changing nature of the site. In this way, St. Ann's began "gathering" to itself participants, actions, behaviors, and more stories in the form of *memorates*, other local legends (such as Hecate), and even national panic rumors (such as devil worship). If performative commemoratives are per-formative because they "make something happen" (such as a change of atti-tude) in political and social realms, a performative landscape is an emergent entity that blurs boundaries between physical reality and narrative. They are less concrete in the change they effect than either Austin's performative utterances or Santino's performative commemoratives. They do not accom-plish goals, but instead are the instruments of their own change and growth, a change that can be described as "ever-becoming." Narratives (and, more broadly, belief) play a role in this process, but it is the conjoining of belief, narrative, landscape, and behavior in particular ways that conditions possi-bilities of performativity for a site itself.

The concept of ostension has been used to explain legend-questing behavior and goes a long way in clarifying the gross misunderstanding between the caretakers of St. Ann's and the legend questing teens that night. Originally borrowed from semiotics by Linda Dégh and Andrew Vázonyi (1983), ostension refers to the acting out of legendary events—that is, a literal imitation or performance of narrative. Bill Ellis notes that ostension allows oneself to become engrossed in the reality of self-generated plots. Teenagers, for example, may draw on legendary material in order to perform a satanic ritual. They do so not because they are Satanists but to see if anything happens. Ellis (1996) also notes that ostensive behavior can have negative consequences. So-called satanic rituals may be interpreted by adults as real, leading to considerable misunderstandings and perhaps even violence—for example, the case of Bloody Mary in Nebraska (Summers 2000), the incident at Yellowwood Forest in Tennessee (Guinee 1987), and the interaction between the teenagers and men at St. Ann's.

Ostension, however, does not fully explain the seductive fluidity between narrative, reality, and landscape that occurs in legend questing and that brought the men and teens together at St. Ann's in such a horrific manner. To say, for example, that legend questers "perform" the narrative suggests participants bring the narrative to life in the manner of Schechner's "reenactment of the event" (1988). This framework also implies that people consciously take on the roles of actor and audience, that they have appropriated some kind of script and act accordingly. This model is useful, but it leaves the physical landscape akin to the role of the theater black box, a passive participant and an object to be acted upon or within (the conventional role assigned to landscape in the *Oxford English Dictionary* definition).

In contrast, consider for a moment that legendary landscapes are essentially liminal, supernatural places that operate outside of the boundaries of everyday reality.[18] Arnold van Gennep ([1909] 1960), who developed the notion of liminality, pays specific attention to the importance of space in his discussion of ritual practices, including the crossing of thresholds. Others have also pointed to legendary landscapes as somehow liminal because liminal spaces are frequently where this world and the Otherworld meet: examples include bridges, which connect this side to that side; cemeteries, which connect the living and the dead; and forests, which connect the civilized and the wild. As a camp (i.e., an impermanent dwelling) in the woods, St. Ann's is doubly liminal and therefore an excellent place for Otherworldliness.[19]

For example, it is an essential component of a legend quest that one must *travel* to these landscapes. Legend questers are like folktale heroes: teens leave the safety of home and travel to a remote geographical locale where odd things occur, frequently aided by consciousness-altering substances such as drugs and alcohol. Like folktale heroes, teens deal with issues pertaining to growing up during their sojourn abroad. But the ritualistic nature of legend quests (noted by a variety of scholars[20]) does not solely lie in the fact that teens address adolescent problems, fears, or concerns, though those things certainly occur. Rather, much like religious rituals allow people to tap into a larger mythical realm, by traveling to and entering a legendary or supernatural landscape participants ritually transform themselves into story characters and then wander around in a performative supernatural realm. The communal narrative is an always-ongoing drama and, as people enter the scene, it is the actors who are transformed to fit the narrative. The alternate reality produced is one in which the landscape of legend becomes real and actual people become characters in a story they already know. Participants know what happened at this place and what *might happen again* if they only look hard enough. If they act ostensively— if they enact the elements of the story—it is because this is their duty as characters in an ongoing plot. Collective narrative becomes embodied, lived experience, not so much because legend has been transformed into fact but because the participants have become storied.

As people enter a site and become storied, they respond to cues that fit the narrative (as Linda Dégh [2001, 386] points out, spooky noises are heard and mysterious things are seen, but no one is absolutely sure it might not have been the imagination), allowing the narrated event and the narrative event to merge (or come very close) (Bauman 1986). This merging produces the conditions of felicity that allow performativity to arise, creating an ever-expanding/emerging/living event that generates new narratives and new happenings and entices new participants for future growth. This combining of narrative event and narrated event for participants is what differentiates legendary performative landscapes from the sites that Santino examines. Performative sites of commemoration also invite participation from the audience and become self-generating events, but people who participate by commemorating the dead or contemplating the political and social conditions of the untimely death are commenting on the original event rather than participating in it. They are not reliving the so-called "scene of the crime" over and over again. In legendary performative landscapes, however, people leave their own reality and insert themselves into another, participating in not only the "original" event but also becoming part of the ongoing one. The consequences of doing so, however, are clearly unpredictable.

CONCLUSION

The case of St. Ann's is quite sad on the one hand, since a once-beautiful development was transformed into a place where nuns were harassed, property was damaged, and teenagers were terrorized. On the other hand, the case does illustrate that the melding of reality and legend that occurs in legend quests depends on site, location, and landscape for efficacy. The landscape plays an active role—it is a primary context, not secondary. Once put into motion by an array of forces that produce conditions of felicity, performative landscapes take on a life of their own. No amount of barbed wire, armed guards, or "no trespassing" signs have yet stopped St. Ann's becoming; these elements, along with the newer stories about the terrorized teens, simply become part of the larger event.

The case of St. Ann's also illustrates both Santino's and Foote's point that such sites are polysemous: they are open to multiple interpretations and are frequently a source of conflict. The legend questers viewed St. Ann's as a site of adventure, exploration, and possible encounters with the supernatural, while the sisters experienced fear, harassment, and anti-Catholic sentiment as a result. The caretakers interpreted themselves as the site's guardians and viewed the legend-questing teens as trespassers who needed to be taught a lesson. The sheriff's department apparently agreed with them, and the community was divided vociferously on the issue. The prosecutor ultimately disagreed with the police and pressed charges against the men, which resulted in felony convictions and jail time.

Foote (2003) suggests that obliterated sites must be razed entirely off the face of the planet and "started over" in order to become once again useful to society. It is unclear yet whether that is to be the fate of St. Ann's. What Foote doesn't recognize, however, is that obliterated sites may also be performative, and at the folk level they may have other uses other than the merely utilitarian. The actors involved here—nuns, teens, caretakers, townspeople—whether intentionally or not, were drawn to St. Ann's as storied characters in an ongoing event that intimates a variety of larger issues, including religious belief, morality, gender, and property rights (Arnlkóts

2000; Thomas 1991). Although this event may not have utilitarian or practical ends, it is certainly not without cultural and scholarly significance.

NOTES

1. Terry Gunnell's (2010) anthology, enticingly called *Legends and Landscape*, presents analyses of legends located in place but does not discuss the role of landscape itself. Other scholars such as Max Lüthi (1982) and Linda Dégh (2001) broach the subject, but the role of landscape as a primary context in legendry among folklorists has largely escaped close scrutiny.
2. Fife Folklore Archives, folk collection 8, box 71, 01–019.
3. According to Foote's (2003) schema, landscapes that are sanctified are ones in which those who have died are memorialized in some kind of positive way. Activities usually include the erection of a memorial or plaque, as well as public recognition. Designated landscapes are frequently on their way to being sanctified, but have not quite gotten there. The violence is recognized, but has not been officially acknowledged. Rectification means the site is cleaned up and put back to use, in contrast to obliterated sites, in which the area is simply abandoned.
4. See also Hunter (2013).
5. Information taken from a folder of materials on St. Ann's, Archives, Roman Catholic Diocese of Salt Lake City.
6. Fife Folklore Archives, folk collection 8a, group 7: SNL box 8, folder 9.
7. Personal communication with Sister Anges Richelin, June 28, 2013 at St. Gertrude's Monastery, Cottonwood, Idaho.
8. Anna-María Snaebjörnsdóttir Arnlkóts (2000), for example, points to a newspaper article published in 1986 about the ghost legends of St. Ann's that "created an emotional response from the Logan Catholic community, who took the article as an intentional provocation" (4).
9. Fife Folklore Archives, folk collection 8, box 8, 81–003, item number 7. For other examples see folk collection 8, box 28, 84–050, item number 2; folk collection 8a, group 7: SNL, box 8, folder 10.
10. See Fife Folklore Archives, folk collection 8A, group 7, "Supernatural Non-Religious Legends," box 8; folk collection 8, box 8 and box 28. For a full explanation of the history of Hecate from the classical period, see Thomas (1991) and Arnlkóts (2000).
11. Thank you to Dr. Christine Cooper-Rompato for pointing me to these medieval and early modern sources.
12. Fife Folklore Archives, folk collection 8, box 20, 84–050, item number 5 and 10.
13. Fife Folklore Archives, folk collection 8A, group 7: SNL, box 12, folder 10, item 2.5.5.7.
14. For examples, see Fife Folklore Archives, folk collection 8A, group 7: SNL, box 8, folder 10.
15. Information taken from a folder on St. Ann's available in the archives of the Catholic Diocese of Salt Lake City.

16. Information taken from the following newspaper articles: Paul Allen, "Thrill-seekers Steer Clear of Canyon Site," *Utah Statesman*, 15 October 2000; Kelly Palmer, "St. Anne's Nunnery has a history of haunting," *Utah Statesman*, 29 October 2004; Phil Jensen, "Nightmare in Logan Canyon," *Herald Journal*, 12 October 1997; Ryan Robb Oliver, "Canyon Watchmen Identified," *Herald Journal*, 13 October 1997; Phil Jensen, "Canyon Scare Charges Likely," *Herald Journal*, 14 October 1997; Ryan Robb Oliver, "St. Anne's Trio Not Paid Guards," *Herald Journal/Bridgerland*, 14 October 1997.

17. The term "spacing," according to Crouch (2012, 46) emphasizes changes that are abrupt and non-linear, as well as influences that are other-than-human.

18. Linda Dégh (2001) points to a similar claim by Peuckert, who suggests that legend landscapes exist outside the boundaries of the community—in other words, they are liminal places. I think Peuckert, however, believes legends come from a pre-rational, mythical age (an opinion drawn from a book review, since the book is not translated).

19. My thanks to an anonymous reviewer for pointing out these examples.

20. Bill Ellis (1983) has suggested that legend trips are teenage "rituals of rebellion," since activities such as drinking and drug-taking are often part of the expedition. Patricia Meley (1991) also suggests that legend trips are ritualistic. Drawing on van Gennep ([1909] 1960), she says the sites of legend trips are zones of liminality for teenage initiation rites in which teens assert independent identities from adults, confront common fears, and become part of a peer group. S. Elizabeth Bird (1994), in her study of the Black Angel in Iowa City, also suggests that legend trips function as initiations into adulthood. Men experiment with masculinity—testing themselves in terms of bravery and sexual prowess, for example—while women undergo trials of a sexual nature. And indeed, as far back as 1969, when Linda Dégh first identified legend trips, she interpreted them as initiation rituals for young males. Over time then, scholars came to a consensus that legend trips are ritual in nature, and that they offer a way for teens to confront concerns such as sex, death, mortality, gender roles, and an emerging adult identity.

WORKS CITED

Archives. Roman Catholic Diocese of Salt Lake City.

Arnlkóts, Anna-María Snaebjörnsdóttir. 2000. "Legend Tripping at St. Anne's Retreat and Hecate in Logan Canyon: Origin, Belief, and Contemporary Oral Tradition." Master's thesis, Utah State University. Folk Coll. 3, no 356.

Austin, J. L. 1975. *How to Do Things with Words*. Cambridge, MA: Harvard University Press.

Basso, Keith. 1996. *Wisdom Sits in Places: Landscape and Language among the Western Apache*. Albuquerque, NM: University of New Mexico Press.

———. 2007. "Wisdom Sits in Places: Notes on an Apache Landscape." In *Senses of Place*, edited by Steven Feld and Keith Basso, 53–90. Santa Fe, NM: School of American Research Press.

Bauman, Richard. 1986. *Story, Performance, and Event: Contextual Studies of Oral Narrative*. Cambridge, UK: Cambridge University Press.

Ben-Amos, Dan. 1969. "Analytical Categories and Ethic Genres." *Genres* 2: 273–301.

Bird, Elizabeth S. 1994. "Playing with Fear: Interpreting the Adolescent Legend Trip." *Western Folklore* 53.3: 191–209.

Boccaccio, Giovanni. 2004. *The Decameron*. Hertfordshire, UK: Wordsworth Editions Limited.

Broschinsky, Korral. 2006. "National Register of Historic Places Nomination Form." Submitted to the United States Department of the Interior, National Park Service.

Casey, Edward. 1997. "How to Get from Space to Place in a Fairly Short Stretch of Time: Phenomenological Prolegomena." In *Senses of Place*, edited by Steven Feld and Keith Basso, 13–52. Santa Fe, NM: School of American Research Press.

Crouch, David. 2012. "Landscape, Land, and Identity: A Performative Consideration." In *Land & Identity: Theory, Memory, and Practice*, edited by Christine Berberich, Neil Campbell, and Robert Hudson, 43–65. Amsterdam, Netherlands: Rodopi.

Dégh, Linda. 1969. "The Haunted Bridges Near Avon and Danville and Their Role in Legend Formation." *Indiana Folklore* 2.1: 54–89.

———. 2001. *Legend and Belief: Dialectics of a Folklore Genre*. Bloomington, IN: Indiana University Press.

Dégh, Linda, and Andrew Vázonyi. 1983. "Does the Word 'Dog' Bite? Ostensive Action: A Means of Legend Telling." *Journal of Folklore Research* 20.1: 5–34.

Ellis, Bill. 1983. "Legend Tripping in Ohio: A Behavioral Study." *Papers in Comparative Studies* 2: 61–73.

———. 1989. "Death by Folklore: Ostension, Contemporary Legend, and Murder." *Western Folklore* 48: 201–20.

———. 1996. "Legend Trips and Satanism: Adolescents' Ostensive Traditions as 'Cult' Activity." Reprinted in *Contemporary Legend: A Reader*, edited by Gillian Bennett and Paul Smith, 167–86. New York: Garland.

Fife Folklore Archives. Utah State University.

Foote, Kenneth E. 2003. *Shadowed Ground: America's Landscapes of Violence and Tragedy*. Austin, TX: University of Texas Press.

Gabbert, Lisa, and Paul Jordan-Smith. 2007. "Space, Place, Emergence." *Western Folklore* 66.3–4: 217–32.

Georges, Robert. 1971. "The General Concept of Legend: Some Assumptions to Be Reexamined and Reassessed." In *American Folk Legend: A Symposium*, edited by Wayland D. Hand, 1–19. Berkeley, CA: University of California Press.

Goldstein, Diane, Silvia Grider, and Jeannie Banks Thomas. 2007. *Haunting Experiences: Ghosts in Contemporary Folklore*. Logan, UT: Utah State University Press.

Guinee, William. 1987. "Satanism in Yellowwood Forest: The Interdependence of Antagonistic Worldviews." *Indiana Folklore and Oral History* 16.1: 3–5, 15–17.

Gunnell, Terry. 2010. *Legends and Landscape: Plenary Papers from the 5th Celtic-Nordic-Baltic Folklore Symposium*. Reykjavík, Iceland: University of Iceland Press.

Hall, Gary. 1980. "The Big Tunnel." In *Indiana Folklore: A Reader,* edited by Linda Dégh, 225–57. Bloomington, IN: Indiana University Press.

Hunter, Jeff. 2013. "Historic Gem of Logan Canyon." *Herald Journal, Bridgerland Edition: Brick by Brick: Historic and Interesting Cache Valley Buildings*, March 31, 27—28, 39.

Jackson, Bruce. 2008. *The Story Is True: The Art and Meaning of Telling Stories*. Philadelphia: Temple University Press.

Lüthi, Max. 1982. *The European Folktale: Form and Nature*. Translated by John D. Niles. Bloomington, IN: Indiana University Press.

Meley, Patricia M. 1991. "Adolescent Legend Trips as Teenage Cultural Response: A Study of Lore in Context." *Children's Folklore Review* 14.1: 5–24.

Nabokov, Peter. 2006. *Where the Lightening Strikes: The Lives of American Indian Sacred Places*. New York: Penguin Books.

Nicolaisen, W. F. H. 1996. "Legends as Narrative Response." In *Contemporary Legend: A Reader*, edited by Gillian Bennett and Paul Smith, 92–101. New York: Garland Press.

Santino, Jack. 1996. "Light up the Sky: Halloween Bonfires and Cultural Hegemony in Northern Ireland." *Western Folklore* 55.3: 213–31.

———. 2004. "Performative Commemoratives, the Personal, and the Public: Spontaneous Shrines, Emergent Ritual, and the Field of Folklore." *Journal of American Folklore* 117.466: 363–72.

Schechner, Richard. 1988. *Performance Theory*. London: Routledge.

Summers, Wynne L. 2000. "Bloody Mary: When Ostension Becomes a Deadly and Destructive Teenage Ritual." *Midwestern Folklore* 26.1: 19–26.

Toelken, Barre. 1976. "The 'Pretty Languages' of Yellowman: Genre, Mode, and Texture in Navaho Coyote Narratives." In *Folklore Genres*, edited by Dan Ben-Amos, 145–70. Austin, TX: University of Texas Press.

Thomas, Jeannie. 1991. "Hecate in Habit: Gender, Religion, and Legend." *Northwest Folklore* 9: 14–27.

Tuan, Yi-Fu. [1979] 2013. *Landscapes of Fear*. Reprint, Minneapolis, MN: University of Minnesota Press.

Tucker, Elizabeth. 2007. *Haunted Halls: Ghostlore of American College Campuses*. Jackson, MS: University Press of Mississippi.

van Gennep, Arnold. [1909] 1960. *Rites of Passage*. Chicago, IL: University of Chicago Press.

Wehmeyer, Stephen C. 1993. "A Place Called Gahaine: The Haunted Hill in Contemporary Seneca Story." *New York Folklore* 19.3–4:75–87.

Yorke, Barbara. 2003. *Nunneries and the Anglo-Saxon Royal Houses*. London: T&T Clark.

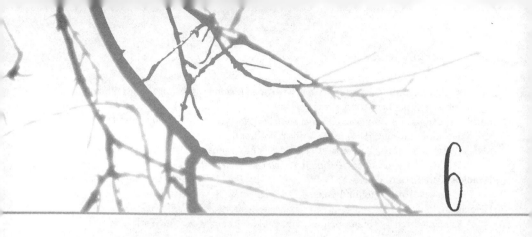

6

Messages from *the* Dead

Lily Dale, New York

ELIZABETH TUCKER

The first time I drove through Lily Dale's gates, I felt as if I had traveled
through a time warp to Limerick, Maine, a tiny rural village where my
parents, sisters, and I spent our summers in the early 1960s. My sisters
and I would have preferred the glamour of New York City. At first glance,
there seemed to be nothing for teenagers to do in Limerick, but we soon
found the village to be a strangely fascinating place. Black cats crouched on
porches, wildflowers blossomed in gardens, hex signs decorated doorbells,
and wind chimes made ethereal sounds. Miss Eva, Miss Frances, and other
white-haired ladies rocked in wicker chairs on their front porches. Miss Eva
brewed dandelion wine and mixed apple cider vinegar tonics; Miss Frances
grew goldenseal, burdock, and other herbs for home remedies. Both ladies
baked light, fluffy pies for baked bean suppers in Limerick's little white
congregational church. My sisters and I liked the pies but avoided the home
remedies, which looked nasty. Late at night, when the heat kept us awake,
we told family ghost stories. Relatives had told us Uncle Glenn's ghost
walked across our dining room at midnight. Uncle Stubby had seen a table
climb up a wall in another Maine village when he was very young.[1] In Limerick in the 1960s, the supernatural became real for my sisters and me.

FIGURE 6.1. Lily Dale angel and gazing globe. (Photo by Geof Gould)

I thought I'd lost that magical place and time until I drove through the gates of Lily Dale, New York, in the summer of 2010.

Like the rural village of my childhood, Lily Dale Assembly, founded in 1879, has many white-haired ladies, cats, wildflower and herb gardens, wind chimes, and delicious pies. Its embrace of the supernatural goes far beyond Limerick's, however. When you walk down Lily Dale's streets, you *expect* to get in touch with ghosts. If you want to lease a house in Lily Dale, you must belong to a Spiritualist church and pass a test to show you have psychic ability. At daily message services, psychic mediums deliver messages from the dead; there are also daily healing services. Since books such as Christine Wicker's *Lily Dale: The True Story of the Town That Talks to the Dead* (2004) and films such as HBO's *No One Dies in Lily Dale* (2010) have recognized Lily Dale's intense focus on communication with the dead, the town has become quite well known. During the summer season, visitors line up for readings with middle-aged and elderly mediums, some of whom have become celebrities through the HBO film. This is a place where people expect boundaries between the living and the dead to shift, stretch, and dissolve: a magical place where amazing things may happen.

Because of this expectation, Lily Dale has become a popular destination for legend quests: trips to discover something mysterious that seems to be of supernatural origin (Dégh 2001; Lindahl 2005; Tucker 2007). Another term frequently used by folklore scholars is *legend trip*. Kenneth A. Thigpen (1971) and Bill Ellis (1983) identify a three-part structure for legend trips: storytelling, rituals to evoke something supernatural, and discussion of what took place. Most folklorists' analyses of legend quests have studied teenagers' drives at night to visit legendary, secluded places. Bill Ellis has analyzed teenagers' rebelliousness on such trips, emphasizing their need to "say 'screw you' to adult law and order" (2003, 188). Legend quests by older people have not been documented as well, although some studies have addressed adults' responses to ghostlore (Bennett 1987; Goldstein 2007). I have chosen to use the term *legend quest* because visitors to Lily Dale put so much emphasis on finding meaning after they hear legends of amazing things that have happened there.

Not all visits to places of supernatural significance are legend quests or trips; some, including post-legend quest visits to Lily Dale, can be better identified as pilgrimages: single or repeated trips to sites that have intense meaning. Not all pilgrimages have a strong connection to religion. Victor Turner observes, "The plain truth is that pilgrimage does not ensure a major change in religious state—and seldom in secular status—though it may make one a better person, fortified by the graces merited by the hardships and self-sacrifices of the journey" (1992, 37). In another important study, *Intersecting Journeys: The Anthropology of Pilgrimage and Tourism* (2004), Ellen Badone and Sharon R. Roseman present analyses of pilgrimages in relation to tourism. Their introduction mentions the concept of tourism as a personal quest, introduced by Edward M. Bruner (1991, 247). This concept is somewhat similar to that of the legend quest, although a tourist's personal quest does not necessarily involve storytelling.

In my research on Lily Dale, I have discovered that many middle-aged and elderly women find visits to this little town to be deeply meaningful. Unlike teenagers driving to haunted locations, these women do not tend to get excited about car travel or expressing rebellion against older people's authority, but they value time with good friends as much as teenagers do. Some women come to Lily Dale with friends; others come with spouses, partners, and/or children. These women tend to follow the classic three-part pattern of a legend quest: storytelling en route to the haunted place, the visit itself, and then storytelling on the way home about what happened (Ellis 1983).

The first part of this chapter explores Lily Dale's unique identity, which has inspired many legend quests. Spiritualist history, mythical space, feminist activism, and local legends have all played a part in the formation of this identity. The chapter's second part explores three Lily Dale legend quests, each with an emphasis on gender roles. Accounts of such quests help us understand how the long tradition of receiving messages from the dead has influenced people's perception of Lily Dale, a community—with many white-haired ladies, both mediums and seekers of messages—that originated from the unusual experiences of two little girls in a small brown house.

A HOUSE THAT HAUNTS:
THE FOX SISTERS' SPIRIT RAPPINGS

Although Lily Dale is one of a number of active Spiritualist communities in the United States, it is the only one that owned the house where Spiritualism began. This is not, like other dwellings associated with the supernatural, a haunted house; instead, we can call it a house that haunts a community. In Hydesville, New York, in 1848, fourteen-year-old Margaret and eleven-year-old Kate Fox told their parents they were receiving messages from the spirit of a peddler who had been killed in their house. These messages took the form of rappings that everyone in the house could hear. Crowds of startled friends and neighbors gathered to hear these mysterious sounds, and both young women rapidly became famous as mediums. With speed that might surprise us in our current era of Internet communication, telegraph messages spread the news of the girls' spirit communication around the world.[2]

Forty years later, in 1888, Margaret confessed that she and her sister had made the rapping sounds by snapping their toe joints. One year after that, Margaret tried to take her confession back, but this effort did not go well. She and her sister died a few years later. Barbara Weisberg, author of *Talking to the Dead* (2005), suggests, "Kate and Maggie, containing worlds within themselves and experiencing many worlds without, were undoubtedly subject to powerful and conflicting impulses. As later events would

demonstrate, they were also endowed with unusual openness and sensitivity, whether to the messages of the spirits or to the spoken and unspoken
wishes of other mortals" (43). Weisberg's analysis expresses both believers'
and nonbelievers' reactions to the Fox sisters' activities. According to Linda
Dégh, author of *Legend and Belief* (2001), expressions of both belief and
skepticism promote legend telling. Such has certainly been the case with
legends about the Fox sisters, and the sequence of confession followed by
retraction has made stories about their childhood experiences especially
intriguing. Sociologist Alan Aldridge (2000) observes, "This pattern of confession followed by retraction, which is not uncommon, has supplied both
true believers and skeptics with material to support their case, so controversy never ends" (58).

One of the most important legends cherished by believers in the Fox
sisters' powers concerns what happened after Margaret and Kate claimed
that a peddler named Charles B. Rosma had died in the cellar of their family's cottage. Although no man by that name had been reported missing,
the girls' story gained credibility when workers found what was supposedly a man's skeleton, along with a peddler's trunk, in the cottage's basement. Because of this discovery, the story of the peddler's death became a

FIGURE 6.2. Postcard with a photo of the Fox cottage and well house. (Photo by
Geof Gould)

foundational legend of Lily Dale. Visitors to the community's museum see a painting of the trunk on the sign that identifies the building. Inside the museum lies the rusty old trunk itself, protected under glass, just as certain saints' relics are protected in Catholic churches. The community's emphasis on both the peddler and his trunk encourages belief in legends about the Fox sisters' first communication with spirits, which continue to circulate in variant versions (Cadwallader 2010; Wicker 2003, 6).

Lily Dale Assembly moved the Fox family's house to its own land in 1916; it stood at the center of the community until it burned down in 1955. Although the house no longer has a physical presence in Lily Dale, a photograph at the spot where it once stood, now occupied by a memorial garden, reminds visitors of its importance. The house's faded photographic image brings to mind the legend of Margaret's and Kate's communication with a murdered peddler; it also commemorates the founding of Spiritualism more than 160 years ago, which the girls' spirit rappings inspired.

MYTHICAL SPACE IN A FOREST:
LILY DALE'S UNIQUE IDENTITY

Besides honoring the Fox sisters' house, Lily Dale expresses its identity through its configuration of space. Folklorist Mary Catherine Gaydos Gabriel (2011), who lived in Lily Dale while working on her master's thesis, eloquently describes this little town surrounded by trees: "Lily Dale exudes a unique sense of place. It is cocooned within a forest, ten square blocks of streets that feel more like sidewalks than roads, snuggly resting inside a space cleared just large enough to accommodate the homes and a few public buildings, just large enough so that it doesn't feel crowded, but rather protected, watched over, and safe" (64). Gabriel's emphasis on smallness, safeness, and snugness captures Lily Dale's appeal very well. Noting that Lily Dale is "cocooned within a forest," she finds its woodland surroundings to be soothing and serene. The old-growth forest known as Leolyn Woods reminds visitors of earlier times. Streets that "feel more like sidewalks" suggest a comfortable, homelike community where people can interact in a friendly way, not worrying too much about vehicles' presence. Gabriel also observes that there are flowers all around Lily Dale in the summer and that the names of houses, such as "Zen Glen" and "Fairy Frond House," reflect the town's fanciful atmosphere (64).

FIGURE 6.3. Lily Dale home. (Photo by Elizabeth Tucker)

When I first visited Lily Dale, I also marveled at the town's homelike atmosphere and the houses' many imaginative names, which reflected the eclectic new age philosophy developed in the 1960s and 1970s. Although many of Lily Dale's buildings date back to the late nineteenth century, its atmosphere seems more new age than Victorian. Looking at a list of upcoming workshops, I noticed that past life regression, dream interpretation, reiki, and holistic health care were all included. Blending Eastern and Western spirituality, Lily Dale welcomes diverse approaches to spiritual awareness.

Lily Dale also has a long, proud tradition of feminist activism. In the late nineteenth century, Susan B. Anthony and other feminists gave speeches that made the town a center of support for women's suffrage. Significant connections between Spiritualism and the nineteenth-century women's rights movement are clarified in Ann Braude's insightful study *Radical Spirits: Spiritualism and Women's Rights in Nineteenth-Century America* (1989). Braude's exploration of the appeal of Spiritualism's heterodoxy to both women and men is especially illuminating (56–81). Another researcher, Cara Seekings, author of *The Ladies of Lily Dale* (2010), tells an amusing legend

FIGURE 6.4. Inspiration Stump. (Photo by Geof Gould)

about a medium informing Susan B. Anthony that she had a message from a deceased aunt. Anthony replied, "I didn't like her when she was alive, and I don't want to hear from her now. Why don't you bring someone interesting like Elizabeth Cady Stanton?" (4).

Although various forms of spirituality converge in Lily Dale, the town has certain sacred sites that provide focal points for both residents and visitors. Within Leolyn Woods stands Inspiration Stump, where mediums and visitors congregate to receive messages at daily services during the summer season. Surrounded by an iron fence, Inspiration Stump has a reputation for being a place of power. Since the nineteenth century, local residents have told many stories about human and animal spirits appearing there. The stump's name suggests that it inspires both speakers and presenters of psychic readings. During the late nineteenth and early twentieth centuries, mediums would stand on the stump to do readings, much as politicians would give a "stump speech" as they moved from town to town, but overuse of the stump caused its gradual decay.

Because residents of Lily Dale feel so much reverence and affection for Inspiration Stump, it serves as a spiritual center for the community. Psychic readings take place there twice a day, and mediums-in-training stand near the stump as they practice summoning spirits. Once a week, members of Lily Dale Assembly lead evening tours that culminate at the stump. Standing under the trees in the dark, the tour guides ask all participants to look closely at the surrounding trees and listen carefully. Perhaps, in this place of power and eloquence, a spirit will come to one of the visitors.

Even though Inspiration Stump has a protective fence around it now, some people stand on it anyway. Daring to defy the town's prohibition of standing on the stump has become a subject of local legend-telling. Anthropologist Joshua D. Rose writes about young campers daring each other to stand on Inspiration Stump, especially after drinking late at night (2011, 65), and the HBO film *No One Dies in Lily Dale* (2010) shows a grieving mother standing on the stump, feeling skeptical and frustrated but hoping, nonetheless, to contact her lost son.

Some of Lily Dale's legends signal Inspiration Stump's potency and potential danger. Journalist Christine Wicker, who interviewed many Lily Dale residents, explains that mediums' use of the stump as a standing place stopped "when one of them had a heart attack in mid-proclamation" (2003, 22). Wicker interviewed medium Betty Schultz, who described her effort to find two boys who had drowned: "their spirits appeared at Inspiration Stump, dripping water" (49). Other legends I have collected describe the stump's power to draw spirits of humans and animals, especially late at night.

The presence of animal spirits at the stump seems appropriate, since part of Lily Dale's space in the middle of Leolyn Woods is devoted to a pet cemetery. Here residents of the community can express their sadness after losing dear cats and dogs. Homemade memorials placed on the gravesites of deceased pets create a sense of family love and devotion. Readers of Stephen King's *Pet Sematary* (1983), in which pets return from the dead in horrible ways, might expect this burial ground to have a macabre edge, but it does not; it is simply a place to commemorate beloved pets.

On the same side of Lily Dale as Inspiration Stump and the pet cemetery, the Fairy Trail contains a wide range of whimsical miniature dwellings. There are dollhouses, bark shelters, birdhouses, beach houses, and many other kinds of homes for fairies. Originally built for the sake of child visitors, the trail has become a favorite destination of adult visitors as well. Although it is more fanciful and less central to Lily Dale's identity than Inspiration Stump, the Fairy Trail satisfies local residents' and visitors'

FIGURE 6.5. The entrance to the Fairy Trail, Lily Dale. (Photo by Elizabeth Tucker)

FIGURE 6.6. A fairy house on Fairy Trail, Lily Dale. (Photo by Elizabeth Tucker)

desire to view and help create dwellings for small supernatural beings. How many visitors believe that fairies actually inhabit the Fairy Trail? During my visits to Lily Dale I have never heard anyone express their belief in fairies, but the site delights visitors and supports a sense of community. Every spring, Lily Dale Assembly organizes an event called "Welcome Back the Fairies," during which local residents freshen up the trail and repair the tiny houses after the long, upstate–New York winter.

Sometimes, as Sabina Magliocco observes in *Witching Culture*, people who work hard and struggle to deal with life's pressures feel a need for re-enchantment (2004, 121). I discuss college students' longing for re-enchantment in *Haunted Halls: Ghostlore of American College Campuses* (Tucker 2007, 21). The Fairy Trail re-enchants everyday lives beautifully, offering a dazzling variety of fairy homes and encouraging visitors to add tiny houses of their own making. Lily Dale's support of this communal process, open to all who wish to participate, has brought joy to many children and adults.

The Fairy Trail, Inspiration Stump, and the surrounding Leolyn Woods all convey a sense of sacredness. One of the reasons why these areas have become so meaningful is their evocation of mythical space. As the geographer Yi-Fu Tuan argues in *Space and Place* (1977), there are two kinds of mythical space: one is "the spatial component of a world view, a conception of localized values within which people carry on their practical activities"; the other is a "fuzzy area" of knowledge that surrounds our empirical knowledge (86). At Lily Dale we find both kinds of mythical space. The first expresses Spiritualist values, which permeate all daily activities in Lily Dale. Since Spiritualism advocates belief that the dead are always with us and that mediums can obtain messages from them, it is not surprising that Lily Dale, owned and governed by Spiritualists, is a place where expectations of supernatural activity seem natural. Myths are foundational, sacred stories that remind people of their cultural and religious roots. In Lily Dale the most important stories are those that describe the Assembly's founding and its early years. Lily Dale's historian tells many such stories during town tours and at the museum. Some describe early psychic readings, during which mediums produced ectoplasm and other signs of spirits' presence for fascinated observers. Another popular story of the Assembly's early years describes Harry Houdini's vigorous efforts to discredit mediums. Going from one medium's house to another, he would try to prove that mediums were fakes—instead, members of the community would slam their doors and shut their windows. These stories and others remind listeners of Spiritualist values and of clashes with nonbelievers.

Besides these specifically Spiritualist myths, there are ancient myths and epic narrative poems that tell of heroes' efforts to enter the land of the dead. Ancient Greek mythology, for example, tells of the gods of Mount Olympus and human or semidivine heroes. In the Greek myth "Orpheus and Eurydice," a husband desperately tries to bring his beloved wife back from the underworld; because he cannot resist looking back at her, he fails (Hamilton 103–4). The ancient Sumerian epic of Gilgamesh, in which the king of Uruk sadly seeks the secret to immortality after losing his friend Enkidu, also does not end with the deceased person's return (Sandars 1972). However, there is a more positive conclusion to book six of Virgil's *Aeneid*. Aeneas, who has lost his father, succeeds in speaking with his father's spirit with the assistance of the Cumaean Sibyl. Afterward, he sees a vision of Rome's future (West 2003). These are just a few of the old stories in which heroes seek contact with lost loved ones. Nowadays, it is common for this kind of search to occur in popular movies such as *Ghost* (1990), in which Demi Moore plays the role of a grieving wife and Whoopi Goldberg plays a medium who delivers messages from the wife's deceased husband.[3] In all of these myths, epics, and films, protagonists struggle desperately to make contact with dead loved ones, but, in Lily Dale, anyone who wishes to talk with the dead can do so by requesting a psychic reading. The easy availability of this kind of communication makes Lily Dale a place imbued with wondrous possibilities.

Lily Dale's psychic mediums receive so many messages that there seems to be a very thin line between life and death. The town has a firm physical boundary, however: a gate that separates Lily Dale Assembly from the outside world. This gate marks the difference between Spiritualist values, which emphasize continuity between life and death, and the values of the surrounding area of New York State. Within Lily Dale, Spiritualism's interest in what happens after death comes through in local legends. According to a local legend recorded by Mary Catherine Gaydos Gabriel (2010), Topsy, a horse buried in the pet cemetery, fell through the ice on Cassadaga Lake and drowned (69–70). Like other spirits of deceased animals, Topsy is still part of the Lily Dale community. Gabriel also tells of the ashes of early Lily Dale mediums who are buried around Inspiration Stump: when the ground freezes in winter, the mediums' urns rise up to the surface (69–70). This slightly gruesome story seems to suggest that early mediums want to be remembered. Visitors to Lily Dale's museum learn about these early mediums' legacies, so the past has not been forgotten.

Lily Dale emphasizes the afterlife, but it is also a place of much lively activity in the "here and now." People attend message services, healing services, workshops, and lectures; they eat healthful food at the Sunflower Cafeteria; they wander by the shore of Cassadaga Lake; and they shop for books, CDs, jewelry, and other products at the bookstore. Although mythical space is a big part of Lily Dale—in its own fashion, it is a land of the dead—there is plenty of involvement in practical, everyday space as well.

THREE WOMEN'S STORIES:
FEMALE NURTURERS, A DARK MALE SHADOW, AND HORSE SPIRITS IN AN INVERTED HOUSE

In the midst of the active, cheerful routine of Lily Dale's summer season, many women come to consult mediums. There is a strong female presence in Lily Dale. As you walk from South Street to Marion Street, you can see middle-aged and elderly female residents chatting with each other, calling

their cats, and picking flowers. Of the forty-one psychic mediums registered in Lily Dale at the time I was writing this chapter, eighty percent were
female. I saw both men and women at message services during my three
visits to the town, but more women attended than men. It does not seem
surprising that the Spiritualist religion, inspired by the spirit communications of two little girls and appreciated by feminist activists, has drawn a
large proportion of female practitioners and clients. Because of this focus on
women's work and concerns, I will analyze the significance of gender in stories about three women's visits to Lily Dale. I have known one of the women
for two years and I talked with the other two during summer visits to Lily
Dale. All of them initially made legend quests to Lily Dale after hearing an
intriguing story from a friend or from a website, and all of them have made
repeated visits to Lily Dale since then. Since all of the women now view Lily
Dale as a deeply meaningful place that provides an important pause from
everyday life, their post-legend-quest visits function as pilgrimages.

According to Jeannie Banks Thomas, ghost legends "present the masculine and the feminine in culturally familiar ways," reflecting stress and
conflict (2007, 83, 89). Thomas analyzes a character in ghost legends that
mirrors perceptions of male behavior: the "Extreme Guy," whose threatening behavior expresses American culture's linkage of masculinity with
aggression and violence. She finds that some female characters in ghost legends provide an intriguing alternative to the nineteenth-century concept of
the "angel in the house," which originated in a poem by Coventry Patmore:
an "ideal, submissive woman and wife" (81). In ghost legends, female characters may nurture others, but they may also disrupt traditional values, act
assertively, and dare to be eccentric.

This approach to gender in ghost legends helps us understand the meaning of male and female characters—as well as characters that appear to be
genderless—in women's stories about legend quests. I have found both
Extreme Guys and assertive, somewhat eccentric women in accounts of
legend quests to Lily Dale. Outside Lily Dale and other Spiritualist colonies,
mediums are often perceived as having eccentric habits as well as unusual
abilities to summon spirits and offer advice; such abilities also belong to
Americans' perception of witches (Adler 1979, 3–14).[4] Perception of mediums
by visitors to Lily Dale tends to emphasize good, assertive advice, which may
greatly improve the life of the person who seeks it.

Many women's stories about their first trip to Lily Dale highlight interactions with a medium or mediums. One such story comes from my friend

Josette, a very kind, insightful person whom I have known since the spring of 2010. In her mid forties, Josette has devoted herself to raising her three children while working full time. It has been a privilege to get to know her and hear her story, which has recently been published (Berardi 2011).

Josette's first visit to Lily Dale took place after a friend told her about her own trip, which included a reading with a medium. Josette believed that visiting this Spiritualist community would help her fourteen-year-old daughter Nicole, who had been conversing with spirits since early childhood. Nicole had had recurrent encounters with a "man at the foot of the bed," a male spirit who hid toys, "was dressed all in black, had long greasy hair, and was not a nice guy." This firmly gendered spirit kept giving Nicole disturbing visions of a hospital ward where a man lay suffering from a head injury (Berardi 2011, 58). Similarly, Josette herself perceived a male spirit when she first arrived in Lily Dale: "I saw a full-body shadow walk towards me on Buffalo St. I don't think it was walking towards me to show himself to me, I think he was just there and I saw him. I don't know why I think he is a 'he' either, but it was big and dark and did not scare me. Almost just a 'Oh, look, a full-bodied figure over there' was my reaction" (Berardi 2012).

Although Josette recalls that the male shadow did not scare her, her emphasis on its being "big and dark" suggests she worried about its size and absence of recognizable features. Both the full-body shadow and the man at the foot of the bed raise the possibility of discomfort and potential danger. They fit Thomas's identification of the Extreme Guy, a volatile, difficult man who inflicts damage and destruction (2007, 83–91). Although neither the man at the foot of the bed nor the male full-body shadow inflict physical damage, we get the impression that both of them could wreak havoc on people around them if they chose to do so. These depictions of dark male figures reflect contemporary American culture's portrayal of men as aggressive figures who are likely to use violence to get what they want. Recent crime statistics show that 88% of those who commit homicide in the United States are male (Homicide Trends 2012). Crime shows on television—such as *CSI*, *Without a Trace*, and *Criminal Minds*—have sensationalized violent crimes committed by men, creating haunting images of danger and distress.

In contrast to these two threatening male spirits, protective, nurturing female spirits have been an important part of Josette's and Nicole's messages from the dead. Josette's maternal grandmother, "Granny Rose," emigrated from Italy to the farming community of Watkins Glen, New York, early in the twentieth century. Rose's parents, Nicolina and Nicholas, had a vegetable stand. When Rose grew old enough, she worked at the Watkins Glen salt mine. Devout Catholics, the family members worked hard and enjoyed celebrating special occasions together. Before Granny Rose died of cancer in 1979, she "would stare off toward one corner near her bed, presumably talking with deceased family members and others whom she called by name" (Berardi 2011, 31). Almost thirty years after her passing, Nicole, who was named after Granny Rose and her great-grandmother Nicolina, told her mother that Granny Rose had visited her as a spirit and had explained that she herself had been a psychic medium, although she had not had many chances to use this ability.

In the summer of 2009, Josette received a message from one of Lily Dale's mediums, Dr. Patricia Bell, who told her that "[her] grandmother was standing in front of [her] holding a tomato and some very green lettuce" (Berardi 2011, 51). Such messages are common in Lily Dale, where spirits of parents and grandparents may encourage their descendants to eat good food, go for walks, and do other things to maintain a healthy lifestyle. With Dr. Bell's guidance, Josette interpreted the message from Granny Rose as encouragement to eat more healthful food and to remember her grandmother's gardens, which had helped her family stay strong for many years. She enjoyed thinking of her beloved grandmother, who reminded her of happy childhood days.

Josette's story about the message from her grandmother's spirit has strong color images. Both red and green traditionally represent the life force in European folktales. Both colors have some ambivalent associations: red can also mean danger, and green can signal decay. But in this story, the red and green vegetables represent a grandmother's nurture of her dear granddaughter. With her bright, healthful vegetables, Granny Rose brings to mind the Greek goddess Demeter, who provides food to nurture growth and also oversees the cycle of life and death. Green, the color of growing plants, has particular strength as a symbol. Like her mother, Nicole perceived green as a positive color. One of her two spirit guides is a caring spirit called the Green Lady; another is a Native American woman named Dove. In Lily Dale, and in other Spiritualist communities, psychics have identified Native American spirit guides, as analyzed in Stephen C. Wehmeyer's dissertation "Red Mysteries: 'Indian' Spirits and the Sacred Landscapes of American Spiritualism" (2002).

Like Josette, I have visited Lily Dale a number of times. Every time I go, I feel the routines of teaching at a mid-sized university recede; what takes their place is a serendipitous sequence of conversations with women who have embarked on meaningful legend quests. One such encounter took place in Lily Dale's historic Maplewood Hotel (founded in 1880) in the summer of 2011. Having learned from my conversations with Josette that the Maplewood Hotel had a reputation both for being haunted by horse spirits and for charging very reasonable rates, I came with my husband and our good friend to stay there for a couple of days.

When we entered Maplewood's lobby, we saw white wicker furniture near a sign that proclaimed "NO Readings, Healings, Circles or Seances in This Area Please." Even though the chairs looked tempting for circle-makers, all guests seemed to be obeying the rules. My husband, our friend, and I walked into the room next to the lobby, which held a collection of paintings known for having been created by spirits. As we gazed at the paintings, I felt as if we had stepped back into the 1880s, when Spiritualism was still new.

The next morning, the sound of geese flying over the hotel awakened me early. I decided to go downstairs to see if any other hotel guests besides me wanted to learn more about Maplewood's famous horse spirits. In the lobby I met Dottie, a woman in her early fifties who wore a white kerchief and carried a sketch pad. On the pad was an unfinished sketch of a horse with a long, ethereal mane.

"Do you know about the horse spirits in this hotel?" Dottie asked me.

"Not very much," I answered. "Let's go ask the desk clerk."

The clerk, a man in his late thirties or early forties, said, "There are supposed to be horse spirits in the attic from about a hundred years ago. The stable was here first. Sometimes people hear the horses; they might even see something."

Dottie answered, "Yes, they lifted each floor up as they built a new one. I think they called it suspension building."

"That's right," the desk clerk replied. "The stable was on the original floor. We're on the fourth floor here. There are ghosts of cats and dogs running around the place too."

Ever eager to seize an opportunity, I asked, "So the stable is up in the attic? Can people ever go up there?"

"No," the desk clerk answered, "only if they have special permission. There are a lot of bats up there."

Dottie and I looked each other in the eye, grimacing slightly. Not wanting to encounter bats, we did not ask for permission to visit the attic. We did, however, spend some time talking as we drank tea sitting in the white wicker armchairs. Dottie told me she had read about Maplewood's horse spirits on the Internet and had been eager to feel their presence.

"Are you going to have a reading from a medium while you're here?" I asked Dottie.

"Yes," she said, smiling, "but the horse spirits are my favorites."

Both Dottie and I found Maplewood's horse ghosts to be enchanting (but not enchanting enough to bring us up into an attic filled with bats). Dottie liked horses and enjoyed drawing them. Looking at her sketch of a ghostly horse, I remembered that many young girls have enjoyed reading books about horses: *My Friend Flicka* (O'Hara 1997), *Misty of Chincoteague* (Henry 2006), and others. Amazon.com is so well aware of the appeal of horse stories to girls that it recommends "the very best horse stories for girls" on one of its web guides (So you'd like to . . . 2012). Maplewood's stories about horse spirits can evoke memories of childhood days when a good book about a horse offered quiet contentment.

The desk clerk's story about the hotel and its horses also helps listeners understand how people built houses in late-nineteenth-century rural America. At that time, it was not unusual for carpenters to hoist a house's first floor higher and higher so it eventually became the top floor. This technique resulted in an inverted house, where, as Maplewood's desk clerk pointed out, guests standing in the lobby were actually standing on the fourth floor. Although this technique was common in the nineteenth century, it is not well known now. Visitors to Maplewood may feel surprised and slightly shocked by the hotel's peculiar floor plan. Like the Winchester Mystery House in San Jose, California, which the heiress Sarah Winchester built over a period of thirty-eight years, the Maplewood Hotel gradually took shape as carpenters hoisted its original floor higher and higher. Knowing that the first floor is really the fourth floor of the hotel gives visitors a pleasant sense of disorientation. Dottie greatly enjoyed this sensation, as did I.

The third woman whose legend quest I was privileged to discover had needed more than a sense of enchantment; she had the desire to recover from both physical pain and domestic troubles. "Lily Dale saved my life," Sylvia, a friendly woman in her seventies, told me when I stopped to talk with her one morning in the summer of 2011. She explained that a badly broken arm had brought her to Lily Dale more than twenty years ago. Having heard stories about Lily Dale healings, she had wanted to travel there to make her arm feel better. Mediums took her pain away by rubbing the arm. Relieved of pain and fascinated by the healers' power, she kept coming back to Lily Dale every summer.

There was, however, more to Sylvia's story than her appreciation of Lily Dale's healers. Before she came to Lily Dale, her husband had set the pace of their lives and had held her back from doing things she wanted to do. She had broken her arm hurrying across a street, trying to keep up with him. Once she arrived in Lily Dale, she found support from psychic mediums to become more independent. "You can stand on your own two feet," three mediums told her during one year of readings. After she received the mediums' support, Sylvia's husband never held her back again. She came to Lily Dale on her own, getting to know other mediums and visitors. As a longtime summer guest, she had become an important part of the community, and she came close to being chosen as one of the central characters in the HBO film *No One Dies in Lily Dale* (2010).

The story of Sylvia's strong attachment to Lily Dale demonstrates the high level of support that women can receive there. Sylvia was in great need of help because of the limits her husband had placed upon her. The story of her breaking her arm while hurrying across a busy street dramatically illustrates her dilemma. Although her husband does not seem to be as aggressively masculine and dangerous as some of the Extreme Guys in ghost legends, he hurts his wife by insisting on dominating her through old-fashioned gender roles. In his own way, by taking away his wife's independence and peace of mind, he takes the role of an Extreme Guy who needs to be stopped. Both physical healing and supportive advice made it possible for Sylvia to become independent, to "stand on her own two feet." This kind of caring support forms an important part of Lily Dale's meaning for female visitors.

THE MEDIUM IS THE MESSAGE

Marshall McLuhan's statement, "The medium is the message" (1964), stresses the importance of modern forms of communication, but it also applies, with a definitional twist, to Lily Dale's unique identity. In Lily Dale, mediums are perceived as having a crucial ability: the power to deliver messages from the dead. Since most of these mediums are female, people's perception of their power has cultural significance. Mediums serve as cultural symbols of women's power. Deeply rooted in Spiritualism, new age spirituality, and rural American folk culture, mediums' revelations become the central aspect of many women's accounts of their legend quests.

Stories about legend quests and subsequent pilgrimages suggest that a medium's supernatural power can change a woman's life in a positive way. Two of the three women described here mention mediums offering key insights, helping a sensitive and talented child, reaffirming family values, and loosening restrictive gender roles. The other woman mentions a medium but pays more attention to animal spirits hearkening back to the nineteenth century: exciting, thought-provoking ghosts that are typical of legend quests. These are only three women's stories, but they strongly represent Lily Dale's Spiritualist and feminist traditions.

Besides focusing on mediums and unusual spirits, stories about legend quests and pilgrimages to Lily Dale provide a glimpse of its unique atmosphere. Its veneration of sacred sites and evocation of old stories about interactions with spirits of the dead make visits there memorable and meaningful. Women who need to get away from tedious or troubling circumstances in their everyday lives can rediscover a childlike sense of amazement and relaxation in Lily Dale. A walk down the Fairy Trail, a veggie burger at the Sunflower Cafeteria, a past-life regression workshop, and a message service at Inspiration Stump can make it easier to re-enter the less-than-enchanting workaday world.

NOTES

1. The family legend of my Uncle Glenn Libby (1886–1961) walking in the dining room at night has a connection to older family members' memories of his being paralyzed and longing to walk for years before his death. The legend of the jumping table, told by Uncle A. S. "Stubby" Treworgy (1907–1999), is part of the table-tipping tradition that was very popular in rural Maine in the early twentieth century.

2. According to Kenneth Pimple, the Fox sisters "were in the right place at the right time, with the right message, at the right time; they introduced spirit rappings to a world that was hungry for spirit rappings" (1995, 81).

3. For an analysis of romantic films involving encounters with ghosts, see Fowkes (2004).

4. One of Lily Dale's legends pokes fun at the perception of mediums as witches: "There was a gentleman who was the librarian for about five years there. He had some visitors asking questions. One of them asked if all the people who lived in Lily Dale were witches. He replied, "There are no witches that live here, but if you change 'w' to a 'b,' we have a few of those" (Pfortmiller 2012).

WORKS CITED

Adler, Margot. 1979. *Drawing Down the Moon: Witches, Druids, Goddess-Worshippers, and Other Pagans in America Today*. Boston: Beacon Press.

Aldridge, Alan. 2000. *Religion in the Contemporary World: A Sociological Introduction*. New York: Polity.

Badone, Ellen, and Sharon R. Roseman. 2004. *Intersecting Journeys: The Anthropology of Pilgrimage and Tourism*. Urbana and Chicago: University of Illinois Press.

Bennett, Gillian. 1987. *Traditions of Belief: Women, Folklore, and the Supernatural Today*. London: Penguin.

Berardi, Josette. 2011. *The Man At the Foot of the Bed*. Frederick, MD: Publish America.

———. 2012. E-mail communication. 7 January.

Braude, Ann. 1989. *Radical Spirits: Spiritualism and Women's Rights in Nineteenth-Century America*. Boston: Beacon Press.

Bruner, Edward M. 1991. "Transformation of Self in Tourism." *Annals of Tourism Research* 18: 238–50.

Cadwallader, Mary E. 2010. *Hydesville in History*. New York: Nabu Press.

Dégh, Linda. 2001. *Legend and Belief*. Bloomington, IN: Indiana University Press.

Ellis, Bill. 1983. "Legend Tripping in Ohio: A Behavioral Survey." *Papers in Comparative Studies* 2: 52–69.

———. 2003. *Aliens, Ghosts, and Cults: Legends We Live*. Jackson, MS: University Press of Mississippi.

Fowkes, Katherine A. 2004. "Melodramatic Specters: Cinema and *The Sixth Sense*." In *Spectral America: Phantoms and the National Imagination*, edited by Jeffrey Andrew Weinstock, 185–206. Madison, WI: University of Wisconsin Press.

Gabriel, Mary Catherine Gaydos. 2010. "Ordinary Spirits in an Extraordinary Town: Finding Identity in Personal Images and Resurrected Memories in Lily Dale, New York." All Graduate Theses and Dissertations. Paper 79. http://digitalcommons.usu.edu/etd/792.

Ghost. 1990. Paramount Pictures. Directed by Jerry Zucker.

Goldstein, Diane. 2007. "The Commodification of Belief." In *Haunting Experiences: Ghosts in Contemporary Folklore,* edited by Diane Goldstein, Sylvia Grider, and Jeannie Banks Thomas, 171–205. Logan, UT: Utah State University Press.

Hamilton, Edith. 1969. *Mythology*. New York: Penguin.

Homicide Trends in the U.S. Bureau of Justice Statistics. 2012. http://bjs.ojp.usdoj.gov/content/homicide/gender.cfm.

Henry, Marguerite. 2006. *Misty of Chincoteague*. New York: Aladdin.

King, Stephen. 1983. *Pet Sematary*. New York: Doubleday.

Lindahl, Carl. 2005. "Ostensive Healing: Pilgrimage to the San Antonio Ghost Tracks." *Journal of American Folklore* 118.468: 164–85.

Magliocco, Sabina. 2004. *Witching Culture: Folklore and Neo-Paganism in America*. Philadelphia: University of Pennsylvania Press.

McLuhan, Marshall. 1964. *Understanding Media: The Extensions of Man*. New York: Mentor

No One Dies in Lily Dale. 2010. HBO. Directed by Steven Cantor.

O'Hara, Mary. 1997. *My Friend Flicka*. New York: Buccaneer Books.

Pfortmiller, Sandra. n.d. "A 'Dale' by Any Other Name." *National Spiritualist Association of Churches*. http://www.nsac.org/LilyDale.aspx (accessed June 21, 2012).

Pimple, Kenneth D. "Ghosts, Spirits, and Scholars: The Origins of Modern Spiritualism." 1995. In *Out of the Ordinary: Folklore and the Supernatural*, edited by Barbara Walker, 75–89. Logan, UT: Utah State University Press.

Rose, Joshua D. 2011. "What is New Age?" Master's thesis, George Mason University.

Sandars, N. K., ed. 1972. *The Epic of Gilgamesh*. London: Penguin Books.

Seekings, Cara. 2010. *Ladies of Lily Dale*. Lily Dale, NY: Lily Dale Assembly.

So you'd like to . . . read the very best horse books for girls! *Amazon.com*. http://www.amazon.com/gp/richpub/syltguides/fullview/2XH46FIBWoI82 (accessed June 22, 2012).

Thigpen, Kenneth A. 1971. "Adolescent Legends in Brown County: A Survey." *Indiana Folklore* 4.2:141–215.

Thomas, Jeannie Banks. 2007. "Gender and Ghosts." In *Haunting Experiences: Ghosts in Contemporary Folklore,* edited by Diane Goldstein, Sylvia Grider, and Jeannie Banks Thomas, 81–110. Logan, UT: Utah State University Press.

Tuan, Yi-Fu. 1977. *Space and Place: The Perspective of Experience*. Minneapolis, MN: University of Minnesota Press.

Tucker, Elizabeth. 2007. *Haunted Halls: Ghostlore of American College Campuses*. Jackson, MS: University Press of Mississippi.

Turner, Victor. 1992. "Death and the Dead in the Pilgrimage Process." In *Blazing the Trail*, edited by Edith Turner, 29–47. Tucson, AZ: University of Arizona Press.

Wehmeyer, Stephen C. 2002. "Red Mysteries: 'Indian' Spirits and the Sacred Landscapes of American Spiritualism." PhD dissertation, University of California at Los Angeles.

Weisberg, Barbara. 2005. *Talking to the Dead: Kate and Maggie Fox and the Rise of Spiritualism*. New York: HarperOne.

West, David, ed. 2003. *The Aeneid*. New York, NY: Penguin Classics.

Wicker, Christine. 2003. *Lily Dale: The True Story of the Town That Talks to the Dead*. San Francisco: Harper SanFrancisco.

The Haunted Asian Landscapes
of Lafcadio Hearn
Old Japan

BILL ELLIS

Lafcadio Hearn (1850–1904) was a "man without a country" for much of his life: born the result of a transient affair of an Irish doctor and a Greek peasant woman, he spent his childhood shuffled among relatives in Ireland, England, and France before arriving in the United States as a teen. His polyglot upbringing, however, gave him unique insight into ethnic communities, and his early observations of Creole folklore in both New Orleans and the Caribbean were decades ahead of their time. His most lasting literary work was his turn-of-the-century series of travel sketches of Japanese culture, a nation only recently reopened to the West. These detailed translations of supernatural beliefs and legends were not only popular among English-language readers but they were also quickly back-translated into Japanese, making him one of the country's formative nationalist writers.

Hearn's initial purpose, as he states in the preface of *Glimpses of an Unfamiliar Japan* ([1894] 2012), was to use his observations to define "the rare charm of Japanese life, so different from that of all other lands" (ix). Thus, his versions of legends, at least superficially, are filled with "picturesque" details intended to place the Japanese common people's quaint customs in a romantic Otherworld well suited for the cultural tourists for whom he was writing. It would thus be easy to dismiss his work as part of the nostalgic

Lafcadio Hearn and his Wife.

FIGURE 7.1. Lafcadio Hearn, ca. 1896, after he had accepted Japanese citizenship and taken the name Yakumo Koizumi, with his Japanese wife, Setsu Koizumi. (Wikimedia Commons, from the Mary Louise Vincent Lafcadio Hearn Collection, Hiram College, Hiram, Ohio)

romanticism that informed the work of many European and American folklorists who were contemporaries of Hearn. They often saw folklore in terms
of "survivals" or "antiquities," seeing value in quaint and marginal customs
found in marginal cultures and ignoring the much larger and more important traditions that affected the everyday lives of most people.

But Hearn's approach to folklore was revolutionary; it was intimately
tied to the contemporary significance of the lore he observed, rather than to
its usefulness in celebrating quaint antiquities that were fast passing away.
His versions of Japanese legends are much fuller and richer than European
supernatural legend texts, often digressing to "unpack" the implications
of narrative details for their original narrators and giving fuller weight to
the performative context of the stories. By making use of internationally
circulated print media, a novelty in his time just as the Internet is in ours,
he placed Japanese traditions in a global context. This, of course, highlighted the distinctively "Japanese" texture of these narratives. But, paradoxically, it also revealed the ways their content and structure are typical of
narrative traditions that are neither old nor uniquely Japanese but instead
are vitally active in the contemporary cultures of his readers worldwide.

In structuring his work this way, Hearn anticipates the work of folklorists a century later, who also view "contemporary" legends as crucial to seeing the dynamics of social change during a specific period. For *contemporary*
does not simply mean "the decade during which this article was published":
it means whatever period a tradition was actively circulating and seen as
relevant to that present moment (Ellis 2001; 2003, 46ff.). And so *hypermodern* can mean not only typical of the early twenty-first century but also
the way a culture is influenced, for better or worse, by the impact of a newly
introduced, consumer-oriented mass media. This is especially true when
it enables and encourages readers to indulge in a form of cultural tourism,
if only remotely (as with web-mediated material) through the mass medium
of printed text.

As Charles R. Frederick observed, folklore has a dual nature, "simultaneously illustrating singularity and evoking commonality" (1990, 171). This
chapter will explore this double significance in three of Hearn's supernatural legend texts. The first, "Mujina," ([1903] 1971), is a brief and enigmatic
encounter with a "faceless" entity, which links to an international tradition
of especially uncanny phenomena that cannot be described in words. The
second, "Furisodé" (1899) tells of a beautiful woman's robe that carries a
curse, bringing misfortune to each of its owners and ultimately to the entire

community. The last and most intriguing, "In the Cave of the Children's Ghosts" ([1894] 2012), is an account of a legend trip, complete with a core narrative that is reinforced by cautionary stories and validated by Hearn's own account, in which he describes seeing with his own eyes the footprints left by the little spirits.

This chapter will acknowledge Hearn's keen ethnographic sense, which was influential in encouraging native Japanese academics such as Kunio Yanagita to document local traditions in a culture-specific way that highlighted the distinctive traits of that country's spirit. But I also argue that by documenting traditions in a manner that was hypermodern for his day, Hearn located esoteric, globally common structures and universal human reactions to life's mysteries. By taking care to observe and record these legends' *singularity* in the context of an exotic setting, Hearn captures the elements that most strongly illustrate their *commonality* within the international realm of contemporary folklore. And by using a newly available mass media, he showed that Japanese folklore had vital connections to the rest of the world, thus spurring Japanese writers and scholars to rethink their own esoteric structures and ideas in an international perspective.

HOW IS "PLACE" IMPORTANT FOR HEARN AND FOR CONTEMPORARY FOLKLORISTS?

Traditionally, folklorists studying the supernatural have focused on the dialectic of "legend" and "belief." Legends comprise a wide range of socially constructed verbal expressions, ranging from words or phrases identifying uncanny phenomena ("It's a ghost!") to elaborate accounts of experiences ordinary people have had that seem to require paranormal explanations. As a whole, legendry makes up a cultural grammar of belief-language, which allows people to generate an endlessly variable set of stories on this perennially intriguing topic. Belief, or the degree to which individuals accept these explanations, is quite variable. Some stories argue strongly for the presence of the miraculous, while others debunk such a claim, instead showing that there are simple explanations for every "paranormal" event. Still others hesitate between these poles of belief and disbelief, presenting witnesses as careful and cautious observers willing to seek natural explanations for events, yet unable to account for each and every strange detail. Overall, legendry enables a community to agree to disagree about the nature of the world they live in and what may be possible in it. Thus, all levels of belief—from enthusiastic advocacy to cynical skepticism—are equally part of this sociolinguistic system.

"The supernatural is born of language," structuralist critic Tzvetan Todorov perceptively noted, for the implied structure of a fantastic experience has to be constructed after the fact using culturally shared words, statements, and concepts (1973, 82). This does not mean that folklore, in and of itself, generates supernatural experiences, as some skeptics have claimed. But those who have witnessed events that they sense are extraordinary are compelled to talk to others about them, and in so doing they use cultural concepts that they and their audiences share. As these stories are told and retold, they tend to conform more and more to traditional content and structure. For this reason, folklorists have analyzed the supernatural as a social phenomenon, located in the context of a verbal performance and metanarrative reaction rather than an existential one. This is appropriate, as we have no certain way to determine what reality lies behind any given story, nor whether informants in fact do believe the stories they tell or if they are simply relating them in a naturalistic way to involve an audience.

For this reason, discussing "place" as part of the dynamics of legend can be problematic. The supernatural is not "out there," but rather it is "here among us" in the shared milieu that allows legends to be told and actively discussed. But this context also includes ways in which we socially construct the space around us, both the landscape and the ways in which humans alter it for their use. Seen that way, "place" is like the supernatural in that it is an experience filtered into discourse with the help of previous stories of its history, use, and social significance. We experience a place not just in terms of sensory impulses, but also as the most recent unfolding of the spot's ongoing history. Any visit to a noteworthy place, in other words, is born of language, just like any legendary encounter of the supernatural. So perhaps legendry should be seen more dynamically as a threefold interplay, with the ongoing social history of the place engaging with the culture's definition of the supernatural and with the ways we emotionally respond to the world we live in.

Lafcadio Hearn, a lifelong wanderer, experienced the places in which he lived with unusual objectivity and sensitivity. Even in his childhood in Wales, a biographer noted, he eagerly sought out fishermen as sources of legendary tales and watched in fascination as they pointed out landmarks on the rocky coast as the actual locations of their tales (McWilliams 1946,

38). His 1870s sketches of crimes and sensations in the ghettoes of Cincin-
nati likewise showed a similar vividness and attention to detail. In his jour-
nalism, he frequently assailed modern industrialism for exploiting minori-
ties and marginalizing their cultural heritage. And so he became a practical
ethnographer, holding up the oral and material culture of the communities
he encountered as a sign of their suppressed creativity (Bronner 2005, 161).
He similarly celebrated the Creole subcultures he studied in New Orleans
and the West Indies during the next period of his life, publishing studies of
proverbs and foodways that were ahead of their time, placing these traditions into their original cultural contexts.

However, when Hearn was sent to Japan by *The Atlantic Monthly* in 1890,
he fell in love with the culture, eventually becoming a citizen of the country,
marrying, and adopting the name Yakumo Koizume. Japan, like the United
States, was undergoing rapid industrialization, a trend that Hearn decried.
But "Old Japan," the subculture that retained a pre-industrial rural structure
and maintained many old customs, was still very much alive. To be sure,
his understanding of Japanese culture was, like those of many early folklorists, warped by a romantic view of "the folk." In the preface of his first
collection of travel sketches (1894), he praised the rural Japanese for their
"delightful old customs," "picturesque dresses," and "simple happy beliefs,"
and expressed concern that many traditions that were "primitive" yet
"comparable for beauty of fancy to . . . Greek myths" were being consigned
to the dust heap by modernization (1894 [2012], ix). Still, for all his social
Darwinist rhetoric (he was an ardent admirer of his contemporary Herbert
Spencer), his multicultural background made him a keen and sympathetic
observer of tradition and its context.

At the end of a lengthy description of the shrines at Enoshima, he imag-
ines the reader summing up the bare facts of the visit and saying, "And this
is all that you went forth to see . . . ?" Hearn admits this is true, but adds,
"And nevertheless I know that I am bewitched. There is a charm indefinable
about the place—that sort of charm which comes with a little ghostly thrill
never to be forgotten" (1894 [2012], 109). His choice of words—"bewitched,"
"charm," "ghostly"—evokes the presence of the supernatural, though he
concedes that the magic is worked not by occult means but by "numberless
subtle sensations and ideas interwoven and inter-blended." Chief among
these are the acts of smelling and touching things in the present moment,
while simultaneously recognizing that one is walking on a path considered holy for over a thousand years and visibly worn down by the feet of

countless pilgrims. In a later sketch, he witnesses the enactment of an
ancient rural dance and finds himself thinking he is watching something
both contemporary and at the same time "immemorially old, something
belonging to the unrecorded beginnings of this Oriental life" (1894 [2012],
155). The same images recur:

> Under the wheeling moon, in the midst of the round, I feel as one
> within the circle of a charm. And verily this is enchantment; I am
> bewitched, bewitched by the ghostly weaving of hands, by the
> rhythmic gliding of feet, above all by the flitting of the marvelous
> sleeves—apparitional, soundless, velvety as a flitting of great tropi-
> cal bats. No; nothing I ever dreamed of could be likened to this. And
> with the consciousness of the ancient hakaba behind me, and the
> weird invitation of its lanterns, and the ghostly beliefs of the hour
> and the place there creeps upon me a nameless, tingling sense of
> being haunted. (156)

In neither situation does Hearn *literally* feel he is in contact with supernatural forces: rather, he is metaphorically "haunted" by the "ghosts" of the
past being reenacted in the present moment. Yet the emotion, he argues,
is the same as being literally bewitched, enchanted, or confronted by a paranormal force. And indeed, from a contemporary folkloristic perspective,
the supernatural experience is not just a scary happening, but one that has
been given structure and meaning by the equally uncanny immanence of
tradition.

History does "haunt" places, in more ways than one. Locations where
murders, memorable disasters, or military battles took place attract ghost
stories, and the link between place and tragic history is so widespread in
legendry that it merits a series of entries in the *Motif-Index of Folk-Literature*
(Thompson 1960): "E.334 [Ghost haunts scene of former misfortune, crime
or tragedy]," "E337 [Ghost reenacts scene from own lifetime]," "E411.10 [Per-
sons who die violent or accidental deaths cannot rest in grave]." As Jeannie
Thomas has noted, ghost stories are dramatic attempts to preserve the culture of past eras in a way that audiences find both interesting and relevant
to their own lives (Goldstein, Grider, and Thomas 2007, 31). And such stories
often preserve a contrahegemonic edge as well. In analyzing the universal appeal of campus ghosts, Elizabeth Tucker (2007) unpacks the ways in
which these accounts preserve the disconcerting sides of these institutions'

official history: racist or sexist episodes in its history, or the actual but unrecorded stories of women whose rape or physical abuse went unaddressed at the time.

In this volume, Frank de Caro shows how legends featuring the revenants of tortured slaves, notably those attached to the haunted Lalaurie House in New Orleans, are "part of a larger trend by which ghost stories can be used to call attention to the horrors of slavery and how we are still haunted by a past that has not simply been left behind" (chapter 1). Such a "dark history" also seems present in Grider's historical analysis of the stereotypical "haunted house," which she links to architectural styles favored by the "super-rich" who were blamed for the economic exploitation of their communities (Goldstein, Grider, and Thomas 2007, 146). This does not mean that the place-related details of the alleged ghost story have to literally be true; only that the impact of the story should convey an alternative way of seeing the world that challenges "common sense" (i.e., majority culture) norms.

And legends make a more direct impact than other forms of discourse. As Iwasaka and Toelken point out, they dramatize issues that matter very much to us but also produce anxiety because they are ambiguous and difficult to resolve rationally. In fact, legends emerge and compel people's imaginations—even those who are skeptical about their literal truth—precisely because they are concrete embodiments of concerns that would otherwise remain abstract and unexplored (1994, 58). The authors point to the nature and location of the recently dead as one such area: a person who is physically alive in this world is, as the Japanese put it, resident in *konoyo*: "this world here." Someone who has died is no longer with us, but is in *anoyo*: "that world way over yonder." The logic of Japanese grammar suggests there would be an interstitial zone, *sonoyo*: "that place nearby." But none of Japan's dominant religions—Shinto, Buddhism, or Christianity—give believers a reason for believing in an intermediary stop for spirits on their way to their final destination. Nevertheless, supernatural legends abound in that country that suggest the world of the dead, especially the recently dead, is in fact very near to the everyday land of the living (1994, 14–15).

One aspect of this, Iwasaka and Toelken observe, is the tendency of legends to congregate around aspects of the physical landscape that are *liminal*, a term derived from the Latin word for threshold, the part of a doorway that is neither inside nor outside, but is an ambiguous space in between

(1994, 74). Crossroads, bridges, gates, tunnels, seashores, riverbanks, and the like are commonly defined as uncanny places where the supernatural may manifest. Likewise, roads passing through mountains or dense forests are liminal: paths constructed by humans in a "wild" terrain that are intended for nothing more than swift travel (1994, 87–88). Perceptively, Iwasaka and Toelken note that many of the situations in these legends involve irresolvable conflicts in the social world—that is, the eerie ambience of a liminal landscape parallels an ambiguity in moral values that provokes anxiety and fear.

Hearn was keenly sensitive to details in the landscapes he visited, and he was perspicacious about the social contours of the communities he came to know. This made him a shrewd ethnographer in this new world, as he had already proved in the United States. We turn now to some of the places he visited.

"MUJINA": NAMING THE NUMINOUS

The first example comes from *Kwaidan: Stories and Studies of Strange Things* ([1903] 1971), Hearn's best-known anthology of Japanese tales. He gives unusual attention to the location of the story, beginning, "On the Akasaka Road, in Tōkyō, there is a slope called Kii-no-kuni-zaka,—which means the Slope of the Province of Kii." Then, for no particular reason, he adds, "I do not know why it is called the Slope of the Province of Kii."[1] On one side of the slope, he explains, there was "an ancient moat, deep and very wide," while on the other there were the "long and lofty walls of an imperial palace." Before modern times, he adds, the spot was lonesome after dark and residents would walk miles out of the way to avoid it—"all because of a Mujina that used to walk there."

A pause. Legend scholars recognize this lead-in as Hearn's adaptation of the first section of an oral legend, often called an "orientation." It places the story in a very specific setting, telling the reader that the story to follow is no third- or fourth-hand tall tale that happened to some guy somewhere. It is a way of establishing credibility for a particular flavor of supernatural story, one that Gillian Bennett (1988) termed "told for true." In addition, it tells enough that the audience understands the place is liminal in more ways than one: it bears a puzzling name and lies in a dark area, close to the busy capital but outside of its business district. In addition, the road cuts between the walls of a palace and the deep moat constructed in ancient times to defend it. There is a bank and a body of water. Just the place for . . .

A "Mujina"? Hearn uses this term for his title and capitalizes it where it is used in the story. But, significantly, he never explains what it means. Is it a kind of ghost or monster? A personal name? What tradition lies behind the name? Hearn does not tell us, and so "a Mujina" remains a puzzling, exotic detail, which is exactly what the author intends.[2] "The last man who saw the Mujina," Hearn continues, "was an old merchant of the Kyōbashi quarter, who died about thirty years ago." One evening this person was heading up the slope when he saw a woman on the edge of the moat, immaculately dressed in noble garb and weeping bitterly. Concerned that she was intending suicide, he went over to her and said, "O-jochū, do not cry like that! . . . Tell me what the trouble is; and if there be any way to help you, I shall be glad to help you." Accosting a woman in a dark, lonely spot like this could be construed as an attempted sexual adventure, so Hearn hastens to assure the audience that the merchant was being sincere, "for he was a very kind man." But the woman continued to moan and sob, hiding her face behind one of the long sleeves of her kimono. The traveler persisted, telling her that this was no place to linger after dark and finally touching her shoulder, repeating "O-jochū!—O-jochū!—O-jochū!"

We are reminded again and again that this story takes place in "Old Japan" by Hearn's repeated and emphatic use of this exotic Japanese title, which (unlike the enigmatic "Mujina") he does explain in a footnote as the polite Japanese way to address a young lady that one does not know. Many North American folklorists would nevertheless recognize the scenario as a common situation in the "La Llorona" tradition, one of the most widespread contemporary legends in Latino cultures. Many of these variants describe a young male finding a woman in some liminal spot, typically on the edge of a body of water, weeping and moaning. "This happened to Tio Lencho, uncle of Pancho, my husband," one Mexican variant begins, in exactly the same place-focused way as Hearn's story (Glazer 1984, 115). It continues, "he was coming from the town of General Teran, near Montemorelos, state of Nuevo Leon . . . [and] in order to get to his ranch, he had to cross a bridge called 'el Puenton.'" There, the text tells, he saw a beautifully dressed woman sitting on the bank of the river "playing with her feet in the water." As with Hearn's kind-hearted merchant, he rushes up to the lady, touching her beautiful blonde hair with his hands, and asks, "What are you doing here all by yourself?"

By now, though, the audience knows that some shock is in store: a lovely woman in a liminal place is always more than meets the eye. And indeed, Hearn's "O-jochū" turns to the man, wipes her face with her hand, "and the man saw that she had no eyes or nose or mouth" ([1903] 1971). Likewise, when the Mexican rancher sees the beautiful woman by el Puenton bridge clearly, she has no face, just the features of a skull (Glazer 1984, 115). Similar shocks are reported elsewhere. "In May of 1959," for instance, "a young woman headed out for a night at the movies at the Waialae Drive-in Theater in Kaimuki," a suburb of Honolulu (yet another place-heavy lead-in) (Hanamoto 2011). Around midnight she went to the restroom (a liminal place in youth culture, where pools of water abound) to refresh her makeup. There she found another girl, combing her long black hair in the mirror like a mermaid. Then the girl slowly turned her face to the intruder, revealing "a smooth, white surface, like an egg-shell," where her face should be. The terrorized young woman, in some variants, had a nervous breakdown and was hospitalized (2011).

But Hearn is not finished. The merchant, frantic with fear, ran toward town until he came to the stand of an itinerant soba-seller. Out of breath and barely able to speak, he told the owner, "I saw . . . I saw a woman— by the moat;—and she showed me . . . Aa! I cannot tell you what she showed me!" The stand's proprietor, unperturbed, said, "Hé! Was it anything like THIS that she showed you?" And so he too wipes his face with his hand, and it also becomes featureless, like an egg. "And, simultaneously, the light went out," Hearn's story abruptly ends.[3]

This "double climax" is found in other contemporary legends, in which the protagonist runs to a safe place only to receive a second shock. Around the time of the first Gulf War, a legend circulated in Saudi Arabia about two young girls, out after dark in Suleimaniya, a suburb of Riyadh. They heard music coming from a palace building, peeked through a window, and saw "almost a hundred elegant unveiled women dancing to tribal wedding music" (Theroux 1991, 15–17). One of the dancers invited the two to join them, but one of the girls grabbed her friend's elbow and pointed at the strange women's feet: they all had "the legs and hoofs of donkeys." In panic, they rushed out of the palace and hailed a taxicab, urging him to call the police, as well as a sheikh, to expel the demons. "How do you know they were demons?" the driver asked "placidly."[4] "They were dancing, and had donkey legs!" they reply. Blandly, the taxi driver pulled up his robe to reveal his own donkey hooves, asking, "Like this?" (17).

Interestingly, all of these stories are very specific about the place, and many of them give variations on a theme openly expressed in Hearn's version: "This is no place for a young lady at night!" The Mexican *Llorona* tradition often depicts the young man who accosts the woman by the water as planning a quick sexual conquest, for a young woman out alone in the frontier is virtually "asking" to be molested. And a teenager at a drive-in theatre as late as midnight (long after most parents' curfews) likewise looks to be engaging in risky sexual play. Theroux observed that men who heard the Riyadh legend often asked out loud what two young women were doing out walking by themselves after dark. So a common theme, both in Old Japan and in other cultures' parallel stories, is that women—and men—need to know their "place" in society.

But Hearn's story has a second interesting point. While the setting is very closely defined, the supernatural is much less so. We aren't told what a Mujina is, and the story tells us only what she does *not* have. She is like the many haunts that are especially frightening because they cannot be described in words, or even counted. This aspect is dramatically realized in the coda, when the frightened merchant tries to explain to the soba-seller what has happened:

> "Aa!—aa!!—aa!!!" . . .
>
> "Koré! koré!" roughly exclaimed the soba-man. "Here! what is the matter with you? Anybody hurt you?"
>
> "No—nobody hurt me," panted the other—"only . . . Aa!—*aa!*" . . .
>
> "—Only scared you?" queried the peddler, unsympathetically. "Robbers?"
>
> "Not robbers,—not robbers," gasped the terrified man. . . . "I saw . . . I saw a woman—by the moat;—and she showed me . . . Aa! I cannot tell you what she showed me!" (Hearn [1903] 1971, 205–207)

As folklorists note, one of the key psychological functions of legendry is to allow individuals to put disorienting experience—*numens*, as Lauri Honko (1964, 16) termed them—into words. The ability to *name* such experiences gives us control over them and allows the story to be told. The merchant, sadly, cannot *tell* his story, and thus he is doomed to repeat it. And so, all of a sudden the lights go out, on him and on us.

"FURISODÉ": PERSONALIZING CATASTROPHE

This narrative is the first story in Hearn's 1899 (2005) collection *In Ghostly Japan*. In contrast with "Mujina," it begins with deliberate vagueness: Hearn says that, while he was visiting some shop in some little street, he happened to see a formal long-sleeved robe—or *furisodé*—for sale and he was reminded of a legend about "the daughter of a rich merchant" in Edo,[5] the old name for Tokyo. Attending "some temple-festival," she noticed an anonymous young man pass in a crowd. She instantly fell in love with him, and hoping to attract his attention she had a robe made for herself in the style called furisodé, or "long-sleeved," using the same color and design of the mysterious samurai's clothing. However, she never saw the young man again, and, languishing for love, she devoted herself to worshiping the garment, repeating the Buddhist "Lotus mantra"—*nam myō hō rengé kyō*—before it and hoping the gods and Buddhas would help her find and win the young man.

Instead, as the story goes, she died, and the robe was, according to old custom, donated to some Buddhist temple. The priest would customarily resell costly garments such as these, Hearn explains, and use the money for the shrine's upkeep. Since the dead woman's furisodé was made of the best silk and was in perfect condition, it quickly sold for a good price. Unfortunately, (as you can probably guess), the woman who bought it wore it for only one day before she became haunted by the image of a beautiful man, weakened, and died. The robe once again was donated to the temple and sold to another young girl, who likewise wore it for one day and suffered the same fate. After this happened two more times, the priest realized the robe held some evil influence.

So far we can identify many traditional elements in this narrative. The cloak that brings death to its wearer dates back to classical times: Medea, jealous of her lover Jason's new bride, infused the wedding gown with a poison that burned the poor woman to death. As Adrienne Mayor (1995) has noted, this and related narratives may have been based on rumors that devastating plagues had been caused by enemies of the Greeks, who traded clothing taken off the bodies of dead victims. Similar legends circulated in the 1800s about European settlers killing off Native Americans with smallpox-infected blankets, and Dionizjusz Czubala, collecting contemporary legends in Mongolia during the early 1990s, found a similar belief that the Chinese had deliberately poisoned the silk they sent overseas to trade (1993, 5). Maskiell and Mayor (2001) also found many narratives in East

FIGURE 7.2. Yūrei (ghost)
by Sawaki Sūshi, from *Hyakkai
Zukan* (*The Illustrated Volume
of a Hundred Demons*), 1737.

Indian tradition in which ceremonial robes of honor were poisoned and then
ritually presented to unwelcome guests.

However, the most detailed parallel is the mid-twentieth-century "Poisoned Dress," first documented by Ernest Baughman in 1945,[6] though it
probably circulated a decade earlier. These accounts also begin with the same
studied vagueness as Hearn's text: "One particular girl" wants to attend
"a banquet at a prominent hotel in a certain city." So she buys a gown at
"a local department store." This store is sometimes identified as the Chicago-
based Marshall Field's, but most recorded variants leave it unnamed. She
wears it once, then faints and mysteriously dies. Police investigate and find
that the dress had previously been purchased to clothe the corpse of a dead
woman at her viewing and then returned to the store for a refund. Toxic
chemicals used to embalm the corpse seeped into the dress and, when its
second owner became warm from dancing, they soaked into her body with
lethal results (Brunvand 1984, 112–14).

All these versions, however, imply a scientific explanation for the deadly
properties of the clothing: a poison deliberately or accidentally soaked into
the fabric. Hearn's narrative stresses that the deadly influence of the robe
is supernatural: the young woman who had it made died with an unfulfilled
wish, one made all the more dangerous because of her sacrilegious use of a
powerful religious text to worship the memory of the godlike young man
she desires rather than Buddha. And so, after death, she becomes what Japanese tradition describes as a *yūrei*, a malicious revenant. Such souls, art historian Tim Screech (2002) notes, remain earthbound until they achieve the

unsatisfied desire that possessed them when they died. Further, they do not roam freely, but are bound to the place associated with their untimely death. "Rising up from the darkness," Screech says, "*yūrei* reanimate themselves with the flame of their passion." However, their utter concentration on their unfulfilled goal prevents them from becoming fully human, so, rather than being a personality, he concludes, "A *yūrei* is a purpose."[7]

We now understand why Hearn's story began in such general terms: the furisodé is itself the central space in the story, the liminal spot in which the young girl's vengeful spirit, caught between worlds, has taken its home. And, as exotically "Old Japan" as the *yūrei* concept is, some versions of the Western "Poison Dress" include a parallel motif. The raconteur Bennett Cerf added a supernatural detail to the torments of the dying girl: she hears the "harsh and bitter" voice of a woman whispering, "Give me back my dress!" (Brunvand 2004, 48).

As unsettling as the legend is to this point, its next episode defines place in yet another way, making it even more horrific. The priest decides to destroy the cursed garment, and his acolytes build a bonfire in the temple courtyard. But when it is placed in the flames, its *yūrei* nature becomes manifest: the silk bursts into a cluster of sparks, which sets the temple's wooden roof on fire. Driven by a strong wind, the blaze spreads from roof to roof, street to street, district to district, until the entire city of Edo is consumed. "And this calamity," the story concludes with austere precision, "occurred upon the eighteenth day of the first month of the first year of Meiréki" (Hearn 1899, 14). A legend that began as a tragic love story, and continues in the form of a contemporary legend, ends as a historical legend about the most devastating catastrophe in Japan's history.[8]

The legend thus *humanizes* the catastrophe by making it the result of a personal act. We see the same impulse in the immediate and long-term constructions of similar disasters in other cultures. For instance, a persistent rumor that circulated in the wake of the Chicago fire of October 1871 held that it had begun in the barn of Catherine O'Leary, an Irish immigrant. Supposedly, she had carelessly placed a lighted kerosene lantern on the floor behind a cow she was milking. The nervous animal kicked it over, and the fire quickly spread from the neighborhood to the center of the city. Factually speaking, the O'Leary barn was the first structure consumed, but an intensive, official investigation exonerated Mrs. O'Leary from blame. Nevertheless, she made a convenient scapegoat for the catastrophe. An example of the lower class that was frequently blamed for shoddy living places,

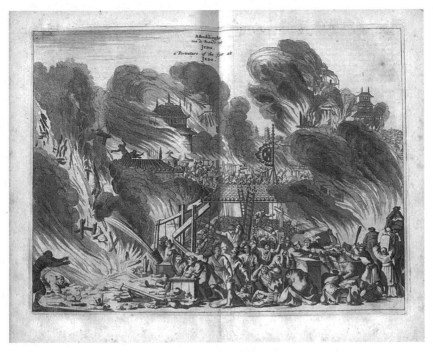

FIGURE 7.3. The Great Fire in Edo, 1657. Engraving in Arnold Montanus's (1669) book, *Gedenkwaerdige Gesantschappen der Oostindische Maatschappy in't Vereenigde Nederland aan de Kaisaren van Japan.* (Courtesy of the Collection of Wolfgang Michel, Fukuoka, Japan)

a shiftless lifestyle, and un-American beliefs associated with Catholicism, she was essentially powerless to rebut the charge that she was personally responsible (O'Leary Legend 2011). In much the same way, the lower-class "Typhoid Mary" Mallon became a convenient scapegoat for the frequent outbreaks of typhoid fever that affected New York City in the early twentieth century. The city's primitive water and sanitation system was a more likely cause for the spread of this disease, but an Irish immigrant was a more satisfying cause, especially since she was also female (Fine and Ellis 2010, 87–88).

Gary Alan Fine and Irfan Khawaja (2005) saw the same tendency in the aftermath of the September 11 terrorist attacks, in which a range of Middle Easterners were identified as complicit with the al-Qaeda conspirators. Interestingly, for some time the narrators continued to speculate on what terrorists were like personally. While some of the immediate reactions to the attacks imply that the event was simply an expression of existential evil, the more enduring narratives described terrorists as solicitous boyfriends or random shoppers who reciprocate a small act of kindness with advance warning about the next strike. Those who pass on such rumors do not see ethnic Middle Easterners as any less to blame for 9/11; they just think they understand them as human beings a little better. As with Chicagoans' stories of Mrs. O'Leary, the rumors did not address the real cultural roots of terrorism, but instead reinforced common stereotypes about Middle Easterners. Thus, Hearn's legend looks backward to classic myths and forward to contemporary legend, finding transnational roots in the impulse to blame tragedies on individual humans.

Hearn ends his account—with a hint of apology for its opening vagueness—by adding the supposed names and addresses of the characters in the story, as well as the location of the temple. But, he concludes skeptically, there are many variations on the story, and in any case the source that gives the most exact details also claims that the young samurai who inflamed the passion of the furisodé's owner was not really human. According to this account, he was actually "a transformed dragon, or water-serpent" who lived in the bottom of Shinobazu Pond, a popular park in Edo/Tokyo. Hearn (1899, 16) ends on this note, leaving readers uncertain what to believe. Was the cause of the great fire the young girl's fatal attraction or the malice of a local *yōkai* (monster)? In typical legend fashion, the final choice is left to the individual, but Hearn's skepticism implies that the mysterious samurai was no goblin. If the furisodé's owner had become a single-minded *yūrei* capable of death on the megascale, then it makes narrative sense that the flame of the lovesick girl's passion, finding literal expression in the blaze that destroyed Edo, could not be controlled until it tracked down the lad and claimed his life. That would never happen, of course, if he were a dragon living under a lake. As "The O'Leary Legend" (2011) concludes, "Given that the catastrophe could not be undone, there was even something imaginatively satisfying in the tale that this epic fire had such a humble beginning."

"IN THE CAVE OF THE CHILDREN'S GHOSTS": CULTURAL TOURISM AS PILGRIMAGE

The third and most interesting of our texts appeared in Hearn's first anthology of Asian sketches, *Glimpses of an Unfamiliar Japan* ([1894] 2012). During his first days in Japan, Hearn was taken to a Buddhist cemetery in

FIGURE 7.4. Jizō statue at Mount Osore, Japan. (Courtesy of Japanexperterna, www.japanexperterna.se)

Yokohama, where he saw a statue of Jizō, a divinity who protects human souls as they traverse the realms of the afterlife toward enlightenment. Hearn's informant explained that Jizō's particular role is to protect the spirits of little children. Too weak to cross the swift river that separates this world from the first realm of the afterlife, the children are condemned to build towers of stones as an act of penance, which the demons constantly knock down as fast as the children can build them. Hearn saw, with fascination, how little stacks of stones stood around all six statues, with more pebbles placed in cotton bags around their necks. The acolyte assured him, "Every stone one lays upon the knees or at the feet of Jizō, with a prayer from the heart, helps some child-soul in the Sai-no-Kawara to perform its long penance" (Hearn [1894] 2012, 52).

This place between realms was "beneath us, below the ground," Hearn was told, but when he settled in the town of Matsue he learned that a place on the nearby coastline was reputed to be an earthly Sai-no-Kawara. He quickly made arrangements to visit the spot, a shoreline cavern called Kyū-Kukedo ("ancient sea cave") on the Shimane Peninsula, close to the fishing town of Kaka. Arriving by boat, he saw first a pale statue of Jizō, then, all around him, "hundreds and thousands of . . . little towers of stone and pebbles deftly piled up by long and patient labor" (Hearn [1894] 2012, 255). "Shinda kodomo no shigoto," his tour guide muttered with a kindly smile, which Hearn translates: "all this is the work of the dead children." Leaving the boat, Hearn walked cautiously into the cave along a narrow path between the piles of stones. His guide warned him to be careful not to knock down any of the towers, for doing so makes the children cry. Eventually, they arrived at a clear, flat beach of sand, and there among the little towers were "light prints of little feet, children's feet, tiny naked feet, only three or four inches long—*the footprints of the infant ghosts*" (emphasis original). If they had come earlier in the day, his escort said, there would have been more, for they fade as the sun dries them out. Nevertheless, Hearn says, the footprints were "singularly distinct."

In that place, standing beside the telltale prints, his guides told Hearn a series of legends. When a storm comes, waves crash into the cave "like raging Oni," scattering all the stone towers. But after the first calm night, the piles or rocks are mysteriously rebuilt. Hearn again quotes his guide in Japanese: "Hotoke ga shimpai shite: naki-naki tsumi naoshi-masŭ"; then he translates: "They make mourning, the hotoke [spirits of the dead]; weeping, they pile up the stones again, they rebuild their towers of prayer" (Hearn [1894] 2012, 258). At that point, Hearn accidentally upset two of the little stacks of pebbles surrounding them, and even his careful attendant knocked down another, which gave her a chance to explain that they were now obliged to construct six new stone piles, two for each one they had upset. That provided an opportunity for another legend, one about two fishermen who spent a night in the cavern and heard the sounds of a great crowd of little children humming and murmuring. Every night, she concluded as they returned to the boat, the piles of stones are rebuilt in different shapes.

Contemporary folklorists see that Hearn has been taken on a legend trip. The combination of oral storytelling and ostensive enactment make this clear, as does Hearn's comment that at the time he could not get a clear answer to why the children's ghosts haunt that particular site in the first place. But while the legends that motivate these visits are notoriously unstable, the trip remains the thing, and the same place may be frequented over generations (Ellis 2003, 187). Hearn's account makes it clear that the shrine was well visited in the 1890s. He noticed several additional statues in the back of the grotto, kept in reserve to replace the ones in front as they became damaged by storm waves. And visitors had brought offerings, such as little sandals to keep the ghosts' feet from being hurt on the sharp rocks.

Its impressive location on the shore of the pounding Sea of Japan, aided by stories about the mysterious phenomenon, made it a popular destination for pilgrims and curious tourists like himself.

And it remains one. A local tourism board still advertises charter boats that will take contemporary visitors to the site, where a convenient tunnel has been constructed so tourists no longer have to squeeze in among the rock towers built by the children's ghosts. Its website (Matsue Tourism Association, Shimane Branch 2013) adds new stories to the ones recorded by Hearn. The most dramatic one tells of a sailor who put in to the nearby fishing port, went to a tavern, and overheard the legend of the children's ghosts rebuilding the towers after a storm. How silly, he thought, and he took a rowboat over to Kyū-Kukedo and knocked down every tower with an oar. But that night, when he tried to sleep, the sound of weeping children kept him awake. And when he revisited the cave, the towers were rebuilt—yes, every one of them—just as they'd stood before. When the sailor's boat went on its next voyage, a great storm came and sank it. He survived, but he'd learned his lesson, and when he returned he brought more statues of Master Jizō, which replenished the reserve in the back of the Sai-no-Kawara grotto.

Other contemporary stories on the website confirm that the place really is the residence of children's ghosts. According to one account, a mother printed Jizō's image on a thousand sheets of paper and set them adrift in the ocean, saying, "Show me where my child has gone!" (Matsue Tourism Association, Shimane Branch 2013).[9] Many of them came ashore at Kyū-Kukedo. In another, a couple arrived from Tokyo claiming their lost child had appeared to them in a dream, saying, "I'm at Kukedo, near Kaka. Please come visit me." They had never heard of the place, and it took them a long time to track it down. When they found it, they brought their child's favorite toys and offerings for Jizō. Photographs on the website and visitors' videos uploaded to YouTube[10] show that the mysterious stone towers still stand in every direction around a statue of the benign deity, accompanied by plastic toys, plush animals, and flowers. Where Hearn had seen pairs of straw sandals, now child-sized sets of sneakers are provided for the little spirits' feet.

North American folklorists who have investigated San Antonio's "Gravity Hill" (Glazer 1989; Goldstein, Grider, and Thomas 2007, 54–57; Lindahl 2005) will recognize many of these same motifs. This complex of stories is focused on an isolated railroad crossing on the southern side of the city, where cars parked on the tracks appear to be "pushed" off by unseen hands. Tradition has it that the agents are the ghosts of children, victims of a fatal school bus accident on the spot, who use their supernatural force to prevent any similar tragedy. Visitors commonly dust the backs of their cars with baby powder to reveal the prints of small hands, thus providing evidence for the ghostly children's presence. Carl Lindahl (2005) describes many of the same features that Hearn recorded: a liminal location, ostensive actions, and particularly the interest in physical and emotional proof that children's spirits do live on in a mystical space between this world and the next.

Lindahl argues that Gravity Hill is a "semi-sacred site," particularly for Latino participants, and thus a focus for a kind of pilgrimage. Ethnographers describe this activity, common to many religious traditions,[11] as a visit to an interstitial space, one that lies between one's normal cultural landscape and one that is essentially mythological in nature. Victor and Edith Turner (1978) suggest that pilgrimage is a mild form of cultural rebellion. In everyday religious life, believers engage in ritual activities that are prescribed and supervised by authorities, while pilgrimages by contrast are motivated by individual choice and personal involvement in the mythos that informs religious life. Pilgrims, they argue, are free to choose the time and place of their journey, and, while completing such a trip may enhance one's social standing in the community, its primary function is to escape from a culturally prescribed structure, enter a metaphorical space that is "betwixt and between" cultures, and return with a deeper personal appreciation of religious beliefs (7–11).

The Turners add that such an activity comes very close to tourism, particularly as the motives for visiting a faraway place may not derive from religious motives but rather from wanting to temporarily escape a constricting social milieu. The place visited may, for historical or natural reasons, be felt to be "a life source," and co-travelers often experience "an almost sacred, often symbolic, mode of communitas" during a trip that is otherwise seen as a secular form of recreation (1978, 20). In the same way, Graburn (2004) sees tourism as a kind of "sacred journey" that occupies the same role as a pilgrimage. In Japan, the boundaries between the two categories become still more blurred, since visits to historic Shinto and Buddhist temples may be viewed simultaneously as a form of tourism as well as an observation of religious duties.

Much the same blurring of motives occurs during legend tripping, a common custom among adolescents and young adults. Though the activity involves a much smaller time and travel commitment than either pilgrimages or tourism, it is structurally similar and it also seems to stem from a desire to rebel against cultural restrictions by visiting a liminal spot. As folklorists have noted, participants could be motivated by an even wider range of nonreligious motives, such as a desire to "trip out" (i.e., experience an altered state of consciousness with or without the help of drugs) or encourage a reluctant girlfriend to engage in sex (Ellis 2001, 189). Lindahl nevertheless cautions against seeing such locations as no more than a congregating spot for adolescent troublemakers. A legend trip may attract some participants seeking a "pious thrill," he concedes, but others come as sincere pilgrims affirming "a constellation of culture-specific beliefs," including the immortality of the soul, "hoping to achieve for even one second the complete communion of the living and the dead" (2005, 180–81). Graburn likewise notes the way in which Buddhism has become for Japanese (of all faiths) a religion negotiating death and the afterlife. Temples, he says, frequently include small altars where bereaved parents are encouraged to bring toys and plush animals to offer to the spirits of absent children (2004, 128).

Consequently, it is no surprise to find that the various narratives and customs Hearn found in Kyū-Kukedo are part of a much larger Japanese supernatural tradition. Museum curator Gabi Greve finds that custom is very much alive in contemporary times. Browsing the websites of regional shrines and the blogs of Japanese tourists, he located twelve additional places—mostly in Hokkaido and northern Honshu—that were being visited as Sai-no-Kawara sites (Greve 2004; Schumacher 2012). Tourist photographs show that the offerings left by the small statues of Jizō parallel those left at North American memorial sites: pinwheels, toys, plush animals, etc.[12] Such visits, and the time spent building or rebuilding the towers of rocks, create an opportunity for storytelling and for feeling—at least temporarily— at one with the spiritual presence of the site. Hence the two traditions, one Japanese and one North American, seem to reflect common impulses for creating semi-sacred places and maintaining them, both in physical space and, with ostension, in time.

CONCLUSION

Hearn's observations, though describing an exotic "Old Japan" that was passing away, were in fact hypermodern in his era. In the stories and customs he chose to observe, we see Hearn discovering elements of contemporary legend and international traditions in "Old Japan." "Mujina" reflects

the human need to gain psychological control over the memory of a numi-
nous encounter, whether with an angel, demon, animal spirit, or ghost.
Ironically, it describes a case in which the witness is successfully punished
by the supernatural for not being able to reduce it to words. In contrast, folk
traditions create and communicate sociolinguistic systems that allow a community to discuss such encounters and connect them to other beliefs about
their natural (and supernatural) world. "Furisodé" reflects a similar quest
to grasp the significance of dehumanizing tragedies like the Meireki Fire by
humanizing its roots. The legend puts a face, a motive, and—in the object
of the cursed furisodé—a literal space on the cause of this catastrophic fire.
And "The Cave of the Children's Ghosts" brings together legend, custom,
belief, and ritual in a way that is simultaneously an adventure and a quasi-
religious experience. All can be understood in terms of the broader dialectic
of collective legend and individual belief/experience, which, as we have
seen in past decades, is not just metacommentary but an integral part of
legendry.

Hearn's emphasis on the social construction of *place* adds a new hypermodern element to our understanding of the supernatural. Paradoxically,
the texture of his sketches seems to highlight the Otherworldly and yet
distinctively Japanese qualities of these stories. Stylistic devices such as
translated or untranslated vocabulary and strange place names heighten the
apparent distance between his urbanized Western reader and the age-old
Asian customs and beliefs he describes. And yet the dynamics of the stories, text and texture both, impact readers because they speak to *universal*
functions of folk narrative, present not just in Old Japan but in many world
cultures. "Place" is not only a physical locale but also the aura of social implications that humans invest in it. Unlimited to any specific time and space,
it becomes a part of the imagination through discourse and can be visited by
many people over centuries.

This aspect of Hearn's ethnography was clearly felt by his contemporaries, both European and Japanese. John Erskine (1922), an early biographer
of Hearn, observes that most people seek the exotic "in remote places and in
exceptional conditions"; however, Hearn's genius was that he cultivated in
his readers a sharper alertness to emotionally powerful aspects of life that
are part of the everyday. It was not just that Hearn captured the Otherness
of Japan, an unfamiliar and then distant country, but that "he finds for
us the exotic in ourselves" (vii–viii). In a similar way, Ellen Badone (2004)
argues that ethnography itself is structurally identical to both tourism and

pilgrimage—it involves travel to an exotic space, a quest for experience and knowledge not available at home, and an intellectual re-creation of one's worldview. Citing Geertz, she concludes that such a newfound perspective is "a peculiar manner of construing the world,"[13] much like religious experience (181).

Hearn's Japanese contemporaries also recognized his work as immensely important. Shortly after his death, the influential poet and author Yone Noguchi (1911) wrote, "We Japanese have been regenerated by his sudden magic," reminded of ancient beauties and narratives that Hearn revived "with a strange yet new splendor." Nevertheless, Noguchi adds, "what impressed us most was that he was a striking figure of protest" (17). He was, in fact, a contrarian advocate for folklore studies in Meiji-era Japan (just as his rejection of segregation politics was crucial to his advocacy for Creole folkloristics in New Orleans). By calling attention to folk culture and its importance in daily life, he led the way for the indigenous development of folkloristics as a serious academic field. And, more than a half century before the text/context dispute emerged in American folkloristics, his emphasis on textual and performance details is visibly more linked to modern folklore scholarship than the colonialist speculations of the discipline in his time.

Kunio Yanagita, Japan's most successful advocate for folklore research, was strongly influenced by Hearn's attention to rural storytelling and customs. It is true that Yanagita dissented from Hearn's habit of presenting texts in his own voice rather than using authentic records of what his Japanese sources had in fact told him. Yanagita's landmark *Tōno monogatari [Legends of Tōno]* (2008) was compiled as a corrective to Hearn's texts: dry and flatly descriptive, his versions of the narratives he collected reflect the rhetoric of rural villagers who took their supernatural traditions as a fact of everyday life. His grim, minimalist approach to folk narrative proved to be, like Hearn's work, a hypermodern attack on the sentimentalism of Meiji-era scholarship and literature. *Tōno monogatari,* cultural historian Leith Morton (2003) concludes, was for Yanagita's contemporaries "the beginning of an entirely new way of thinking about Japan, of imagining how a modern Japan may differ from its European rivals" (57). Yet, David Hufford (1994) observes that the dynamics of the marvelous encounters Yanagita recorded, though they were placed in a Japanese rural context, were the same as those recorded from many other parts of the world. Further studies like his, he concludes, "will enrich our appreciation both of the distinctive qualities

of cultures around the world and the common humanity of those who create, maintain, and live within them" (xvi).

Yanagita and Hearn, in fact, were of one mind in viewing "things
felt"[14]—the activities that are emotionally "haunted" by a pervasive sense of
collective history and significance—as central to a community's definition
of who and where they are. By paying attention to the complex interplay
between individuals and the group, Leith Morton (2003) says, Yanagita
advocated developing an "art of listening" rather than simply a craft of finding etic meaning in objective field notes (80). Yanagita's emphasis on the
folklore of isolated rural places, Michael Dylan Foster (2012) argues, is not
simple romanticism but—as with Hearn's approach—is a means of reviving
places in Japanese readers' imaginations that were in danger of being overwhelmed by modernity. Yanagita's focus on describing the physical landscape of the mountain village of Tōno, Foster argues, is a way of using newly
adopted forms of mass media to transport urbanized readers to the landscape he observed and make its patterns of thinking accessible to a much
wider audience. Landscape, Foster suggests, is "really a matter of language"
(2012, 22). Which is the spot where this essay began.

Western folklorists, generations later, are now beginning to see that to
comprehend a supernatural story means becoming literate in the worldview
and knowledgeable about the terrain of the culture that produced it. Yet,
our journey's end is not the exotic Otherworld of "Old Japan" but a better
perspective of our own contemporary landscapes. And in order to arrive,
we often travel, as did Hearn's contemporary audience, on the wings of
hypermodern communication.

NOTES

1. A modern guide to the places mentioned in Hearn's sketches explains that this
   palace was once used as the Edo residence of the underlord of Kii Province,
   a strategic region to the south of the capital. Such underlords were required
   to live in the imperial capital for part of each year to ensure centralized control of the nation. See "Ki-no-kuni-zaka," Exploring Lafcadio Hearn, http://web
   .archive.org/web/20120906191128/http://lafcadiohearn.jp/tokyo/kinokuni.html
   (as archived on June 24, 2002).
2. Hearn's use of the term has puzzled Japanese readers as well. In some localities,
   it is used to name a tanuki, a canine mammal native to Japan, while in others it
   refers to a badger. Both animals, along with foxes, are said to develop into yōkai
   as they age and gain experience; these yōkai, like the fairy-folk in European lore,

can shapeshift into human form and play pranks on humans. But there is no strong tradition associating either *tanuki* or badgers with a prank of this specific sort. A *yōkai* that more closely fits this tradition is called *Nopperabo,* and some commentators think Hearn simply mixed up the two traditions. Or maybe not. See Yoda and Alt 2012a, 126–29 (*Tanuki*) and 166–69 (*Nopperabo*) for an effort to straighten things out.

3. The 1994 Japanese anime film *Pom Poko* includes a variant of this story. The plot describes the rebellion of a group of *tanuki* against the destruction of their habitat, during which they play this prank on a passerby. It is extended by a third incident in which the terrorized victim runs from the soba seller into a crowded store and tries to tell his story to the clerks and customers there. Predictably, all of them react by wiping their faces into blanks.

4. Theroux interjects here that Riyadh taxi drivers are stereotypically skeptical about any kind of rumor.

5. Hearn used the now obsolete variant "*Yedo,*" but I've substituted the more familiar, Westernized form of this place name.

6. Charlton (1945), followed up by another correspondent in subsequent issues of *Hoosier Folklore Bulletin.*

7. See also Yoda and Alt (2012b, 7–8).

8. More commonly known as the Meireki Fire, the conflagration began on March 2, 1657, and raged for three days, during which approximately half of the great city's population (well over one hundred thousand lives) were lost. The total loss of life was comparable to that of the two modern-day Tokyo disasters, the 1923 earthquake and fire and the 1945 bombing by Allied air forces. However, in the seventeenth century Japan's population was only about a third of its modern size; the cultural impact of this catastrophe was, in effect, two to three times greater than either of the two recent calamities.

9. This website is in Japanese. I'm indebted to Casey Schoenberger of the University of the South, Suwanee, TN, for providing a translation of these legends.

10. An especially effective one titled "*Kaka no Kukedo*" [加賀の旧潜] was published on YouTube as recently as July 9, 2012, by hiro ada (http://www.youtube.com /watch?v=rsGsacuwqKk). It shows the visitor proceeding through the new tunnel (punctuated by lighted niches with flowers) and into the cavern, where stacks of rocks, along with memorial offerings, crowd the space. This video, which visibly reflects the visitor's heavy heartbeat, ends poignantly as the tourist picks up two fallen stones and restores them to one of the cave's towers.

11. As noted by Badone (2004, 181).

12. Yvonne Milspaw (2004) has also described a less elaborate but similar complex of narratives and customs associated with a little girl's grave in a cemetery near Hummelstown, Pennsylvania. "It is always covered," Milspaw says, "with animal toys and figures, pretty stones, flowers, butterfly images, pinwheels, and especially ceramic or stone images of angels" (52). As the grave stood near an elementary school, she says, beliefs and customs quickly arose among the children who passed. "If you put something on her grave," one told her, "like another toy or something, she brings you good luck, she helps you out. I put some quarters in her frog bank that was on the grave. I think it helped me" (54). Similarly, desecrating the display troubles the girl's spirit, just as wantonly disturbing the stone towers in the cave is thought to lead to supernatural retribution.

Furthermore, offerings left at spontaneous memorials of more public tragedies, such as the Vietnam Veterans Memorial in Washington, DC (Fish 1983) or the 9/11 Memorial in New York City (Grider 2001), are often assumed to be semi-sacred and cautiously preserved in some way.

13. Badone (2004) cites Clifford Geertz's classic essay, "Thick Description: Toward an Interpretive Theory of Culture," in *The Interpretation of Cultures*.

14. Iwasaka and Toelken (1994, 55) render this part of Yanagita's famous three-part subdivision of folklore as "things believed" (the others being "things seen" and "things heard"). I've followed Morton's (2003, 79) translation here, since it is more faithful to Yanagita's conviction that these traditions were so subjectively complex that they could not simply be observed and transcribed, but they needed to be experienced on an emotional level as well. For this reason, unlike Western folklorists, Yanagita encouraged his students to become involved in the practice and performance of such traditions, and to record their personal reactions to what they experienced. Such traditions were not matters of the brain, he argued, but of the heart.

WORKS CITED

Badone, Ellen. 2004. "Crossing Boundaries: Exploring the Borderlands of Ethnography, Tourism, and Pilgrimage." In *Intersecting Journeys: The Anthropology of Pilgrimage and Tourism,* edited by Ellen Badone and Sharon R. Roseman, 180–90. Urbana, IL: University of Illinois Press.

Bennett, Gillian. 1988. "Legend: Performance and Truth." In *Monsters with Iron Teeth: Perspectives on Contemporary Legend III,* edited by Gillian Bennett, Paul Smith, and J. D. A. Widdowson, 13–36. Sheffield, UK: Sheffield Academic Press.

Bronner, Simon. 2005. "'Gombo' Folkloristics: Lafcadio Hearn's Creolization and Hybridization in the Formative Period of Folklore Studies." *Journal of Folklore Studies* 42.2: 141–84.

Brunvand, Jan Harold. 1984. *The Choking Doberman and Other 'New' Urban Legends.* New York: Norton.

———. 2004. *Be Afraid, Be Very Afraid: The Book of Scary Urban Legends.* New York, NY: Norton.

Charlton, Virginia. 1945. "The Poisoned Dress." *Hoosier Folklore Bulletin* 4: 19–20.

Czubala, Dionizjusz. 1993. "Mongolian Contemporary Legends: Field Research Report, Part Two. Political Rumors and Sensations." *FOAFTale News* 29: 1–7.

Ellis, Bill. 2001. "Hæc in Sua Parochia Accidisse Dixit: The Rhetoric of 15th-Century Contemporary Legends." *Contemporary Legend* n.s., 4: 74–92.

———. 2003. *Aliens, Ghosts, and Cults: Legends We Live.* Jackson, MS: University Press of Mississippi.

Erskine, John. 1922. "Introduction." In his *Books and Habits: From the Lectures of Lafcadio Hearn,* v-xv. London: William Heinemann.

Fine, Gary Alan, and Bill Ellis. 2010. *The Global Grapevine: Why Rumors of Terrorism, Immigration, and Trade Matter.* New York: Oxford University Press.

Fine, Gary Alan and Irfan Khawaja. 2005. "Celebrating Arabs and Grateful Terrorists: Rumors and the Politics of Plausibility." In *Rumor Mills: The Social Impact of*

Rumor and Legend, edited by Gary Alan Fine, Véronique Campion-Vincent, and Chip Heath, 189–205. New Brunswick, NJ: AldineTransaction.

Fish, Lydia. 1983. *The Last Firebase: A Guide to the Vietnam Veterans Memorial*. Shippensburg, PA: White Mane Publishing.

Foster, Michael Dylan. 2012. "Yōkai and Yanagita Kunio Viewed from the 21st Century." In *Yanagita Kunio and Japanese Folklore Studies in the 21st Century*, edited by Ronald A. Morse, 20–35. San Francisco: Japanime.

Frederick, Charles R. 1990. "Family Folklore." In *The Emergence of Folklore in Everyday Life: A Fieldguide and Sourcebook*, edited by George H. Schoemaker, 171–73. Bloomington, IN: Trickster Press.

Goldstein, Diane E., Sylvia Ann Grider, and Jeannie Banks Thomas. 2007. *Haunting Experiences: Ghosts in Contemporary Folklore*. Logan, UT: Utah State University Press.

Glazer, Mark. 1984. "Continuity and Change in Legendry: Two Mexican-American Examples." In *Perspectives on Contemporary Legend*, edited by Paul Smith, 108–27. Sheffield, UK: CECTAL.

———. 1989. "Gravity Hill: Belief and Belief Legend." In *The Questing Beast: Perspectives on Contemporary Legend IV*. Edited by Gillian Bennett and Paul Smith, 165–77. Sheffield, UK: Sheffield Academic Press.

Graburn, Nelson H. H. 2004. "The Kyoto Tax Strike: Buddhism, Shinto, and Tourism in Japan." In *Intersecting Journeys: The Anthropology of Pilgrimage and Tourism*, edited by Ellen Badone and Sharon R. Roseman, 125–39. Urbana, IL: University of Illinois Press.

Greve, Gabi. 2004. "Sai no Kawara, the Limbo for Children." *Darumasan-Japan: Daruma san in Japanese Art and Culture*, http://groups.yahoo.com/group /Darumasan-Japan/message/502.

Grider, Sylvia. 2001. "Spontaneous Shrines: A Modern Response to Tragedy and Disaster." *New Directions in Folklore*, volume 5, https://scholarworks.iu.edu /dspace/handle/2022/7196.

Hanamoto, Ben. 2011. "Faceless Ghost at the Drive-In." *National Japanese American Historical Society* [blog]. February 8, http://njahs.blogspot.com/2011/02/faceless -ghost-at-drive-in.html.

Hearn, Lafcadio. [1903] 1971. *Kwaidan: Stories and Studies of Strange Things*. Rutland, VT: Tuttle Publishing.

———. 1899. *In Ghostly Japan*. Boston: Little, Brown, and Company.

———. [1894] 2012. *Glimpses of an Unfamiliar Japan: First Series*. Auckland, NZ: The Floating Press.

Honko, Lauri. 1964. "Memorates and the Study of Folk Beliefs." *Journal of Folklore Research* 1: 5–19.

Hufford, David J. 1994. "Forward." In *Ghosts and the Japanese: Cultural Experience in Japanese Death Legends*, edited by Michiko Iwasaka and Barre Toelken, xi–xvi. Logan, UT: Utah State University Press.

Iwasaka, Michiko, and Barre Toelken. 1994. *Ghosts and the Japanese: Cultural Experience in Japanese Death Legends*. Logan, UT: Utah State University Press.

Matsue Tourism Association, Shimane Branch. 2013. 加賀の旧潜戸 [Kaga no kyū kugurido], http://www.kankou-matsue.jp/shimanecho/kukedo22.html.

Lindahl, Carl. 2005. "Ostensive Healing: Pilgrimage to the San Antonio Ghost Tracks." *Journal of American Folklore* 118: 164–85.

Maskiell, Michelle and Adrienne Mayor. 2001. "Killer Khilats, Part 1: Legends of Poisoned 'Robes of Honour' in India." *Folklore* 112: 23–45.

Mayor, Adrienne. 1995. "The Nessus Shirt in the New World: Smallpox Blankets in History and Legend." *Journal of American Folklore* 108: 54–77.

McWilliams, Vera. 1946. *Lafcadio Hearn*. Boston: Houghton Mifflin.

Milspaw, Yvonne J. 2004. "Ghosts and Grave Offerings: Legends from South Central Pennsylvania: A Case Study in the Intersection of Stories and Stone." *Contemporary Legend* n.s., 7: 44–66.

Morton, Leith. 2003. *Modern Japanese Culture: The Insider View*. New York: Oxford University Press.

Noguchi, Yone. 1911. *Lafcadio Hearn in Japan*. New York: Mitchell Kennerley, http://ebook.lib.hku.hk/CADAL/B31414813/.

O'Leary Legend, The. 2011. *The Great Chicago Fire and the Web of Memory*. Chicago Historical Society and Northwestern University, http://www.greatchicagofire.org/oleary-legend.

Schumacher, Mark. 2012. "Sai no Kawara." *Japanese Buddhism Dictionary Project*, http://www.onmarkproductions.com/html/sai-no-kawara.html.

Screech, Tim. 2002. "Japanese Ghosts." *Mangajin* 40. April 6, http://web.archive.org/web/19990203172419/http://www.mangajin.com/mangajin/samplemj/ghosts/ghosts.htm (As archived on February 3, 1999).

Theroux, Peter. 1991. *Sandstorms: Days and Nights in Arabia*. New York: W. W. Norton.

Thompson, Stith. 1960. *Motif-Index of Folk-Literature: A Classification of Narrative Elements in Folk Tales, Ballads, Myths, Fables, Mediaeval Romances, Exempla, Fabliaux, Jest-Books, and Local Legends*. Bloomington, IN: Indiana University Press.

Todorov, Tzvetan. [1970] 1972. *The Fantastic: A Structural Approach to a Literary Genre*. Ithaca, NY: Cornell University Press.

Tucker, Elizabeth. 2007. *Haunted Halls: Ghostlore of American College Campuses*. Jackson, MS: University Press of Mississippi.

Turner, Victor, and Edith Turner. 1978. *Image and Pilgrimage in Christian Culture: Anthropological Perspectives*. New York: Columbia University Press.

Yanagita, Kunio. [1908] 2008. *The Legends of Tono*. Translated by Ronald A. Morse. Lanham, MD: Lexington Books.

Yoda, Hiroko, and Matt Alt. 2012a. *Yokai Attack! The Japanese Monster Survival Guide*. North Clarendon, VT: Tuttle.

———. 2012b. *Yurei Attack! The Japanese Ghost Survival Guide*. North Clarendon, VT: Tuttle.

FRANK DE CARO is a professor emeritus of English at Louisiana State University in Baton Rouge and currently lives in New Orleans. He received his MA from the Writing Seminars at Johns Hopkins University in 1964 and his PhD in folklore from Indiana University in 1972. He was on the faculty at LSU from 1970 until 2001 and taught courses in literature, writing, and folklore. He is a Fellow of the American Folklore Society. His essays and reviews have appeared in a wide variety of publications, and his most recent books include *Folklore Recycled: Old Traditions in New Contexts* (2013) and *Stories of Our Lives: Memory, History, Narrative* (2013); he also wrote the foreword for a new edition of Jeanne deLavigne's *Ghost Stories of Old New Orleans* (2013).

BILL ELLIS is a professor emeritus of English and American studies at Penn State University. His academic publications include *Raising the Devil: Satanism, New Religions, and the Media* (2000), *Aliens, Ghosts, and Cults: Legends We Live* (2001), *Lucifer Ascending: The Occult in Folk and Popular Culture* (2003), and, with Gary Alan Fine, *The Global Grapevine: Why Rumors and Legends about Immigrants, Terrorists, and Foreign Trade Matter* (2010). He has also published articles on the role of the Internet in the spread of topical jokes and legend parodies, as well as on the development of folklore as a means of maintaining online communities. A Fellow of the American Folklore Society, he has served on that organization's executive board. Fans of Japanese popular culture recognize him more readily as the creator and curator of *Sensei's Anime Gallery*, a permanent online display of Japanese animation art.

LISA GABBERT is an associate professor of English and director of the folklore program at Utah State University; she also has served on the executive board of the American Folklore Society. Her research interests include folklore and landscape, festivity, and ritual and play in medical contexts. Her work has appeared in a variety of journals, including the *Journal of American Folklore, Western Folklore, Contemporary Legend, CUR Quarterly, Glimpse:*

The Art and Science of Seeing, and others. Her book, *Winter Carnival in a Western Town: Identity, Change, and the Good of the Community* (2011), inaugurated the Ritual, Festival, and Celebration series edited by Jack Santino at Utah State University Press.

MIKEL J. KOVEN is a senior lecturer and course leader for film studies at the University of Worcester. Holding a doctorate in folklore studies from Memorial University of Newfoundland, he is the author of *La Dolce Morte: Vernacular Cinema and the Italian Giallo Film* (2006), *Film, Folklore, and Urban Legends* (2008), and *Blaxploitation Films* (2010). Zombies are currently taking over his life.

LYNNE S. MCNEILL earned her PhD in folklore from Memorial University of Newfoundland and is currently the director of online development for the folklore program at Utah State University. Her research interests include digital culture, legends, and folk belief. She is the author of the introductory textbook *Folklore Rules* (2013), as well as several articles and book chapters on topics ranging from ghost hunting to Internet memes. She currently serves as the review editor for the journal *Contemporary Legend*. She has appeared on Animal Planet and the Food Network, and she has been a guest on public radio's RadioWest.

JEANNIE BANKS THOMAS is a professor at Utah State University, where she is also head of the Department of English. She received her doctorate in folklore and English from the University of Oregon. Her feminist study of women's stories and laughter, *Featherless Chickens, Laughing Women, and Serious Stories* (1997), received the Elli Köngäs-Maranda Prize. Gender and the oral narratives (including legends) about material culture are the subjects of *Naked Barbies, Warrior Joes, and Other Forms of Visible Gender* (2003). *Haunting Experiences: Ghosts in Contemporary Folklore* (2007), co-authored with Diane Goldstein and Sylvia Grider, won the Brian McConnell Book Award in legend studies. She is the former editor of *Midwestern Folklore* and has been a member of the editorial boards of *Western Folklore* and *Folklore Historian*.

ELIZABETH TUCKER, professor of English at Binghamton University, is the editor of *Children's Folklore Review* and president of the International Society for Contemporary Legend Research. She received her doctorate in folklore from Indiana University, where she specialized in children's and adolescent folklore, folklore of the supernatural, and legends. She has written five books: *Campus Legends: A Handbook* (2005), *Haunted Halls: Ghostlore of American College Campuses* (2007), *Children's Folklore: A Handbook* (2008), *Haunted Southern Tier* (2011), and *New York State Folklife Reader: Diverse Voices* (2013). She feels very lucky to have gotten to know people who have generously shared stories of their spiritual experiences.

INDEX

Numbers in *italics* indicate figures.